Developing People and Organisations

Edited by Jim Stewart and Patricia Rogers

Chartered Institute of Personnel and Development

Published by the Chartered Institute of Personnel and Development,

151, The Broadway, London, SW19 1JQ

This edition first published 2012

Styled by Exeter Premedia, India

Printed in Great Britain by Bell & Bain, Glasgow

British Library Cataloguing in Publication Data

A catalogue of this publication is available from the British Library

ISBN 978 1 84398 313 2

The views expressed in this publication are the authors' own and may not necessarily reflect those of the CIPD.

The CIPD has made every effort to trace and acknowledge copyright holders. If any source has been overlooked, CIPD Enterprises would be pleased to redress this in future editions.

Chartered Institute of Personnel and Development,
151, The Broadway, London, SW19 1JQ
Tel: 020 8612 6200
Email: cipd@cipd.co.uk
Website: www.cipd.co.uk
Incorporated by Royal Charter.
Registered Charity No. 1079797

Contents

List of Figures and Tables

Contributor Biographies

Jim Stewart is Professor of HRD at Coventry University. He is also chief examiner of learning and development for the CIPD as well as visiting panel chair and external moderator. Jim is chair of the university forum for HRD and author and co-editor of 16 books including, with Clare Rigg, *Learning and Talent Development*, also published by the CIPD.

Patricia Rogers is head of HRM and Organisation Behaviour and the HR Research and Consultancy Group at Coventry University. She is a Fellow of the CIPD and a member of a US forum developing HRM standards. Prior to working at Coventry University she was head of Business School in further education and worked in management and HRM in industry.

Jill Ashley-Jones is an accredited executive, leadership coach and coach supervisor with a particular interest in the development of women leaders and the use of shamanic practices within a coaching context. Formerly a public sector executive director in HRM/OD, she is now a part-time lecturer at Coventry University delivering on the CIPD postgraduate programmes.

Susan Barnes is programme manager and lecturer for CIPD programmes at City College, Coventry, and part-time lecturer in HRM at Coventry University. She is a Chartered Member of the CIPD and has been an HR and management consultant in the public and voluntary sectors. Research interests include mentoring, performance management, recruitment and selection and management development.

Terrence Wendell Brathwaite is a programme manager (MBA degree in Global Development and Comparative Law) and strategic support co-ordinator (teaching, learning, quality and student experience) at Coventry University's Business School, where he lectures and publishes in international and comparative employment law, international HRM and organisational behaviour. He is also a published senior Creative Arts Psychotherapist, an accredited clinical supervisor and executive coach in private practice, and a chartered marketeer, a certified mediator, an IiP adviser and a professional member of the Society of HRM (USA).

Gary Connor is a senior lecturer at Coventry University. Prior to working at Coventry, Gary spent over 20 years working in the steel industry. These 20 years coincided with a revolution of organisational design within manufacturing. He is currently studying for his PhD; his key areas of research are organisational fit, absenteeism and student assessment methods.

Amanda Lee has 15 years' experience as a generalist HRM practitioner, gained within the NHS, construction and retail sectors, and over 10 years' experience managing and delivering management and HR programmes at undergraduate and postgraduate level. She is currently programme manager for full-time MA HRM and MSc International HRM programmes at Coventry University. Her research interests include work–life balance and issues associated with remote/home working, and she is currently exploring issues associated with academic employees following the introduction of location-independent working contracts as part of her doctoral research.

Rosalind Maxwell-Harrison is an executive and performance coach with a background in public sector leadership programmes. She has a particular interest in working with doctors in training and is a coaching provider for the NHS East Midlands Deanery and the NHS East Midlands Leadership Academy. She is an accredited coach supervisor and part-time lecturer at Coventry University, in addition to her private practice .She delivers CIPD postgraduate programmes.

Michael McFadden began his career completing an apprenticeship with Rolls-Royce's Aero Engines Division. He subsequently held teaching and management roles in further education before moving into curriculum development with the Open College Network. Michael's experience of higher education was initially as a project a manager before moving into business development for Coventry University. In this role he developed successful partnerships with HR practitioners from national employers in the design and management of their organisations' training programmes. He is currently a lecturer at Coventry University for the Department for Human Resources and Organisational Behaviour.

Sharon McGuire's work experience in a hospital and an international environment led to her passion for equity in the workplace. Following the completion of an MA in industrial relations she worked through policies for expatriates, defining their roles and recruiting, hiring and managing the redundancy processes worldwide. This also encompassed working with many countries in shaping organisations' HRD, and understanding the differences at the micro and macro levels, before joining Coventry University. Her research interests lie at the intersection of sociology and HRM; this informs her current doctoral study, which investigates equality and the transition from education to work.

Michelle McLardy is a Chartered Member of the CIPD and a lecturer in HRM at Coventry University. She currently teaches various HR modules on several full- and part-time programmes such as the BA HRM degree, the CIPD Postgraduate Diploma in HRM and MA HRM. She is programme lead on the Intermediate CIPD qualification. Previous experience has included various roles within the private sector.

Ian McLean is a Chartered Fellow of the CIPD and a senior lecturer at Coventry University. He has over 40 years' practical business experience in both line management and HR as well as having run his own consultancy practice for 17 years, providing services for organisations as varied as FTSE-100 financial services organisations, retail, automotive and manufacturing. Ian lectures in leadership and management development topics for the HR/OB department.

Sophie Mills is a Chartered Fellow of the CIPD. She is programme manager for full-time postgraduate programmes within the HR and OB department at Coventry

University. She specialises in the areas of people and organisational development and is module leader for the CIPD-accredited Level 7 Organisation Design and Development, Learning and Talent Development modules. She is currently working towards a PhD, and her research involves the analysis of the relationship between critical reflection and emotion in doctoral students. Her other research interests include innovative approaches in teaching and learning, and action learning.

Graham Perkins is a PhD student at Plymouth University. His PhD is focused on how idea generation can best be enabled within SMEs. Alongside his studies Graham works as an HR consultant for a variety of organisations and has a broad spectrum of experience from learning and development projects through to facilitating and analysing staff surveys.

Krish Pinto is a lecturer in HRM and OB at Coventry University. Her main areas of interest include organisational development, organisational behaviour and management development with a special interest in the development of emotional intelligence in leaders, managers and practising HR professionals. Prior to starting at Coventry, Krish was an HR consultant and worked in senior HRM positions in the NHS.

Raymond Rogers is a senior lecturer at Coventry University and supports the teaching and development of accounting and statistics on the CIPD postgraduate and Master's programmes. Prior to working at Coventry University he worked in industry in operations and supply chain management. His current research interests include financial performance models and HRM in the NHS.

Dalbir Sidhu works as a consultant in industry specialising in organisation development. She has a breadth of experience in the learning and development field, where she offers a solution-focused consultancy service which includes diagnosing, designing and implementing a wide range of formal and informal learning and development interventions to meet organisational needs. In addition to her progressive career in industry, Dalbir is a part-time lecturer and module leader at Coventry University, delivering various modules on the CIPD postgraduate programmes.

Dr Kirsten Stevens is a senior lecturer in HRM, teaching at both undergraduate and postgraduate level. Kirsten is joint programme manager for the CIPD-accredited postgraduate diploma in HRM/HRD. Prior to becoming an academic, Kirsten undertook a variety of HR practitioner roles both within the public and private sectors.

Dr Carol Woodhams is a Senior Lecturer in Human Resource Management at the University of Exeter Business School. She has held a number of positions within CIPD including National Examiner for Designing and Delivering Training, External Moderator for the Advanced Qualification and Editor of the flexible learning materials at Intermediate and Advanced levels. She has previously taught at Plymouth University and Manchester Metropolitan University. Her specialist teaching subjects are employee resourcing and equality and diversity. Her research topics include studies of gender and disability discrimination in the UK and China. Prior to her academic career she held posts in management in the hospitality sector.

Acknowledgements

We would like to thank a number of people without whom this book would not exist. At the CIPD, Heidi Partridge and especially Katy Hamilton deserve our gratitude for their patience and support. We also thank our co-editors of the series: Stephen Taylor and Carol Woodhams at Exeter University. Our contributors, who are all colleagues at the Department of HR/OB at Coventry Business School, are thanked for their support of the project and not taking our increasingly strident demands for final versions of chapters too seriously. We would like to give a special thanks to Barbara Madzima, Leila Shokoufandeh, Yu Fu and Simranjit Bhanwra who supported the department by gathering information. And finally, we both thank our families for their patience and support. Domestic duties will now be resumed.

Developing People and Organisations: An Overview

Jim Stewart and Patricia Rogers

INTRODUCTION AND OVERVIEW

Developing and managing people is a theme in the CIPD Intermediate-level qualifications. Those qualifications are composed of a number of units, or modules, which can be studied singly and lead to a CIPD award, or in combination to lead to a CIPD Certificate or Diploma qualification. These combinations may be offered by providers such as universities or colleges and those courses may lead to an award of the provider which is accredited by the CIPD. Certificate- and diploma-level qualifications can be themed as either Human Resource Management (HRM) or Human Resource Development (HRD), and the CIPD applies 'rules of combination' to determine whether the qualification will be themed and so named as either HRM or HRD. This book is intended to support learning associated with the modules required for HRD-themed qualifications.

The book is one of a series of three which between them cover all of the CIPD Intermediate-level units and related qualifications. Here, we introduce the subject and the chapters of this particular book.

We should perhaps say a brief word at this point on the term 'HRD'. It is used infrequently in the CIPD units – for example, only one has the term in its title. Many other units, such as those on organisation development and coaching and mentoring, are directly related to HRD. Even though it is a term more commonly used by academics than by practitioners, you will find it used throughout the book. It can be assumed in this context to be synonymous with terms used more frequently in practice such as 'learning and development'.

PURPOSE, AIMS AND OBJECTIVES

Our purpose, then, in producing this book is clear and unambiguous: it is to help learning and teaching of CIPD intermediate units associated with the HRD stream in professional qualifications. Following good practice in supporting learning and teaching, we also list below some more specific aims. These will hopefully help to guide you through the book and also provide a basis for assessing whether the book is successful in achieving the overall purpose. These additional aims are to:

- introduce and explore concepts associated with, and relevant to, the syllabus of the CIPD Intermediate HRD-related modules
- provide a practical and accessible exposition of key theories informing the professional practice of HRD at Intermediate level
- provide a useful and usable resource to support the teaching and learning of HRD as an academic subject at Intermediate level

- facilitate and support a critically informed examination of the theory and practice of HRD.

It is worth expanding on these aims. They deliberately suggest a clear connection with the CIPD syllabus for each of its Intermediate level modules. The book is intended to cover the ground indicated in the CIPD module descriptors. However, this does not mean that those descriptors have determined the content, or that we have provided either *all* the information or *only* information relevant to each syllabus. The book has an openly declared purpose of preparing students for assessment. This purpose is achieved, however, by our interpretation, and that of our contributors, of the descriptors in terms of the *key* or *critical* concepts, and in terms of the understanding required to utilise and apply those concepts in professional practice.

This raises a second important point about the aims of the book. While the final aim explicitly assumes a separation between theory and practice, we do not believe such a separation is either valid or useful. We share the CIPD philosophy that professional certification must mean the ability to practise in the profession. A key purpose of the book is therefore to help equip individuals to meet the expectations placed upon them in performing specialist roles in developing people and organisations.

A final point on the CIPD connection is to recognise that the book is intended to have relevance to, and application in, the study of HRD as a subject. This means that its content is not restricted to the CIPD modules but is intended to have value in any module concerned with developing people and organisations. Particular chapters will, of course, have greater or lesser relevance to particular modules. In this book, each chapter is associated with a specific CIPD Intermediate module. However, the book is intended to support the teaching and learning of HRD as a subject rather than being restricted to one specific syllabus or qualification.

Two more points are worth considering. First, we have attempted to create a resource which is valuable both to those teaching and to those learning HRD. Although the book is written primarily for those learning to practise, we believe and hope that the content includes some insights and perspectives which will give pause for thought on the part of experienced teachers of the subject. The final point to make about the aims of the book is that we and our contributors wish to encourage alternative paradigms and perspectives to be applied to support critical thinking about the subject.

We are now able to articulate some clear objectives. Again reflecting what is considered good practice in HRD and, indeed, in teaching and learning practices in higher education, these are expressed in terms of what readers can expect to be able to achieve through using the book:

- to explain and analyse the organisational context of HRD practice
- to describe, compare and critically evaluate a range of theories, concepts and methods related to organisation and individual development

- to describe, compare and critically evaluate a range of approaches to, and methods of applying, HRD in practice
- to identify, explain and critically evaluate the connections between HRD theory and practice.

READERSHIP

It will be clear by now that a primary readership for the book is anyone studying HRD-related Intermediate modules as part of a CIPD qualification programme. This includes those studying in universities which provide their own CIPD-accredited courses, as well as those studying for CIPD qualifications in approved centres. However, the book has not been written exclusively for this audience and other readers are envisaged and expected. In fact, all those who 'study' HRD constitute the intended readership. It is, however, possible to identify some specific audiences.

It seems to be an increasing trend to include HRD in undergraduate studies. We have in mind all potential readers at undergraduate level, whether studying CIPD-accredited or approved courses, or not. As already stated, the book is concerned with application. Its value to undergraduate studies therefore requires that they can relate personal experience of work organisations to the content. This experience does not have to be in professional roles. However, the book has not been written to consider the subject at a purely or exclusively conceptual level, and achievement of its aims and objectives assumes and requires regular interaction between reader and text based on personal experience.

Although CIPD Intermediate level equates to second- or final-year undergraduate studies, there are a number of postgraduate programmes to which the book is relevant. Perhaps the most obvious of these is a Diploma in Management Studies and MBA programmes which include HR and/or HRD content, either as mandatory or elective modules. The book assumes no prior specialist knowledge or experience and is therefore appropriate for non-specialist readers. In addition, many universities offer well-established Master's degrees in the professional areas of HRM and HRD. Some of these specialist programmes may require CIPD membership at the point of entry, and this book is aimed primarily at those studying for such membership. However, the book is valuable for students on specialist and post-CIPD Master's programmes who are not specialist development practitioners and may not have studied the subject at CIPD level.

A final group of readers is professional practitioners not involved in a formal course of study. It is not assumed that all readers are students, and the practice orientation of the book makes the book relevant to practitioners. We hope the book reaches such a readership.

STRUCTURE AND CONTENT

The book follows a straightforward structure. Each chapter is focused on a single CIPD module and generally adopts the title of the module. Thus, chapters of most relevance to a particular course and/or reader are easily identifiable. We have not assumed that all courses include all modules, and so each chapter can be viewed in isolation. This does mean that there is some overlap of content between chapters – for example, on evaluation of learning and development. This is necessary to meet the key content of each individual CIPD module. So readers can be assured that their needs related to specific individual modules are met. However, we have minimised overlap as far as possible and have also signposted where additional content on a specific topic can be found in different chapters.

The order of modules and chapters progresses logically. We begin in the first four chapters with organisation-level topics such as organisation design and organisational development and then move to where organisation and individual level meet though needs for development and coaching and mentoring. We then move on to more contextual factors such as contemporary developments in HRD, knowledge management and improving performance. This is intended to provide a meaningful structure for those who will use the book in its entirety in their studies, or who simply wish to further understanding of all elements of HRD. The book's concluding chapter-as well as attempting to draw together some threads-speculates about future directions for the subject and the profession.

There is also a common structure to the chapters. Chapters 1 to 7 have a set of common features. These include the following:

- introduction
- learning objectives
- main content
- reflective activities
- case studies
- summary
- final case study with discussion questions
- further reading and references.

The introduction sets the scene for the chapter and outlines its main purpose. This is then translated into a set of specific objectives. Readers are encouraged to check and assess whether these are achieved as they work through a chapter. The main content of each chapter is interspersed with reflective activities. These are designed to encourage exploration and application of the concepts discussed in the main content. They are also, in some cases, sequential and cumulative; that is, in any given chapter, the third activity (for example) will assume that the first and/or second activities have been completed. However, they are not sequential and cumulative in terms of the book, although the main content is intended to have that feature. Chapters adopt some variation in these activities with some including reflective questions as well as application tasks. All chapters require some form of reader interaction with the content and this interaction also commonly requires some interaction with others, e.g. fellow students or work colleagues.

Completing the activities within each chapter is essential if the chapter objectives are to be achieved. It is possible to read the main content and ignore the activities. However, this will not serve or help to meet any of the purposes of the book. Many activities refer to 'your organisation' or 'an organisation you know/are familiar with'. This can be taken to mean any organisation; it is not necessary to be employed by the chosen organisation. As indicated above, many activities also refer to 'a colleague', sometimes with an instruction that this means a work colleague. In the absence of this instruction, 'a colleague' is meant to indicate someone with whom you are studying and who also carries out the activity. If either of these presents a problem (that is, you are not a student and/or you do not have work colleagues) then any other person can and will serve a valuable purpose. The important and critical requirement is that you *discuss* your responses to activities with some other person who will have views on the topic.

Each chapter closes with a summary of the main arguments and an application case study. All case studies present actual scenarios experienced by professional practitioners. The intention is to encourage identification with the problems and issues encountered in professional practice. The purpose of the case studies is to facilitate discussion at least of applying the concepts examined in the chapter. They also serve the purpose of illustrating the practical implications of theoretical concepts. Some chapters end with a final case study. These are intended to give more life to the concepts discussed in the chapter. All forms of in-text activities serve a similar purpose and so those chapters not containing a final case study should not be seen as being less concerned with practice.

It will be clear that reflective activities and case studies are an essential and integral component of the book. They are certainly important in achieving the objectives of the book and those of individual chapters. The book as a whole has a logical structure and sequence. But, particular parts and/or combinations of chapters may have specific relevance for particular modules or courses of study or issues being faced in practice. So, we expect that readers will make their own sense of the book as they develop their own understanding of the subject.

A FINAL THOUGHT

We have encouraged readers to evaluate the worth of the book and provide features such as learning objectives to help do so. This is because evaluating the worth of investment in HRD is considered good practice. However, it is harder to find that element of good practice being applied than other elements. That is no doubt one reason why evaluation is included in the indicative content of more than one CIPD module; the argument supporting that feature is probably that the more good practice can be encouraged, the better. Evaluation is clearly of relevance to all topics covered in this book. So, as a final comment we wish to encourage readers to have evaluation at the forefront of your mind as you read this book. Evaluate the book and its content but also think about how you might evaluate the methods, techniques and procedures you read about if you applied them in your professional practice.

CHAPTER 1

Organisational Design

Gary Connor, Michael McFadden and Ian McLean

CHAPTER CONTENTS

- Introduction
- What are organisations?
- The evolution of organisation design theory
- Common forms of organisation structure
- Factors influencing organisation design
- Organisational culture
- Other internal organisational factors
- Organisation design models and tools
- The role of HR in organisation design
- Summary

KEY LEARNING OUTCOMES

By the end of this chapter, you will be able to:

- Understand the historical and theoretical basis of organisation design and the relationship between organisational elements and the business strategy.

- Understand the key factors to be considered in the design of organisations and the implications for the management and development of people and resources.

INTRODUCTION

Organisation design is not simply about mapping out an organisational structure, but also about how the organisation is aligned with all other aspects, functions, processes and strategies within the business. When looking at organisation design, the context within which the business exists must be taken into consideration.

The chapter begins by discussing what an organisation actually is before looking at how organisation designs have evolved over time. The chapter then considers various forms of design, factors that influence design, and a range of tools and models you can use to understand how organisation design fits together. The chapter concludes by investigating what role HRM plays within organisation design.

Throughout the chapter there are questions and case studies. We strongly urge you to take time out to try to answer the questions. Only by doing so can you fully understand the complexity and relevance of organisation design.

WHAT ARE ORGANISATIONS?

Whether we are aware of it or not, we have at some stage in our lives belonged to at least one organisation. We also can quite easily identify organisations. These organisations can be international (e.g. the World Bank), national (e.g. Parliament and the National Health Service), or local (e.g. a local charity). But what exactly is an organisation? Most of us would consider it to be composed of a number of people, but would we say it also consists of the buildings that the group of people use?

Naturally there are many definitions. McNamara (2012) suggests that 'in its simplest form' an organisation is 'a person or group of people intentionally organised to accomplish an overall, common goal or set of goals'. Note that this definition accepts that a single person can be an organisation and that the critical factor is that there are *intentionally* established goals. Katz (1966, p18) also recognises the goal-oriented aspect of organisations but suggests that an organisation comprises 'a group of people who work interdependently toward some purpose'. There is no room for a single individual here; individuals are grouped together working with each other. Huczynski and Buchanan (2007, p6) introduce another condition to the definition: one of *control*. For Huczynski and Buchanan, organisations are 'a social arrangement for achieving controlled performance in pursuit of collective goals'. So we have a group of individuals working together to achieve a particular goal, and the engagement of the individuals is not indiscriminate but co-ordinated in a controlled manner. The engagement then has structure; it has design.

A further consideration in defining an organisation is that it usually does not exist in isolation but engages with an external environment. Even a small community organisation often has money placed in a bank; the use of a room as a venue to meet; and possibly interaction with other community groups. The relation with the environment is central in Daft's definition of an organisation. He states that 'an organisation cannot exist without interacting with customers, suppliers, competitors, and other elements of the external environment' (Daft 2007, p11).

We can thus arrive at a working definition to assist us in understanding what an organisation is. We can say that organisations 'are (1) social entities that (2) are goal-directed, (3) are designed as deliberately structured and co-ordinated activities systems, and (4) are linked to the external environment' (Daft 2007, p10).

REFLECTIVE ACTIVITY

1   Is the family unit an organisation? If so, what objective does it have, and how does it engage with the environment?

2   Identify two organisations to which you have belonged. Do they have all four features identified by Daft above?

3   Can you think of two organisations which have not been 'deliberately structured' or which do not have 'co-ordinated activities systems'?

THE EVOLUTION OF ORGANISATION DESIGN THEORY

WEBER'S BUREAUCRACY

We saw in the previous section that organisations are deliberately structured and have design. A particular design of an organisation might be described as bureaucratic – that is to say, it has *bureaucracy*. What do we mean by this, and how does it relate to organisation design? Our understanding of bureaucracy generally comes to us through the work of the German sociologist Max Weber (1864–1920), who uses the term in relation to his discussion of authority. Weber explores why it is that we obey other people and suggests three types of authority: traditional, charismatic and legal-rational.

It is the legal-rational authority that applies to bureaucracy. This type of authority depends not on tradition, as in the case of monarchy, or on the charismatic qualities of a person. The reason we tend to obey this authority is because it has been defined, structured and limited by certain rules designed to achieve specific goals. Thus, within a company managers ought to be obeyed because they occupy the 'office' of a manager, and there are restrictions to the extent of their authority, which has been rationally determined. This would be a different situation from, for example, a young child who obeys the parents purely because they are the parents and because parents are traditionally obeyed.

Legal-rational authority tends to co-exist within certain types of organisations referred to by Weber as having 'bureaucratic administration'. What he means by this is that organisations develop robust processes, structure and rules for workers to follow. It is these features that, when they are put together in an organisation, we refer to as bureaucracy. Weber then goes on to say that organisations adopting the 'bureaucratic administration' type are 'superior to any other form in precision, in stability, in the stringency of its discipline, and in its reliability' (Weber 1947, p337). Moreover, he suggests that the capturing of technological knowledge is the 'source' of the bureaucratic administration. In other words, following industrialisation, developing organisations increased the number of managerial workers who were responsible for capturing, measuring and evaluating work practices. This new knowledge needed to be formulated in a structured way so that organisational processes could be followed, measured and understood. This in turn facilitated an element of control, which in Weber's view contributes to the efficiency of the organisation. Thus for Weber the most effective design for an organisation is one where its structure is bureaucratic. It is this structure that allows greater control of the organisation and in turn leads to greater efficiencies.

TAYLOR AND SCIENTIFIC MANAGEMENT

Frederick Taylor (1856–1915) had considerable personal experience of manufacturing organisations in the USA having served an apprenticeship as a machinist before moving on to become a shop superintendent in the 1880s. He is considered the founder of what we now refer to as **'scientific management'**, which complements several aspects of Weber's rational-legal bureaucracy. From his experience Taylor became aware of the various ways in which workers engaged in the same or similar tasks. He noticed that some methods employed by the workers were more effective than others. If, then, an organisation wants to improve its efficiency, a way forward would be to adopt the most effective method in performing each particular task. It was Taylor's aim to discover what the most effective method in completing particular tasks would be through the use and application of principles of scientific enquiry (Taylor 1947).

Taylor's scientific method

Taylor outlined his scientific method setting out four principles:

1   The 'gathering in' of the knowledge from workers on how they do each task and formulating this into rules, laws and possible mathematical formulae.

2   'Scientifically selecting' the appropriate worker(s) for each task and providing any necessary skill development. For example, if the task requires a lot of manual work, an unfit individual would not be the best choice.

3   The bringing together of the 'gathered in' and the 'scientifically selected'. In other words, ensuring that the most appropriate individual is employed to do each particular task using the 'scientific' method that has now been discovered.

4   Increasing the size of the management workforce as a result of the observing, recording and planning of the work function.

Taylor provides an illustration of good shovelling from the Bethlehem Steel Corporation plant. Shovelling is, according to Taylor, a simple task. From this he concludes that the individual performing this task is of limited intellectual capability. This person would not be a position to work out the most effective way of shovelling. Taylor, however, points out that by methodically studying this task and then selecting able and capable individuals to do it, he will be able to improve the net output. He first selects a few individual workers to extract their knowledge. He then has managers conduct several 'experiments' in which they modified several factors such as the shape and size of the shovel. Next, he demonstrates that by varying the amount of coal on the shovel one could maximise the workers' final output. As much as 38 pounds, for example, would be too great, whereas 16 pounds would be too small; the optimal amount is 21½ pounds.

Taylor's work had a profound influence on work organisation in the early years of the twentieth century, his ideas being most notably adopted by the Ford Motor Company. The most obvious manifestation of these ideas comes in the form of the assembly line, where each worker is given a designated task to perform repeatedly and to maximum efficiency all day long (hence 'Fordism'). To this day there are organisations which have been described as operating on Fordist principles, notably fast-food restaurants and call centres.

TOM BURNS' MECHANISTIC AND ORGANISMIC STRUCTURE

Tom Burns' (1914–2002) brief account of the history of organisation design observes that industry continued to develop from the early crafts industries to the first factories. This development advanced further where organisations adopted a design which Burns refers to as the 'growth of bureaucracy within organisations'. In his observations this design was increasingly undermined by the need for organisations to meet new challenges. These challenges were varied and included a requirement for organisations to adapt to changes to their environment, such as technological changes. They also included the necessity of meeting the needs of consumers. From his observations he concluded that organisations were tending to fall into what he suggested were two 'ideal types' of organisational structure: mechanistic and organismic.

Mechanistic structure

This is characterised as an organisational structure in which job functions have been broken down into specialist tasks that are 'precisely defined'. Workers complete these tasks with little knowledge as to the overall product and are supervised by their immediate superiors. The management structure tends to be vertical whereby the person 'at the top' knows 'all about the company' and 'therefore knows exactly how the human resources should be properly disposed' (Burns 1963, p103). This organisation type adopts this form because of the relatively stable environmental conditions in which it operates and corresponds to the rational bureaucratic and scientific management form described above.

Organismic structure

Organismic (or 'organic') organisations, on the other hand, have adapted to meet unstable environmental conditions. Job functions are less easily defined and supervision is often horizontal or 'lateral'. Demarcation of the job function in this organisational type is blurred, so that many job responsibilities may have to be redefined to meet the changing environment in which the organisation operates. Knowledge and skills expertise are not assumed to reside with 'the boss' but are located anywhere across the organisation. The organisation structure is more open and complex, having to adapt to an unstable environment (Burns 1963, p104).

From Burns' point of view, unless we acknowledge and accept the increasing variables and complexities affecting organisations we will continue to adopt designs that are no longer 'fit for purpose' (Burns 1963). A bureaucratic/mechanistic structure, for example, may suit one type of organisation, but with complexity of technologies emerging and, increasingly, the external environmental impacting on organisations, it cannot meet all organisation designs.

In moving forward, then, we can see that earlier accounts of organisation design were perhaps adequate in explaining early industrial organisations. Today we need better explanations of organisation design which embrace the increasing complexity of markets, customers and technologies.

COMMON FORMS OF ORGANISATIONAL STRUCTURE

Although we now understand that organisational design is far more than simply creating a diagrammatic structure, it is in this way that we most easily recognise the outcomes of design. Following on from the work of Weber (1947), a number of alternative classic types of organisational structure have arisen. These types should not be seen as sequential, but as a range of alternatives which are the subject of deliberate management choice.

All of these types of organisation reflect what might be described as a structuralist view of organisation design, offering a clear chain of command and reflecting in many ways the military model of a hierarchical organisation.

FUNCTIONAL ORGANISATIONS

This type of structure reflects the different functions present within organisations. Thus the marketing, finance, sales, production, research and HR specialties each have their own sub organisation which is (usually) represented at board level. This is shown diagrammatically in Figure 1.1.

Figure 1.1 A typical functional organisational structure

The size of each department varies according to business needs. For example, most manufacturing organisations have a large production department compared to the size of other functions. Some organisations merge sales and marketing. The general point is that such a structure allows employees with specialist skills to deploy these to their best abilities.

Functional organisational structures work best when the organisation or business unit is self-contained, such as a small company or an autonomous unit, such as a subsidiary company. The downside of this type of structure is the easy development of a 'silo mentality', by which issues escalate rather than enabling lateral communication to be brought to bear in order to solve problems.

GEOGRAPHICAL ORGANISATIONS

As organisations expand – particularly when they develop their operations across national boundaries – it is common to observe an organisational structure which reflects this. There is thus a distinct variant on the functional organisation, as shown diagrammatically in Figure 1.2.

Geographical organisational structures work best when local decision-making is required to tailor the product or service to a regional market. For example, a brewery company expanding into an overseas market would have to take local tastes into account.

Figure 1.2 A typical geographical organisational structure

For an organisation which has a strong brand identity where consistency of offer is at a premium, however, geographical organisation requires considerable control. This can depress local initiative, or at the very least, create tensions between the head office and the branches.

ORGANISATION BY PRODUCT

There are many examples of structures which reflect the product line(s) or services which the organisation offers. For example, a passenger transport company may be organised into bus services, coach tours and package holiday products, each with their own dedicated operations. This is shown diagrammatically in Figure 1.3.

Note that some aspects of the functional organisation still remain in this example, but the dominant model is by product line.

Figure 1.3 A typical product-based organisational structure

Product-based organisations work best when there is a need to promote entrepreneurial behaviour. Each of the business areas pursues the development of its products around the organisation's core competencies. One disadvantage of such a structure is that rivalry can develop and a distinct 'pecking order' can be discerned – for example, between coach and bus drivers (Blake 2010). This rivalry can spill over into competition for resources between product groups.

ORGANISATION BY CUSTOMER/MARKET

Examples exist of organisations in which the structure most closely reflects the markets in which they operate. For example, some organisations rely heavily on a small number of important customers who account for most or all of their business. Automotive component manufacturers often organise themselves in this way, with perhaps a dedicated production area, or even a separate plant which produces only for Toyota, another for BMW, another for Tata etc, as shown in Figure 1.4.

Figure 1.4 A typical customer-market-based organisational structure

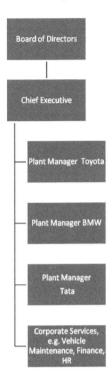

Customer-facing organisations have attracted considerable approval in recent decades, partly spurred by such influential works as *In Search of Excellence* (Peters and Waterman 1982). Being close to the customer and able to respond quickly to their changing demands requires an organisation to uphold the primacy of the customer relationship and give autonomy to local staff to make deals and decisions. Customer-facing structures work less well in organisations where a consistent service delivery against tight contractual requirements is paramount, such as a university.

MATRIX STRUCTURE

A matrix structure is one which sets out to reconcile the competing demands of customers and the need for a strong bureaucratic and efficient functional presence. This type of structure is commonly observed in organisations which are highly project-based – for example, civil engineering companies.

Obviously, there are greater tensions between the requirements of different projects and functions, but the idea is to enable employees to locate themselves within a strongly multi-project environment. This is shown diagrammatically in Figure 1.5.

Figure 1.5 A typical matrix organisation

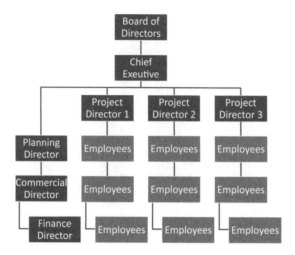

Matrix structures work best in project-based environments, such as engineering and construction, where each project runs for a long period. Each team involved can concentrate their energies upon their designated project, drawing across the range of central services as needed. The major drawback of the matrix design is that everyone appears to have two bosses, which can (and frequently does) lead to role conflict and tensions.

It is important to stress that the common types of organisational structure described above can co-exist within one corporation at one time. For example, a multinational may operate different organisational structures in different markets, or a manufacturer may have one dedicated customer-oriented plant while running the rest of the business on functional lines.

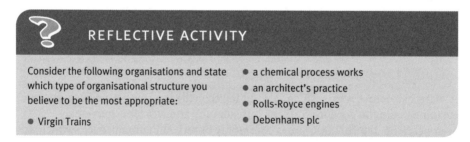

REFLECTIVE ACTIVITY

Consider the following organisations and state which type of organisational structure you believe to be the most appropriate:

- Virgin Trains
- a chemical process works
- an architect's practice
- Rolls-Royce engines
- Debenhams plc

FACTORS INFLUENCING ORGANISATION DESIGN

A number of elements have to be co-ordinated by managers in order to design an effective organisation which can satisfy its overall purpose and objectives. The effective orchestration of these can have a significant impact on the success or otherwise of the organisation. At the heart of this process lies the relationship between organisational **strategy** and organisation design.

'Strategy and structure are jointly determined by more fundamental variables like the firm's technology (economies of scale and scope), the availability of efficient projects, and the profitability of successful projects' (Berkovitch *et al* 2010).

BUSINESS STRATEGY

Organisational strategy is the articulation of the vision, mission and competitive position of a business. The concept also applies to not-for-profit organisations. The whole organisation has a strategy but, in a number of organisations, parts of it will also have a strategy. It therefore follows that the design of an organisation should serve the overall strategic purpose. For example, if a retail organisation wishes to develop a new product line, people and resources must be deployed to achieve this, and an impact will be felt on the organisational structure.

The steps to realising a strategy is summarised in Figure 1.6.

Figure 1.6 An iterative approach to organisational strategy

1 **Mission and vision**

2 **Develop strategy**

3 **Organise and resource**

4 **Execute**

5 **Review and evaluate**

Mission and vision

The mission of any organisation is an articulation of the common purpose which informs the organisation's members and binds them together in the enterprise. Many organisations express this in the form of a mission statement, as a way of communicating to both employees and other **stakeholders** the purpose of the organisation. In some cases, the mission remains in the head of a few people and, if not shared, can lead to confusion and conflict later on.

The vision differs from the mission in that it is future-oriented, setting out a description of where the organisation will be in a defined number of years. The vision statement will probably also address the look and feel of the organisation. If a chief executive does not have a sense of mission and vision, the organisation will probably remain mired in the past without a sense of forward movement.

George H. W. Bush (US President 1989–93) was quoted as saying that he had trouble with 'the vision thing', and was one of the few incumbent presidents in US history to fail to gain re-election to the White House.

In simple terms, the mission should answer the question 'What do we do?' and the vision should answer 'Where do we want to get to in *n* years' time?'

Develop strategy

If the vision is about *where* an organisation wants to get to, then business strategy is all about *how* it gets there. Strategy is not simply long-term planning – it represents the means by which the aspirations of the organisation are realised. Bloisi (2007, pp91–2) summarises this as follows:

'Strategies pertain to those destiny-shaping decisions concerning:

- the choice of technologies on which products and services are based
- the development and release of new products and services
- the processes for producing products and services
- the way products are marketed, distributed and priced
- the ways in which organisations respond to rivals.'

The decisions listed above drive the sub strategies of the organisation – i.e. the marketing strategy, the customer-service strategy, the product-development strategy, the financing strategy and the people-resourcing and development strategy.

Organising and resourcing

This stage is all about the realisation of the strategy. One key output is the design of an organisational structure in order to fulfil its strategic plans. A series of example structures is shown below, but at this stage it is important to remember that strategy should drive organisational structure.

Execution

Self-evidently, execution of strategy is about action and making things happen at all levels of the organisation. It is also the time when the first effects of the strategic plan are seen and therefore feedback loops and management information systems should form an essential part of the execution of strategy.

Review and evaluation

The vision, mission and strategy should be subject to periodic review. This should be done firstly to review **organisational performance** against the goals which the organisation has set; secondly, to ensure that there is still consistency between vision, mission and strategies; and thirdly, to ensure that the organisational structures and systems are still fit for purpose. Such reviews can also lead to a reorganisation in order to maintain the momentum of the organisation.

EXTERNAL ENVIRONMENT

Strategy, as described above, cannot exist within a vacuum. Continuous scanning and review of the environment within which the organisation operates is an essential contributor to organisation design.

A key tool for scanning the environment is known as PESTLE analysis. PESTLE is an acronym for:

- Political
- Economic
- Social
- Technological
- Legal
- Environmental.

The analysis, which can be done by an individual but is better done by a group, consists of reviewing each of these factors in so far as it affects the organisation. PESTLE is also used to generate ideas of opportunities and threats which face the organisation. For example, a solar power manufacturer may find that its sales are affected by government policy on electricity feed-in tariffs.

Alongside environmental scanning, organisations should regularly carry out stakeholder analysis, both when discussing strategy and also when a major project is being developed. Stakeholders can be defined as any individual, group or body who has an interest in the organisation's success. Stakeholders are not confined to owners or shareholders but include employees, suppliers, customers, unions, government (both local and central and agencies) and partner organisations.

Stakeholder analysis is a matter of:

- listing each stakeholder
- identifying what the stakeholders' needs are in relation to the organisation
- identifying the extent to which the stakeholders' needs are currently met
- making decisions about how to close the gap (including whether it is viable to do so)
- considering the organisation design and resourcing implications of closing the gap(s)
- taking action.

 REFLECTIVE ACTIVITY

Consider the university or institution in which you study. Carry out a stakeholder analysis as described above. What changes in the organisation design of this institution would you recommend?

ORGANISATIONAL CULTURE

WHAT IS 'ORGANISATIONAL CULTURE'?

Schein (1990) defines **organisational culture** as having three key elements.

The everyday cultural manifestations of organisational culture are described as 'artefacts'. Cultural artefacts are diverse and can include staff facilities, the availability of car parking spaces (and who gets them!) or modes of mutual greeting in speech. Essentially, artefacts can be seen or heard.

Norms are less obvious, but examples include whether meetings always start and finish on time, methods of communication (e.g. face-to-face, telephone, email) and whether there is an expectation that colleagues will be available outside normal working hours.

Values are hardest of all to identify, although in recent times organisations have been more overt in the publication of their values. However, in certain cases the publication of values creates tensions if employees perceive that they are not being adhered to by management. In connection with this, Argyris (1980) distinguishes between what he calls 'espoused theory', which is the value set declared publicly by management, and 'theory-in-action', which is how management actually behaves.

Handy's cultural typology

Handy (1999) identified four main types of organisational culture: power, role, task and person.

Power cultures are typical in small entrepreneurial companies, although they are certainly not confined to them. Such organisations tend to be dominated by one individual or a small group. Handy likened this type of culture to a spider's web, the owner/manager or entrepreneur in the centre, controlling the organisation by the exercise of power. In start-up companies this is not necessarily a bad thing, but the persistence of such a culture can be a brake on the organisation's development.

Role cultures correspond quite closely to the functional organisation referred to above. Handy likened these to a Greek temple, in which each column represents one of the functions, and where the role of senior management is to co-ordinate the efforts of the various functions. Such cultures are highly procedural and can be very efficient at dealing with business in a mature organisation, including the public sector. The drawback of such a culture is what is commonly referred to as a 'silo mentality' in which the different functions of the business tend to see things their own way, and procedures and rules are continually referred to in order to resolve the inevitable disputes. Such organisational cultures are rarely agile in responding to customer needs.

Task cultures most closely resemble the matrix organisation referred to above. The task culture can be likened to a network of connections in which the delivery of project or task requirements is the overriding concern. Such a culture enables considerable sharing of ideas and internal mobility, although it can be difficult for someone coming from a role culture to adjust to one in which they report to multiple leaders.

Person cultures can be likened to a cluster, where reporting lines are muted compared to the importance of key individuals. Although rare, this culture occurs when individual (non-management) employees of the organisation are of particular value for their professional skills. Person cultures tend, therefore, to arise in professional practices such as law or architecture.

 The trouble with Harry

CASE STUDY

Harry Welsh had worked in the buying function of a major retailer for some years before seeing an opportunity to acquire one of its struggling suppliers. Harry was a great deal-maker who was outstanding in his ability to negotiate contracts, both with his former employer and other retailers.

The business grew and Harry took on more staff to service the contracts he had negotiated. However, as the owner-manager of the business, he always kept things close to his chest, even from other directors of the company. Despite repeated requests from his staff for more autonomy and trust, Harry continued to pull all the strings. Whenever there was a need for training or staff performance

management, Harry's attention would always be distracted by any communication from a customer, with which he always insisted on dealing personally. In effect, Harry had made himself indispensable.

Eventually, Harry and his business partner sold out to a larger group, having never made the step to growing the company – and its people – to their full potential.

1   Consider which type of culture was at work here, and what culture might have been more appropriate in order to grow the business.

Tuckman – group dynamics

Organisational culture is rarely static. The very nature of organisations, especially in the twenty-first century, means that the inflow and outflow of individuals constantly causes the organisation's culture to change, sometimes imperceptibly, sometimes dramatically.

Tuckman (1965) postulated a series of stages of group development. Tuckman's original concept was that groups go through four key stages in their development: 'forming, storming, norming and performing', to which he later added a final stage known as 'adjourning'.

During the forming stage, group members tend to be very sociable and appear willing to work well together. This, however, can be a false consensus and as soon as the pressures begin, the group finds that the team spirit breaks down.

Arguments develop and conflict arises: hence the 'storming' name for that part of the process. The outcomes of the conflict produce a real consensus about how the group should proceed – i.e. the norms are articulated and agreed. Finally, the group is now in a position to perform.

The cultural web

Developed by Johnson and Scholes (1992), the cultural web is a diagnostic management tool for identifying the state of an organisation through six perspectives. Each perspective influences what Johnson and Scholes refer to as the organisational paradigm of the work environment. The proposition is that by analysing each of these perspectives, it is possible to take the cultural temperature of an organisation as a prelude to cultural change. The six factors in the cultural web are:

- *Stories* – Every organisation has its folk tales, often referring to past events, such as how the business was set up. Marks & Spencer, for example, has always told stories of how the business started in Leeds market as the Penny Bazaar.
- *Rituals and routines* – The day-to-day ways in which people go about their business in the organisation. Of particular importance here are the behaviours which management reward, and those which they prohibit.
- *Symbols* – Rather like Schein's cultural artefacts above, these are the visible manifestations of the organisation's culture, such as dress codes, quality of office furniture, and who gets what comforts in the office, such as coffee machines, etc.
- *Organisational structure* – Johnson and Scholes mean more here than simply the overt reporting lines in accordance with the organisational chart. This heading also refers to the unwritten lines of power and influence within the organisation.
- *Control systems* – This refers not only to financial controls but also to the systems for rewarding behaviour, and who decides how rewards are apportioned.
- *Power structures* – This category refers to the hidden and informal power structures within the organisation – who really wields the power?

International cultures

As organisations become more global in their reach, some significant work has been done on international business cultures. One key area of debate in this regard is that over *convergence v divergence*.

Convergence theorists argue that with the impact of information technology – most notably the Internet – business cultures are converging and the differences between national cultures pale into insignificance. They cite the case of the IBM executive in his blue suit who, like the Jesuit priest, is at home in any country.

Ranged against this theory are those who argue that national and regional business cultures are pervasive and influence those who enter them. In this respect, the work of Hofstede (1980) is seminal.

Geert Hofstede is a Dutch social psychologist who set out to identify and measure those factors which distinguish one national business culture from another. His research led him to create five indices of cultural norms, which are:

- *Power distance* – This refers to the degree of social distance between senior management and workforce. If there are many levels of management within the organisation, and little contact between those at the top and the bottom of the organisation, power distance can be said to be high.
- *Uncertainty avoidance* – This refers to the appetite for risk which is prevalent in any organisation. A high uncertainty avoidance culture is characterised by low risk-taking, and vice versa.
- *Individualism/collectivism* – This refers to the propensity of the culture to reward individual effort, as distinct from a collectivist approach. This has a clear bearing upon, for instance, reward systems in an organisation.
- *Masculinity/femininity* – This is probably the most controversial of Hofstede's indices: a 'masculine' culture is seen as macho, whereas a 'feminine' culture is seen as nurturing.
- *Long-term orientation* – This was added later to the other four indices, and probably the term needing least explanation. It refers to the distinction between those cultures (such as Japan) which place a premium on long-term investment, and others, such as the USA, where judgements are made on short-term results.

Hofstede took each of these indices and measured them using a survey of managers in one multinational organisation. From these results he discovered that there are regional clusters of business culture which make it easier for those from countries with similar cultures to do business with each other. For example, he identified a Scandinavian cluster which included Sweden, Norway, Denmark, Finland and, interestingly, his own native Holland. The similarities in this cluster set them apart from other clusters.

Critics of Hofstede point out that this represents a limitation in the research, and that it is dangerous to extrapolate these findings without further research. It is certain that there are some researchers who have assumed the veracity of Hoftsede's work to the point of stereotyping – for example, the article by Head *et al* (2010) on 'Global organisation structural design', which exhibits a high dependency on Hofstede and therefore implies a danger of stereotyping.

OTHER INTERNAL ORGANISATIONAL FACTORS

PROCESSES

The organisation's processes impact upon the choice of organisation design.

Midshires Galvanisers

CASE STUDY

Galvanising is a process first discovered in the eighteenth century by which zinc is bonded on to steel in order to increase the longevity of the artefact from which the steel is made. For example, every motorway has crash barriers which are galvanised, thus accounting for their dull pale grey colour.

At Midshires Galvanisers, every plant supports a number of processes: goods reception, stripping impurities, cleaning, pre-flux, immersion in molten zinc at 450ºC, fettling, and despatch. Each of these processes can be undertaken in one of two ways: either a group of workers can follow each piece of work from start to end and conduct all the processes; or each process is undertaken by a different group of workers. Because of the hazards associated with each process, a high level of training and expertise is required, and most galvanising works therefore organise their workforce by process. This is an example of a horizontal process, where each piece of work passes from employee to employee until it is finished.

However, to take the case of an interior design practice, each designer is responsible for each project, and may well see each piece of work 'end to end', from receiving the commission from the client to signing off on the final implementation of the design. This is much more akin to a project management approach and therefore requires a different organisational design from that of the galvanising works.

SYSTEMS

The **systems approach** to organisational design has already been described above. However, systems are also a key element in organisation design. Systems influence, and are influenced by, organisation design.

For example, the national education system can influence the way in which a school is organised. Year groups, subject groups, the division of labour between teaching, administration and senior management structures do not just occur – they are deliberate choices of organisation design by the governors and head teacher. In this way, external systems influence internal organisation.

PERFORMANCE MEASURES

Performance measures are another element in organisation design. After all, the purpose of organisation design is ultimately to improve the performance of the organisation.

There are many ways of measuring organisational performance. For many businesses, financial measures are key, although not exclusive to all other outputs. To quote Simons (2005), 'Organisation design demands the right performance measures. A good measure must be objective, complete, and be responsive to the efforts of the individual whose activities are being monitored. In addition, a measure must be clearly linked to economic value creation.'

TECHNOLOGY

One of the most powerful examples of the impact of technology has been the ease with which senior management can communicate with the workforce, eliminating the need for multiple tiers of management and leading to 'flattening' organisations. In a major piece of research using **data** from approximately 380 US firms, Brynjolfsson and Hitt (1998) found 'greater demand for IT in firms with greater decentralisation of decision rights (especially the use of self-managing teams), and greater investments in human capital, including training and screening by education. In addition, IT has a greater contribution to output in firms that adopt a more decentralised and human-capital-intensive work system.... These findings lend support to the idea that organisational practices are important determinants of IT demand and productivity.'

PHYSICAL ASPECTS

The physical aspects of organisation design – ergonomics, health and safety, well-being, environment and space – should not be overlooked. Depending on the organisation's mission and purpose, these factors may have a greater or lesser impact. Ongoing research demonstrates the effect of technological change, which has been an area of interest since the Tavistock Institute's work on the longwall technique of coal mining in the late 1940s.

For up-to-date advice on ergonomics and job design, see the International Labour Organization's website in the Further reading section.

PSYCHOLOGICAL ASPECTS OF ORGANISATION DESIGN

A range of psychological aspects mediates organisation design. These include the following.

Discretion and autonomy

This refers to the balance to be struck between delivering a consistent, standardised service to customers on the one hand and the degree of empowerment allowed to employees on the other. Much depends upon the service or product proposition to the customer. For example, a branch of McDonalds allows little employee discretion over the product range, whereas an engine designer such as Rolls-Royce offers a great deal of customer input and therefore needs to give its customer-facing staff sufficient discretion to respond to customer requirements.

Job satisfaction and the psychological contract

Job satisfaction is the term used to describe the degree of contentment which an individual has with his or her job. Much of this contentment (or otherwise) stems from the way in which the job is designed, which in turn impacts on organisation design. Thinking back to the work of Taylor, cited above, job satisfaction was imagined to be a result of the extrinsic rewards offered to workers in the form of pay. However, a far better educated twenty-first-century workforce seeks intrinsic satisfaction from the nature of the work itself, recognition, and a sense of achievement, not to mention opportunities for development which a job or an organisation can provide.

Related to job satisfaction is the **psychological contract**. This can be described as a set of unwritten rights and responsibilities which underpin the formal employment contract. These rights and responsibilities work both ways. For example, an employee expects to be treated with respect, to be offered reasonable facilities, and to be able to express his or her views without fear of management reprisal. Equally well, the organisation has a right to expect employees to give of their best while at work and to promote the interests of the organisation.

It is symptomatic of the psychological contract that it is rarely of much interest to either party until one side believes that it has been broken. When this occurs, a sense of betrayal ensues, which can damage or completely break down levels of trust. Such damage can adversely affect employee performance, and therefore organisational performance, remarkably quickly.

The implication for organisation design is that jobs should be designed in such a way that they provide appropriate levels of satisfaction. Attention must also be paid to specialisation or generalisation of skill. Organisation designers should ensure that any changes are carried out, as far as possible, in accordance with the psychological contract as well as with the formal one.

Commitment and employee engagement

Typically, organisations seek a certain level of commitment from their staff, depending on the organisation's strategy. A low-commitment organisation will expect high levels of labour turnover and invest minimally in training. A high-commitment organisation will act in the opposite way. Note, however, that some parts of the organisation may operate a high-commitment strategy while other parts operate a low-commitment strategy.

Employee engagement has aroused considerable interest in recent times and is promoted as a desirable state for organisations to attain. However, employee engagement is a contested topic. When the UK Government sponsored the Macleod Report (Macleod and Clarke 2009), the authors found more than 50 different definitions of employee engagement! To take just two examples, Alfes *et al* (2010) believe that employee engagement consists of a mix of intellectual, affective and social engagement with work. On the other hand, Macey and Schneider (2008) refer to state engagement, behavioural engagement and trait engagement. Many consultancy providers offer to measure levels of employee engagement as a prelude to consultancy **intervention** designed (usually) to increase employee engagement.

Whatever the levels of commitment and employee engagement, organisation designers need to take account of how their work will impact on these factors.

Working with others, communication, power and politics

Organisations are not – despite frequent rhetoric to the contrary – places where everyone uniformly agrees on the ends or the means. They are spaces in which different individuals and factions compete for their own agendas, and where alliances are formed and reformed in order to promote or defend these interests.

Communication plays a key role in helping to resolve some of these tensions, but organisation designers have to be aware of the range of power relationships which exist within the organisation and to develop their negotiation skills in order to achieve their aims and not be blown off course by factional interests.

A key skill here is networking. Networking within and between organisations is seen as an essential attribute in organisation design: 'Without a doubt, collaboration is the most important capability for any organisation to possess today' (Shuman and Twombly 2010, p1). However, as Shuman and Twombly go on to point out, 'Few executives believe their organisations are good at collaborating with other firms, or that they personally have a good understanding of how to create value in networks. By and large they generally understand that they must embrace collaborative networks – they just don't know how. Thus, at present there is a disconnect between what is being said and the reality of what is happening in many organisations. There is no doubt, however, that we are in a time of profound transformation in ways of working, creating value, structuring and managing organisations.'

ORGANISATION DESIGN MODELS AND TOOLS

Many attempts have been made over several decades to show how the factors referred to above can be integrated into an overarching view of organisation design. Such attempts usually take diagrammatic form and can be classified under three broad headings.

STATIC ORGANISATION DESIGN MODELS

These identify a range of factors which can be reviewed as influential on organisation design. As in Figure 1.7 below, such diagrams often position leadership at the centre, suggesting that the role of leadership is to orchestrate the various other factors in order to achieve organisational effectiveness.

Such models are often used by consultancy firms as an overview of organisation design, and each factor is then the subject of a specific diagnostic tool which sets out to identify the current state of the organisation in respect of each factor. Examples of this type of approach include Galbraith's (1995) star model and McKinsey's 7-S model (Waterman *et al* 1980).

Figure 1.7 A typical static organisation design model

DYNAMIC MODELS OF ORGANISATION DESIGN

Dynamic models view organisation design as a transformation process rather than as a series of factors to be orchestrated. The key input in most of these models is organisational strategy, and the key output is organisational performance. The key role of leadership is therefore more cybernetic, using strategy to steer the organisational performance through a range of factors. Examples of this type of model include Weisbord's (1976) six-box model and Burke and Litwin's (1992).

Figure 1.8 An outline dynamic model of

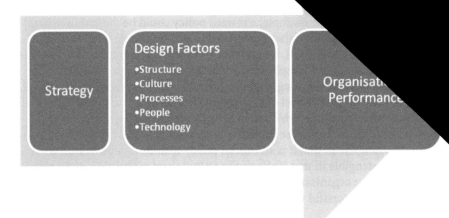

ECOLOGICAL MODELS OF ORGANISATIONAL DESIGN

The starting point for this category of diagrammatic view is that each organisation exists within, and is influenced by, its specific environment. It is also true to suggest that the organisation in turn influences its environment. Organisations can influence the educational environment by providing apprenticeships and placements for students. They can influence the built environment – for example, 'company towns' where they are the dominant employer. They can even, through lobbying activity, influence the legislative environment in which they operate, either directly or through trade associations. Examples of ecological views of organisations include McMillan's (2000) fractal web and the holonic enterprise (Ulieru *et al* 2002).

THE ROLE OF HR IN ORGANISATION DESIGN

Organisation design is a concept that consists of the business strategy, the business structures, processes, systems and performance measures. Many of these aspects are dealt with under the general headings of 'business management'. However, for an organisation to achieve its goals, ambitions, targets, or simply to survive, it requires input in the form of HR functions and processes.

Many organisations, particularly small and medium-sized enterprises (SMEs), do not have an HRM department. However, the same input of HR functions and processes still have to be implemented. So whatever the size, type or location of an organisation, the organisation design within any business requires support from a whole range of HR functions. For example, if an organisation chooses or finds itself controlled by bureaucracy, it will require specific and carefully chosen

ı is cascaded both
ıand, if the
ınication of a more

:t categories. Firstly,
d by HR and can be
: drafted up whereby
dard, they would
;ible aspects that HR
reward strategy,
; methods, which all
rchological aspects all
performance of the
ınd intangible
mal processes. In
ıotivation of employees
ible aspects have strong
gns.

relevant ɪɴɪ⊏
the intranet. In addition, the orgaııɪɒɑ⌐
n an intranet system. All
: business are detailed on
sum of money in a new
piece of IT software that allows employees to upload and share ideas and
information relevant to their job role. However, if employees are feeling
demotivated or are not engaged in their jobs, or do not feel committed to the
organisation, these investments are a waste of money. Employees will not share
their knowledge – they will not even bother looking at the intranet, and they will
often not even read their emails. So whatever processes or systems the business
has in place (tangible), employees need to be motivated to a level where they will
utilise properly (intangible) investments made by the organisation.

Another simple example would be if a company with a matrix structure had a
very important project with tight deadlines. Project management relies heavily on
teamwork, communication, knowledge-sharing and leadership (tangible
processes). It can be argued that how and to what extent these processes are
utilised depends on the attitude of each employee (intangible). An employee with
a positive attitude is far more likely to communicate and work with other team
members than an employee with a negative attitude.

Table 1.1 details the main HR functions and processes that nearly all
organisations have to consider. Some functions are quite obviously a formal
function or process – for example, creating a job description or a formal selection
process. One the other hand, a number of HR responsibilities fall under more
informal criteria. For example, there is no one single process or system that
would commit employees to the organisation. Similarly, there is no one formal
function that ensures that an employee's psychological contract is in place. These

employee attitudes are controlled by a combination of other HR functions. For instance, the reward package, the management style and the job design all have an impact on an employee's level of commitment.

So the column in Table 1.1 headed 'Formal process' indicates whether the HR function involves a tangible process that could be documented and audited to ensure compliance with the process.

The column headed 'Enabling others' refers to functions that affect an employee's attitude and/or behaviour (intangible). These intangible functions can be present within a tangible relationship.

The 'Outline' column identifies a basic description of what the function is intended to do.

The 'Link with OD' column indicates which OD components the function is *most* connected with. This column is subjective and should be viewed as such. It is arguable that most of the functions have a direct or indirect link with all of the components of OD.

To help you understand the importance of the some of these functions, think how an organisation would perform if these function were not in place.

REFLECTIVE ACTIVITY

● Consider how an organisation with a matrix structure would survive if employees refused to communicate and work with each other in teams.

1 What are the implications for an organisation that does not have clear job descriptions?

2 What are the implications for an organisation of having employees who are not committed, engaged or satisfied in their work?

3 What are the implications for an organisation that does not train or develop its employees?

Table 1.1 HR functions and processes

Facet of HR	Formal process	Enabling others	Outline	Link with OD
1 Communication	X	X	Ensure that employees are aware of organisation goals Correct and suitable information timely must be communicated to wherever it is required within the structure of the business Ensure that employees are willing and able to communicate	Business strategy and goals The psychological aspects of OD Structure of the organisation Processes Design model Systems

Facet of HR	Formal process	Enabling others	Outline	Link with OD
2 Teamwork	X	X	Ensure that policies are in place allowing employees to participate in teamwork both between and within departments – e.g. functional or geographical structures Ensure that employees participate in teamwork allowing all to work towards achieving organisational goals	Achieving business goals Supporting the structure Psychological aspect of OD Processes Design model Systems
3 Recruitment and selection	X	X	Ensure that policies and processes are in place guaranteeing that the organisation has the right number of employees with the required capabilities and competences	Achieving the goals of the organisation Processes within the OD Processes Systems
4 Engagement	X	X	Implement policies and practices that allow employees to feel engaged in their jobs	Achieving the goals of the organisation Psychological aspect of OD Processes Systems
5 Performance management	X	X	Ensure that policies and practices are in place enabling line managers to suitably performance manage their employees. Ensure that goals and objectives are aligned with organisational objectives	Business strategy and goals Processes Design model Systems
6 Alignment – internal/ external	X	X	Ensure that all HR functions are aligned with the business strategy and that relevant employees are aware of external influences	Business strategy and goals Design model Systems
7 Authority and leadership	X	X	Depending on the design and structure of the business, HR has to ensure that key employees have the authority they require and ensure that departments are being led in the same direction	Business strategy and goals Supporting the structure Processes Design model

Facet of HR	Formal process	Enabling others	Outline	Link with OD
8 Co-operation or compliance	X	X	Depending on the nature of the job, ensure that employees are at a minimum compliant. Where necessary, HR must ensure that employees co-operate allowing synergy. This can be a source of competitive advantage	Supporting the structure Processes Design model Systems
9 Psychological contract	X	X	The role of HR is to ensure that each employee's psychological contract is in place. This is directly linked to the attitude of the employee that then allegedly controls their behaviour	Psychological aspect of OD Processes Systems
10 Equality, managing diversity, fairness and justice.	X	X	HR should ensure that all employees are treated equally, with fairness and justice. This is required legally and ethically.	Processes Systems
11 Training	X	X	All employees will at some stage require training. HR's role is to determine which employee has what training and who performs the training. This affects the morale, skill and motivation of employees	Business strategy and goals Systems
12 Flexible working	X	X	HR can introduce policies and processes to allow employees to work flexibly. This can include part-time work, working from home or job-sharing. Flexible working also involves implementing a strategy of functional, financial or numerical flexibility, depending on the design, nature and structure of the business	Supporting the structure Processes Systems

Facet of HR	Formal process	Enabling others	Outline	Link with OD
13 Reward	X	X	HR's role is to implement policy and procedures, ensuring that intrinsic and extrinsic rewards are suitably matched to the needs of the organisation and employees. HR would also ensure that the goals and objectives given to employees are directly linked to achieving the organisational goals	Business strategy and goals Supporting the structure Processes Systems
14 Knowledge sharing	X	X	HR would implement processes and ensure that employees are suitably engaged so that employees would share knowledge with other relevant departments and employees	Psychological aspect of OD Processes Systems
15 Change management	X	X	In times of change, HR would ensure that employees are not only able to change their job roles, etc, but that they are willing to change	Psychological aspect of OD Supporting the structure Processes Design model Systems
16 Making a difference	X	X	Part of the psychological contract is that employees want to feel they make a difference. HR's function here is to introduce systems that allow employees to identify the contribution they make to the company	Psychological aspect of OD
17 Job role/ description	X	X	HR needs to identify the specific requirements for each and every job within the organisation. This is then used as a management and legal document to ensure that employees are clear on what their roles are. Job descriptions are also used in recruitment. They allow possible new recruits to clearly see what their role would be within the organisation	Business strategy and goals Supporting the structure Processes Design model Systems

Facet of HR	Formal process	Enabling others	Outline	Link with OD
18 International HR – culture	X	X	With many companies now being global, HR need to ensure staff are aware of cultural issues affecting the business in any one location. HR also needs to identify whether the organisation undertake an ethnocentric, polycentric, regiocentric or geocentric staffing policy	Psychological aspect of OD Supporting the structure Design model Culture
19 Problem-solving	X	X	HR would ensure that processes and rewards are in place which encourage employees to proactively participate in problem-solving. HR would ensure that staff have the correct attitude and ability	Psychological aspect of OD Processes Systems
20 Innovation	X	X	Similar to problem-solving, HR would ensure that relevant staff have the competences to be innovative in their job. HR would ensure that rewards are linked to innovation, as long as the innovation is linked to achieving organisational goals	Psychological aspect of OD Supporting the structure Processes Design model Systems
21 Management	X	X	HR would ensure that training and development policies and processes are in place. HR's role is to recruit and develop staff in such a way that enables them to manage other staff in a suitable and correct manner	Business strategy and goals Supporting the structure Processes Design model
22 Redundancy	X	X	As and when required, HR would oversee any redundancy process. HR would look at redeployment, assistance in locating other work, the levels of redundancy payments and ensure that the remaining workforce remain motivated and engaged with the business	Business strategy and goals

Facet of HR	Formal process	Enabling others	Outline	Link with OD
23 Outsourcing	X	X	The design and structure of the business may make it necessary to outsource particular job roles. HR would oversee this process and ensure that all policies and practices are in line with the needs of the organisation	Business strategy and goals Supporting the structure Processes Systems
24 Health and safety	X	X	This is a crucial aspect of HR. Health and safety only becomes an issue when something goes wrong. HR needs to ensure that all staff are suitably trained and informed on health and safety issues. HR also need to ensure that the organisation complies with all relevant health and safety regulations	Processes Legal requirements
25 Organisational commitment	X	X	Implement policies and practices that allow employees to become committed to the organisation	Psychological aspect of OD Processes

REFLECTIVE ACTIVITY

● From the list of functions described in Table 1.1, for a company that you work for or know quite well, identify the five most important and five least important with regard to affecting the performance of the organisation.

1   Now explain why you have chosen these functions.

2   Does it make a difference which structure or overall design the company has as to what are the most and least important HRM functions?

REFLECTIVE ACTIVITY

As mentioned, many of the functions performed by HR have an intangible affect on organisation design. These effects can be both direct and indirect. For example, a communication process will have a direct effect on the workings of the design of the company. In addition, an employee's attitude to using the communication system will have an indirect effect on the success of the organisational design.

- Have a look at the 25 functions listed in Table 1.1 and identify the ones you think are the top five employee 'motivating' functions.
- Identify five functions in Table 1.1.that Herzberg would classify as 'hygiene' factors. (NB: A hygiene factor is something that does not motivate, but that if it is not there, can

demotivate – for example a faulty flickering light can demotivate you in that it can distract and annoy you. However, a light that does not flicker does not motivate you to work harder. So lights that are in correct working order are hygiene factors.

1   Reviewing your answers to the two Reflective Activities prior to the one immediately above, can you spot any pattern or similarities within your answers?

2   Are formal functions/processes more important to the workings of the organisation design, or are functions that enable employees the more important ones?

SUMMARY OF THE HR ROLE

HR strategies, functions and processes (HRM) have both a direct and indirect effect on how organisations design their business. Additionally, or perhaps more importantly, HRM has both a direct and an indirect influence on whether the organisation design underpins success. It is argued by many that HRM is the last remaining source of competitive advantage. For this reason, HRM cannot be ignored when designing an organisation.

SUMMARY

We started this chapter by considering what an organisation is. We then provided some historical background before highlighting more recent models and explanations for organisation design. Perhaps one point to bear in mind, though, is the application of these models to the contemporary business environment. In the UK, for example, 99% of organisations fall with the category of small to medium-sized enterprises, approximately 70% having fewer than 10 employees. Yet most of the research tends to focus on larger organisations. Also, the increase in the number of companies opting to outsource some functions can also impact on the design of organisations. Core functions which are strategic and essential tend to remain in-house whereas routine, non-core functions are outsourced. Thus, an organisation may well have one type of structure for its core business and another for its non-core business.

As mentioned above, the international dimension is more significant today and organisations will certainly be more global in the years to come. With the emerging economies of India and China it is likely that the structures and designs that emerge in future years will be very different from what we currently see. Our understanding of these new structures will have to take account of cultural differences, and those that do emerge may also have limited application beyond the country of origin. Weber's bureaucracies are no longer fully applicable to effective organisations. We have also a richer understanding of what motivates people at work and how group dynamics affect behaviour and performance, which in turn shapes organisation design. It is probably fair to say that the behaviours associated with shovelling coal is not as simple as Taylor proposed.

 Covmig Retail Ltd

CASE STUDY

A major food retailer is losing market share and has spent large sums of money over the past few years attempting to reclaim it. Changes have been made to its reward, advertising and marketing strategies, all to no avail.

The company has realised that rather than looking at other particular strategies, it needs to overhaul and redesign the organisational structure to meet the demands of the twenty-first century.

The company is structured as follows:

Head office 1,000 employees

Distribution centres × 6 1,500 employees

Retail outlets × 500 25,000 employees

Each subsidiary has its specific type of employees. These include low-skilled and low-paid employees, highly-paid executives, core and periphery workers, part-time and full-time workers and blue- and white-collar workers. In addition, employees fall into a wide demographic continuum. They range from students to more mature workers, male and female, and all form a very diverse workforce. All areas of the globe are represented within the workforce. Some employees are also supplied via agencies and employed on fixed-term contracts.

The new business strategy is based on customer service. Head office has announced that all efforts must be made to provide the best customer service in the food retail industry. Head office has also decided that each distribution centre and each retail outlet must be self-financing and must offer the business a return on its investment.

Sales from the outlets are made up as follows:

Food and grocery 65%

Clothing 20%

Electronic goods 15%

Retail outlets are fined heavily for goods that are returned unsold or sold at below cost price. They are also fined for running out of stock and for having too much stock. Each retail outlet is required to obtain all its produce from one of the six distribution centres.

Questions

1   What form of organisational structure should the company adopt, and why?

2   What are the key internal and external factors that influenced your decision?

3   What should the key business objectives be for:

a)   the distribution centres?

b)   the retail outlets?

4   What are the key HR functions/ roles that the business needs to concentrate on to ensure that the new design has a chance of

succeeding and that each objective is achieved? Think about this from a short- and long-term perspective.

Now that you have answered the above questions, consider the following – there is no need to write anything down, you just need to think about it.

Of all the organisations you know, how many of them do you think were designed in a strategic and well thought out manner – or do you think some organisations evolve into their designs over time?

FURTHER READING

BOOKS

BHATTACHARYYA, D. K. (2009) *Organisational Systems, Design, Structure and Management*. Mumbai: Himalaya Publishing House. An excellent overview of organisation design, and available as an e-book.

HANDY, C. (1999) *Understanding Organisations*. Harmondsworth: Penguin. The ultimate classic study of organisations and a staple for many years. Handy writes in a very accessible yet well-informed way.

MCNAMARA, C. 'Basic Definition of Organization' http://managementhelp.org/organizations/definition.htm#anchor424230 [accessed 10 February 2012]. Provides some of the core fundamentals of organisation design.

SCHEIN, E. (1990) Organizational culture. *American Psychologist*, Vol. 45, No. 2, 109–19. The classic work on organisational culture.

TAYLOR, F. W. (1947) Scientific management, in *Scientific Management*. New York: Harper & Row. 39–73. Taylor's work has been so influential that it is worth looking up the original article to see what it is all about.

WEBSITES

International Labour Organization website: http://actrav.itcilo.org/actrav-english/telearn/osh/ergo/ergonomi.htm. Part of the United Nations, the International Labour Organization is a treasure trove of HRM research

REFERENCES

ALFES, K., TRUSS, C., SOANE, E., REES, C. and GATENBY, M. (2010) *Creating an Engaged Workforce*. London: Chartered Institute of Personnel and Development.

ARGYRIS, C. (1980) Some limitations of the case method: experiences in a management development program. *Academy of Management Review*. Vol. 5, No. 2. 291–310.

BERKOVITCH, E., ISRAEL, R. and SPIEGEL, Y. (2010) A double moral hazard model of organization design. *Journal of Economics & Management Strategy*. Vol. 19, No. 1. 55–85.

BHATTACHARYYA, D.K. (2009). *Organisational Systems, Design, Structure and Management*. Mumbai: Himalaya Publishing House. (E-book)

BLAKE, V. (2010) *In Business, Communication Is Everything*, unpublished MA Dissertation, Coventry University.

BLOISI, W. (2007) *Management and Organisational Behaviour*. Maidenhead: McGraw-Hill.

BRYNJOLFSSON, E. and HITT, L. (1998) *Information Technology and Organizational Design: Evidence from micro data*. Conference paper: MIT.

BURKE, W. and LITWIN, G. A (1992) Causal model of organisational performance and change. *Journal of Management*. Vol. 18, No. 3. 523–45.

BURNS,T. (1963) Industry in a New Age. *New Society*. 31 January. Vol 18, pp17–20, cited in PUGH, D. S. (ed.) (2007) *Organisation Theory: Selected classical readings*. Harmondsworth: Penguin.

DAFT, R. (2007) *Understanding the Theory and Design of Organisations*. Mason, OH: Thomson South Western.

GALBRAITH, J. (1995) *Designing Organisations: An executive briefing based on strategy, structure and process*. San Francisco, CA: Jossey-Bass.

HANDY, C. (1999) *Understanding Organisations*. Harmondsworth: Penguin.

HEAD, T., YAEGER, T. and SORENSEN, P. (2010) Global organisation structural design: speculation and a call for action. *Organization Development Journal*. Vol. 28, No. 2. 41–8.

HOFSTEDE, G. (1980) *Culture's Consequences*. London: Sage.

HUCZYNSKI, A. and BUCHANAN, D. (2007) *Organisational Behaviour*. 6th edn. Harlow: Prentice Hall.

INTERNATIONAL LABOUR ORGANIZATION website: http://actrav.itcilo.org/actrav-english/telearn/osh/ergo/ergonomi.htm [accessed 28 February 2012].

JOHNSON, G. and SCHOLES, K. (1992) *Managing Strategic Change: Strategy, culture and action*. London: Elsevier.

KATZ, D. K. (1966) *The Social Psychology of Organisations*. New York: Wiley.

MACEY, W. and SCHNEIDER, B (2008) The meaning of employee engagement. *Industrial and Organisational Psychology*, Vol. 1, No. 1. 3–30.

MACLEOD, D. and CLARKE, N. (2009) *Engaging for Success: Enhancing performance through employee engagement*. London: Department for Business, Innovation and Skills.

MCMILLAN, E. (2000) *Considering Organisation Structure and Design from a Complexity Prardigm Perspective.* Milton Keynes: Open University.

MCNAMARA, C. (2012) 'Basic definition of organisation' http://managementhelp.org/organizations/definition.htm#anchor424230 [accessed 10 February 2012].

PETERS, T. and WATERMAN, R. (1982) *In Search of Excellence.* New York: HarperCollins.

SCHEIN, E. (1990) Organizational culture. *American Psychologist.* Vol. 45, No. 2. 109–19.

SHUMAN, J. and TWOMBLY, J. (2010) Collaborative networks are the organisation: an innovation in organisation design and management. *The Journal for Decision Makers.* Vol. 35, No. 1. 1–13.

SIMONS, R. (2005) *Leverages of Organization Design.* Boston: Harvard Business School Press.

TAYLOR, F. W. (1947) Testimony before the Special House Committee, in *Scientific Management.* New York: Harper & Brothers. 5–287.

TUCKMAN, B. (1965) Developmental sequence in small groups. *Psychological Bulletin.* Vol. 63, No. 6. 384–99.

ULIERU, M., BRENNAN, R. and WALKER, S. (2002) The holonic enterprise: a model for Internet-enabled global manufacturing supply chain and workflow management. *Integrated Manufacturing Systems.* Vol. 13, No. 8. 538–50.

WATERMAN, R., PETERS, T. and PHILLIPS, J. R. (1980) Structure is not organisation. *Business Horizons.* Vol. 23, No. 3. 14–26.

WEBER, M. (1947) *The Theory of Social and Economic Organisation.* New York: Free Press.

WEISBORD, M. (1976) Organisational diagnosis: six places to look for trouble with or without a theory. *Group and Organisational Studies.* Vol. 1, No. 4. 430–47.

CHAPTER 2

Organisational Development

Sophie Mills, Amanda Lee, Krish Pinto and Kristen Stevens

CHAPTER CONTENTS

- Introduction
- What is OD?
- The historical basis of OD
- The role of the OD practitioner
- Understanding the OD process
- Practices, models and approaches
- The role and purpose of OD interventions
- Summary

KEY LEARNING OUTCOMES

By the end of this chapter, you will be able to:

- Analyse the underpinning history, theories and principles of organisation development.

- Describe and explain the organisation development process.

- Evaluate various organisation development practices, models and approaches.

- Discuss the value of organisation development interventions to business performance and productivity.

INTRODUCTION

This chapter introduces and examines the concept of **organisational development** (OD) and its role within the management of organisational change. It commences by introducing the concept of OD and includes definitions of its characteristics and those required of OD practitioners. The chapter then moves on to provide a historical insight into the emergence of OD, the role of the OD practitioner in greater detail and considerations relating to the place of ethics within OD interventions. Subsequently, the chapter offers a breakdown of a typical OD process, including **contracting**, issue **diagnosis**, intervention planning and evaluation. A series of theoretical approaches and models are included to help demonstrate the operation of the OD process. Finally, the chapter then reflects upon the overall purpose of OD and the importance of the incorporation of performance measurement methods to be able to gauge its overall impact.

Throughout the chapter there are questions and case studies. We strongly urge you to take time out to try to answer the questions. Only by doing so can you fully understand the complexity and relevance of organisational development.

WHAT IS OD?

Progressively, organisations find themselves needing to respond and adapt to ever-changing external environments, whether these changes are associated with customers, suppliers, competitors, legislation, challenging economic conditions, government initiatives/interventions, or a combination of any or all of these. OD can be used to support the management of organisations through change in order to enable them to introduce processes that will optimise their ongoing adaptability and flexibility.

OD, as defined by French and Bell (1999, pp25–6), is:

> a long-term effort, led and supported by top management, to improve an organisation's visioning, empowerment, learning and problem-solving processes, through an ongoing, collaborative management of organisation culture of intact work teams and other team configurations – using the consultant-facilitator role and the theory and technology of applied behavioural science, including **action research**.

Cheung-Judge and Holbeche (2011) used French and Bell's definition and those provided by a number of other authors – Margulies 1978; Beckhard 1969; Schein 1988; Lippitt and Lippitt 1975; Rainey Tolbert and Hanafin 2006 – to identify the following set of OD and OD practitioner characteristics (adapted from Cheung-Judge and Holbeche 2011, p11):

- OD practitioners are 'process experts' who aim to improve organisational processes.
- OD practitioners focus upon the total organisational system, even if only a specific issue has been identified.
- OD practitioners work towards improving organisational problem-solving and renewal processes.
- OD practitioners support organisational leaders.
- Applied behavioural science technology is used to help the organisation strive for healthy development.
- The OD process is 'theory based, process focused' and 'value driven'.

According to Cheung-Judge and Holbeche, the focus of OD is, therefore, on the support of organisational leaders in taking a holistic approach to organisational process improvement and renewal using behavioural science technologies. The incorporation of behavioural science technology is considered a key component of all OD interventions. 'Behavioural science' is a wide-ranging term used to describe the study of people's behaviour in the social sciences. It is often related to issues of management and organisations within a work context. The study of behaviour within behavioural science is predominantly considered using the disciplinary perspectives of sociology (the study of social behaviour), psychology (the study of human behaviour) and anthropology (the study of mankind and the study of social behaviour as a whole) (Mullins 2005, pp29–30).

THE HISTORICAL BASIS OF OD

The emergence of OD as a concept tracks back to the 1940s and 1950s. During this time, US psychologists began to focus their attentions on group dynamics. Exploring the interactions amongst group members, early researchers discovered that individuals responded favourably to participation, resulting in changes in attitude, positive interpersonal relations, increased performance and personal growth.

Stemming from research conducted in the USA in the late 1940s, Kurt Lewin developed a leadership workshop, known as the T-group (a form of sensitivity training), that provided participants with feedback on their behaviour. Lewin and his team of researchers discovered that the provision of such feedback resulted in a rich learning experience. Owing to the success of these initial T-groups, and with financial backing, national training laboratories (NTLs) were formed in 1947. The NTLs were expanded in 1950 to include business and industry, allowing individuals to learn more about themselves and their reactions to given situations. The term 'organisational development' began to emerge as internal professionals and academic scholars applied these participative techniques to organisations (McGregor 1960; Beckhard 1969) to change management styles and overall organisational performance.

Gaining a greater understanding of the impact of management styles on performance, McGregor (1960) discovered two different approaches to management. Based on assumptions made about employees, Theory X managers believe that employees have to be controlled because they avoid responsibility, are inherently lazy and cannot be trusted. In contrast, Theory Y managers assume that their staff will accept responsibility, are committed and will co-operate given the right conditions.

Blake and Mouton's (1981) managerial grid also focused upon management performance, asking managers to pinpoint on the grid their priority for employee or task needs (sometimes referred to as people or production needs). Blake and Mouton concluded that the most effective managers in their roles are those who do not favour production over people and vice versa. Paying the same level of high attention to each aspect (employee and task needs), effective managers inherently promote a higher level of employee participation because communication is greater and employees understand what is being done and why.

The need to be open with staff and provide opportunities for involvement and recognition also forms part of much theory on motivation, most notably

Maslow's 'hierarchy of needs' (1954). When designing jobs, working conditions and organisational structures, Maslow suggested, organisations should bear in mind the full range of needs detailed in his hierarchy – namely physiological, safety, social, esteem and self-actualisation needs. Maslow suggested that people seek to satisfy lower-level needs first (such as the need for food and shelter) before moving up the hierarchy to eventually reach 'self-actualisation' at the top. Maslow argued that as each need is satisfied, it is no longer a motivator. While Maslow's hierarchy was and still is held in high regard in management education, the theory has been criticised. Whetten and Cameron (2005, p318) state that 'The problem with the hierarchical needs theories is that although they help us to understand general development processes, from adult to child, they aren't very useful for understanding the day-to-day motivation levels of adult employees.' Other authors (Kogan 1972; Wahba and Bridwell 1976; Salancik and Pfeffer 1977; Rauschenberger *et al* 1980) concur with the view that there are some problems relating Maslow's theory to the workplace. The main criticisms are that people can satisfy their needs through other areas of their life, not just work; individual differences mean that people place different values on the same need; some rewards or outcomes may satisfy more than one need; and people on the same level of the hierarchy may not have the same motivating factors.

REFLECTIVE ACTIVITY

1   To what extent do you agree with the contention that organisations spend too much time focusing on the lower-level needs of Maslow's hierarchy rather than providing employees with the opportunity to satisfy other higher-level needs?

2   Given the potential diversity of staff working within an organisation, what can HR practitioners do to ensure that they match job requirements with the individual needs of their staff?

Following concerns that traditional approaches to job design, such as Taylor's scientific management (1947), lacked attention to human needs, job design research evolved, giving rise to what became known as the quality of working life (QWL) studies. The QWL programmes worked with managers, unions and staff to design work that offered increased task variety and discretion, higher levels of involvement and the opportunity to gain feedback upon individual performance and contribution. Towards the end of the 1970s, QWL programmes increased in popularity as organisations began to realise the potential for redesigning work flows, reward systems and improved working conditions in order to improve worker productivity. Building on the initial features of QWL programmes, coupled with the emergence of a growing body of 'excellence' literature (Peters and Waterman 1992; Kanter 1983), and the emergence of **total quality management** (TQM) and **human resource management** (HRM) literature, many organisations started to support the notion that employees are an organisation's greatest asset. During this period, contemporary management practice, in post-bureaucratic organisations, sought to utilise more acceptable means of control as workers became more aware of their rights (supported by a plethora of legal instruments now regulating the employment relationship) and sought to fulfil their own needs from the employment relationship. Empowering staff, employers began to provide their employees with greater control over how they achieved their targets. Individual work activities were introduced that aimed to increase job satisfaction and loyalty while at the same time improving the profitability and performance of the organisation. In the early 1990s it was not uncommon for organisations to implement self-managing teams, whose members were responsible for determining their own ways of working within the boundaries set by management. As a consequence of this 'freedom', employers sought to improve job satisfaction, reduce absenteeism and reduce costs. However, Kunda's research (1992) demonstrates that the added pressure to conform to the rules of the team can become far greater and ultimately lead to employee burnout, which can arguably be considered somewhat self-defeating for management.

Continuing to concentrate on the potential value of involving staff in decisions at work, **HR practitioners** recently began focusing their attention on 'engaging' staff who then 'go the extra mile' and surpass the traditional levels of employee satisfaction and commitment. They have aimed to achieve this by introducing employee involvement schemes, improved communication strategies and a culture based on transparency and trust. These initiatives are some of the steps an organisation can take to actively promote high levels of employee engagement.

CASE STUDY

Department for Work and Pensions

In 2008, the Department for Work and Pensions (DWP) implemented an efficiency challenge that involved reducing 30% of its workforce over a period of three years while streamlining and modernising services to customers.

The DWP's 2008 employee engagement survey indicated that 18% of staff were 'disengaged'. This equated to approximately 20,000 employees, most of whom were holding junior grades in front-line delivery roles within Jobcentre Plus offices or contact centres. In response, DWP outlined a series of 'engagement priorities' which looked at increasing the capability, motivation and accountability of first-line and middle managers and the visibility and impact of all senior managers. These engagement priorities were aimed at putting tools in place to involve employees in discussing the vision of DWP and how it could deliver an excellent customer service.

In order to realise these priorities, DWP introduced a number of engagement initiatives, including the 'Making a Difference' programme for first-level leaders and the 'Back to the Floor' programme for senior leaders.

The Making a Difference programme was designed as the catalyst to enable participants to better engage with, lead and deliver business direction. It emphasises that leadership is not just about senior managers; it is about those who have the greatest influence on people within the organisation. Full implementation began in February 2009 and up to 10,000 people are expected to take part in the process. Stephen Hanshaw (Jobcentre Plus manager) believes his Making a Difference journey has better equipped him in engaging people in change: 'We had lots of opportunities to discuss the barriers which can affect our ability to lead our team through change, and share ideas for overcoming these.'

The Back to the Floor programme gives senior leaders the opportunity to experience a customer-facing role for up to a week, working with staff and discovering at first-hand the issues they face in delivering to the organisation's customers. Katherine Courtney (Director of DWP Customer Insight) believes the insights she gained from her Back to the Floor experience have enabled her to influence change for the better: 'In my role it is important for me to see things from the customer's perspective. I try to "walk in the staff's shoes". Seeing the real help we provide customers when they need it most reminded me why I joined DWP in the first place. I was able to influence issues arising from lone parent customers transitioning from Income Support to Job Seekers Allowance.'

The DWP's recent survey results show some positive movement in their engagement scores.

Source: http://www.bis.gov.uk/files/file52215.pdf

REFLECTIVE ACTIVITY

1   In an attempt to measure the levels of engagement amongst their workforce, organisations may decide to distribute an annual satisfaction survey. Compile five to10 questions that you think would be appropriate to include in such a survey. When thinking about the questions, remember to firstly consider what it is you are trying to measure, and why.

2   What can organisations do to maintain morale during challenging economic conditions?

THE ROLE OF THE OD PRACTITIONER

The OD practitioner can be a specialist, thereby concentrating solely on OD, or OD can form part of a more generalist management role. Cummings and Worley (2005, p450) suggest that 'many managers and administrators have gained competence in Organisation Development and therefore apply it to their own work areas'. OD practitioners can also be **external consultants** whose expertise is sought when this does not exist in-house. One distinct advantage of employing an internal OD practitioner is that they are very familiar with the culture of the organisation and the people working within it. However, there is an increased likelihood of bias because such practitioners may find it hard to detach themselves from their predetermined attitudes and assumptions. Conversely, an external OD practitioner may be better placed to make more objective judgements but take longer to form relationships with those with whom they will be working.

Challenging previous and existing organisational behaviours, the OD practitioner can sometimes face opposition because managers and staff may feel threatened or perhaps they may misunderstand the purpose of the OD practitioner's role and contribution. As with much of organisational life, it is essential that lines of communication are kept open and everyone is informed of the nature and likely duration of the OD practitioner's work, so as to optimise transparency and reduce resistance.

Adopting humanist principles, traditional OD practitioners promoted open communication, employee involvement and personal growth and development. However, criticised for sitting on the periphery of an organisation (Bradford and Burke 2005, p19), OD practitioners have since had to expand their skill sets to demonstrate an interest in organisational effectiveness and bottom-line results. Moving from a client-centred to a consultant-centred role, OD practitioners now seek to adopt a more central and strategic role as organisations face increasing change.

ETHICAL CONSIDERATIONS

The role of an OD practitioner is to promote the change that is needed within the organisation they work in or for. Accepting this professional responsibility, OD practitioners have to inspire trust and quickly identify and ascertain organisational norms and values. Needing to form close working relationships with staff, OD practitioners can potentially face myriad ethical dilemmas. Cummings and Worley (2005, p58) state that 'Ethical issues in organisation development are concerned with how practitioners perform their helping relationship with organisation members.'

In order to promote a positive working relationship and reduce the possibility of any misunderstanding, it is essential that both parties are honest with each other from the outset. When working with an organisation, the OD practitioner is responsible for clearly explaining, both verbally and in writing, what it is they will be able to deliver and the timescales to achieve it. Similarly, the client (or organisation) must ensure that it is completely honest with the OD practitioner about the current situation and how the OD practitioner is envisaged to be able to assist it. Under these circumstances it would be considered unethical for the OD practitioner to claim that the adoption of a particular intervention would solve all of the organisation's problems if it was not likely to be the case. The OD practitioner should be clear about the work they think they would be able to carry out within the specified time period and return to the client if this does not turn out to be the case.

Trust is an important aspect of the OD practitioner's role because they will invariably have access to confidential information. It is likely that employees may seek to elicit this information from the OD practitioner as they work on their assigned role. It is therefore imperative that confidentiality is maintained and agreements are made between the client and the OD practitioner in relation to any announcements that are made and access to any sensitive information being collected.

During the course of data collection, an OD practitioner may also obtain additional information which does not specifically relate to their initial brief from the client. For example, the OD practitioner could observe something that could be considered to be inappropriate behaviour at work and may therefore be placed in an uncomfortable situation as they decide whether or not to report this set of circumstances to management. Easterby-Smith *et al* (2008, p134) imply that it is difficult to establish hard-and-fast ethical principles and, consequently, that 'good practice will rely on considerable judgement on the part of the researcher'. Returning to a previous comment relating to the importance of communication in organisations, it is essential that both parties agree upon the information that should be reported, and how. During these initial meetings, both the OD practitioner and the client organisation are required to agree on the point at which the working relationship will cease, because in some situations the client can become totally dependent upon the OD practitioner and reluctant to 'let go' of their support. Paradoxically, the OD practitioner also needs to know when they are required to step back from the organisation and allow the client to take full responsibility of the OD intervention. The OD practitioner may wish to still be involved in the change process, even when their contract deadline has passed – that is, when they have completed the project and/or no longer work for that organisation. The ethics of their continued involvement should ideally be questioned and addressed.

REFLECTIVE ACTIVITY

Imagine you are an OD practitioner for a large multi-site retailer. You have been asked to oversee the relocation of the company's warehouse from Birmingham to a much larger facility in Manchester. The managing director has not yet announced that this move is going to happen and has therefore asked for your discretion as you undertake your preliminary investigations. You are asked to inform anyone who asks that you are doing a review of the health and safety worries within the warehouse. However, after work one evening you decide to join a group of staff that has gone to the pub for a drink. After several hours of chatting, one warehouse operative asks you the real purpose of your work at Birmingham and you let it slip that the Birmingham warehouse is likely to be closing down in six months' time.

Consider the potential consequences of your revelation to: a) the warehouse staff based at Birmingham, b) the organisation as a whole, and c) your role as OD practitioner.

UNDERSTANDING THE OD PROCESS

OD practice has evolved since the 1950s and yet maintained a conceptual core that is still relevant and applicable today. This includes a key focus on improving organisational effectiveness at an individual, group and organisational level, an emphasis on change and a preoccupation with the *process* of change (Schein 1999). The emphasis on *process* has been advanced by OD's humanist values promoting the ideology that *how* things are done between people and in groups is as important as, or more important than, *what* is done (Schein 1999).

Every organisation has its own context and issues, and therefore every OD programme is unique. Yet all OD processes have recognisable frameworks of phases, collections of activities and techniques or identifiable flows of interrelated events helping organisations move towards organisational and/or group and individual improvement (French and Bell 1999). Many authors have advanced slight variations on Kolb and Frohman's (1970) general framework for **planned change** outlining six basic stages. These include scouting, **entry** and contracting, diagnosis, action, and evaluating that action. French and Bell (1999) cite Warne Burke's description of the OD process, which outlines a seven-stage programme: entry, contracting, diagnosis, feedback, planning change, intervention and evaluation.

Although the OD process is described as a sequential, linear and logical progression of events, it is acknowledged that organisational change rarely flows in such a tidy way and in practice the phases are likely to overlap. The importance of paying due diligence to each phase cannot be stressed enough because each stage builds on the foundations for and has an effect on subsequent phases. It is also important to recognise the iterative nature of the OD processes. All organisational change and development programmes are complex and interrelated processes of goals → actions → redefined goals → new actions (French and Bell 1999). Change agents must therefore not only consider the steps required for one entire cycle of OD but also conceptualise and consider how multiple cycles of OD might develop. They also might need to consider how the end of one cycle, and subsequent evaluation, may lead to another iteration of OD (Neumann *et al* 1997). Each stage of the OD process has a set of activities that must be undertaken, and a preoccupation with the process does not negate the importance of the tasks within each stage of the process. It is important, therefore, to examine each of the stages of the OD process in more detail.

ENTRY AND CONTRACTING

Entry into an OD relationship usually starts when an organisational member identifies a problem within the organisation and seeks the help of an OD professional. This contact may come from a **line manager**, an HR professional or other stakeholders within the organisation that will be party to the client–consultant relationship. An OD practitioner may be someone from inside the organisation acting as an **internal consultant**, perhaps an appropriately skilled HR professional, or from outside, an external consultant.

The overall task during the entry phase is to decide whether there is a good match between the client and the consultant and to determine whether the two parties should enter into and establish an OD relationship. An understanding of the organisational problem, clarifying who the client is and understanding their objectives and motives, will help the consultant with this decision. Equally, the client may also want to gather some data about the consultant and be confident that they have the knowledge, skills and experience or the technical, interpersonal and consulting skills necessary to help the client with their problems.

The key purpose of the contracting phase is to reach a formal or informal, verbal or written but explicit agreement about how the OD process will be carried out. The goal of this stage should be clarity about the desired outcomes for the OD process, and the time and resources available, as well as agreeing the rules and boundaries for working together. It is essential that particular attention is paid to establishing a robust understanding of the terms of the informal psychological contract (PC) of mutual needs and expectations that the client and consultant have of each other. A misunderstanding of this could mean someone's expectations are unfulfilled, and a violation of the PC may have serious implications, not least the loss of commitment and support and possibly early termination and failure of the project. It is therefore a critical stage of the process and one that will need to be continually revisited and renewed throughout the life of the project.

DIAGNOSIS AND FEEDBACK

The diagnostic element of the OD process involves collaboratively collecting relevant information and data, analysing it and drawing some conclusions about the organisational **client system**. Consideration needs to be given to the possible courses of action that will address the problems or opportunities and bridge the gap between where the client organisation system is and where they would like it to be. These decisions, however, rely on and cannot be made without collecting and analysing valid information. The values and ethics that underpin OD encourage a collaborative approach to diagnosis as well as to designing and implementing appropriate interventions (Block 2011). Decisions about who, what, when, where and how information will be collected, and the appropriate course of action to be taken, must be arrived at jointly by the client and the OD practitioner. This philosophy is advanced by the belief that only the client owns the problem identified and understands the true complexity of their situation, and only they know what will work for them within their organisational culture (Schein 1999). The role of the OD practitioner is to facilitate the process. Furthermore, the stakeholders within the diagnostic process must not forget the developmental orientation of OD, and improving the overall effectiveness of organisations is as important as uncovering problems and reasons for these problems (Cummings and Worley 1996).

Once the information has been collected, the OD practitioner needs to deploy the appropriate skills and competencies in organising the data to a manageable number of issues. This may involve deductive, inductive and/or statistical techniques to organise and interpret the gathered information. The content as well as the way in which the information is presented will determine if the client is energised towards problem-solving and action. This may therefore involve producing large amounts of information that is properly analysed and presented in a way that the client will understand and find useful. Difficult and unpleasant feedback should not be minimised or avoided. As Block (2011) points out, the client has the right to all the information that has been collected. This will then enable the client to make some informed decisions about the best way forward for the organisation.

PLANNING CHANGE AND INTERVENTION

The purpose of the planning phase is to decide and agree on the action that needs to be taken to address the organisational issues. The OD practitioner's role is to facilitate an arrival at a common understanding of the issues and an agreement on the best way forward. The tasks during this phase may involve critically appraising a number of options and choosing, developing and agreeing a plan of action.

Schein (1999) observes that everything a change agent does is an intervention. You intervene the moment you enter a client system, and sometimes an intervention can be as little as asking a simple question. An OD intervention is defined as '… a sequence of activities, actions, and events intended to help an organisation improve its performance and effectiveness' (Cummings and Worley 1996, p141). Many interventions fail because they do not match the data and diagnosis, have unclear and/or overambitious goals, allow insufficient time for implementation, are poorly designed or because resistance to change has not been dealt with, the organisation is not ready for change and the organisation and/or the OD practitioner do not have the knowledge and skills required to motivate and lead the change process and sustain the momentum required to implement and institutionalise the change (Anderson 2010). For interventions to be successful they must be designed to meet the needs of the organisation, be based on valid knowledge, skills and experience and through active participation in the design and implementation of interventions develop and enhance the organisation's capacity to manage change.

CASE STUDY

Diagnosing issues facing a pathology department within a medium-sized NHS trust

The diagnosis of issues facing the Pathology Department in a medium-sized NHS trust was that it faced a number of problems with its location within the trust. There was, however, strong resistance to change and an equally strong desire to maintain the status quo from some key members of staff within the department. In response to a request for some help with this from the associate director, the internal consultant used Kurt Lewin's force-field model as a diagnostic tool as well as a process that may enable leverage for change.

- Key stakeholders were facilitated to identify and list the driving forces pushing for change on the left side of a page, and the restraining forces that were blocking change down the right side.

- These forces were then given weightings in terms of their power to enable or block the change.

- Totalling the driving and restraining forces showed the driving forces for the change were greater than the restraining forces.

- An action plan addressing the restraining forces and developing the power of the driving forces was developed through facilitation.

Using the force-field analysis had a twofold effect. It enabled the key stakeholders to understand the resistance to change, but also showed the department that the impetus to change was greater than the reasons to maintain the status quo and thus provided a leverage to change.

EVALUATION

Figure 2.1 Kurt Lewin's force-field model

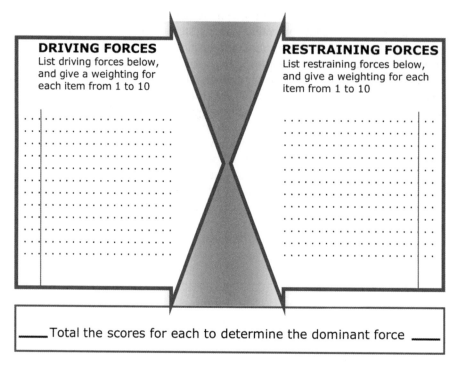

DRIVING FORCES
List driving forces below, and give a weighting for each item from 1 to 10

RESTRAINING FORCES
List restraining forces below, and give a weighting for each item from 1 to 10

_____Total the scores for each to determine the dominant force _____

Evaluation represents assessing what has worked well, what needs further development, and if further diagnosis or intervention is necessary. Evaluation is also about learning from the process and deciding what happens next. It could be the stage at which the OD relationship is ended or a decision is made to enter another iteration of the cycle. In current financially difficult times, managers investing resources in OD efforts would be held to account for results. There are many challenges and barriers to evaluation and many practitioners fail to evaluate. Some of the reasons cited for this are lack of energy and resources, fear of the results, uncertainty about what to evaluate, lack of skills, knowledge and experience of evaluation, and some practitioners viewing it as an optional activity. Evaluation is, however, an essential part of the process and validates OD efforts and enables growth and development for both the client and OD practitioner.

 REFLECTIVE ACTIVITY

Consider the collaborative and facilitative nature of the OD relationship. What do you think are the set of skills and competencies a practitioner needs to facilitate the OD process?

PRACTICES, MODELS AND APPROACHES

ORGANISATION DEVELOPMENT AND CHANGE MANAGEMENT TECHNIQUES

OD models tend to support the premise that in order for change to be successful it should be planned. Additionally, change management programmes should be continuously monitored to take account of internal and external influences. An early popular change model, still in use today, was first proposed by Kurt Lewin in the 1940s. Lewin put forward a three-stage model of change which involves **'unfreezing'** the current state and mind-set to enable change to occur, 'change' or 'transition' to bring about and support the desired change, and finally **'freezing'** or 'refreezing' to reinforce and anchor the change (Lewin 1951). Lippitt *et al* (1958) developed and extended Lewin's ideas into a seven-step planning model. In contrast to Lewin, Lippitt *et al* focused on the role and responsibility of the human players in the change process, rather than the change itself. Figure 2.2 shows the seven stages in the process aligned with Lewin's model of change.

Figure 2.2 Lippitt, Watson and Westley's change model incorporating Lewin's model of planned change

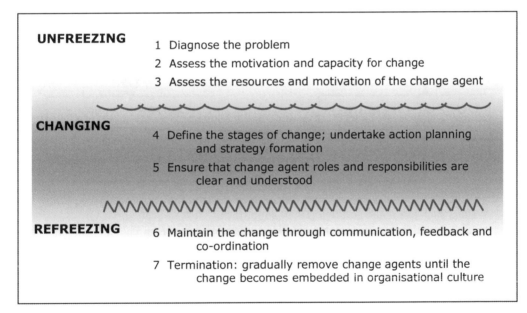

Source: Adapted from Lippitt, Watson and Westley (1958)

Similarly to Lippitt *et al*, Kotter (1996) proposed an eight-stage process for managing change, which can also be compared with Lewin's three-stage process. Kotter proposed: 1) establishing a sense of urgency; 2) creating a guiding coalition; 3) developing a vision and strategy; 4) communicating the change (unfreezing); 5) empowering action; 6) generating short-term wins (changing); 7) consolidating gains and producing more change; 8) anchoring and institutionalising new approaches (freezing).

REFLECTIVE ACTIVITY

The models above assume that successful change is planned change. How realistic do you consider this assumption to be in practice?

ACTION RESEARCH APPROACHES

Action research models are based on a systems approach and tend to be cyclical in design. In this way feedback is possible at each stage and planned actions and outcomes can be used to facilitate further change. It can be argued that models based on Lewin's approach to planned change take an action research approach in the sense that planned input requires 'unfreezing', action requires 'changing', and 'freezing' (or refreezing) requires embedding this change into an output (see Figure 2.3).

Figure 2.3 A simple action research model

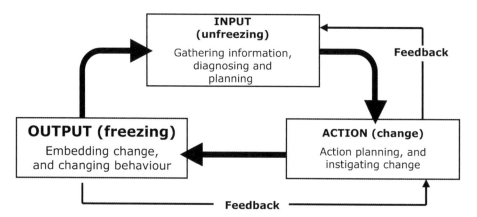

Writers such as French and Bell (1999) support this view and categorise OD as organisational improvement through the process of action research. Cummings and Worley (2008, p25) describe a cyclical eight-step action research model which expands upon the simple model outlined above:

1   problem identification

2   consultation with a behavioural science expert

3   data-gathering and preliminary diagnosis

4   feedback to a key client or group

5   joint diagnosis of the problem

6   joint action planning

7   action

8   data-gathering after the action.

Cummings and Worley argue that although these action research approaches are often associated with organisational change and development, they may not be applicable in all contexts and situations. **Appreciative inquiry** (AI) has been seen as a potential alternative approach and is outlined in the next section.

APPRECIATIVE INQUIRY AND THE POSITIVE MODEL OF PLANNED CHANGE

In contrast to Lewin's change and action research models, the positive model focuses on both challenges/problems (the negatives) faced by an organisation and the areas in which they are doing well (the positives). By identifying both, organisations can build on their strengths and eliminate or diminish their weaknesses. The process by which this type of planned change takes place has been described as 'appreciative inquiry' (Cooperrider and Whitney 2005). In essence AI examines what is going right within an organisation and uses this in order to address what is going wrong. Taking an AI stance towards OD enables a positive approach to change and the way it is managed and encourages wider employee involvement in the process. Cooperrider and Whitney initially proposed a 4-D model of AI but later models have added an initial 'define' stage, as illustrated in Figure 2.4.

Figure 2.4 The 5-D model of appreciative enquiry

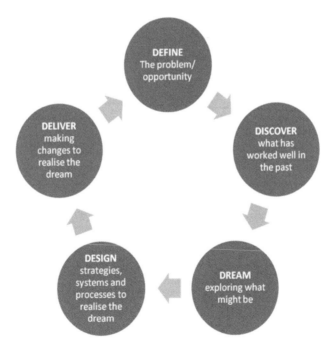

Source: Cooperrider and Whitney (2005)

EMOTIONS IN ORGANISATIONS

Many writers stress the need for employers to consider the role of employee emotions during organisational change (see Bartunek *et al* 2006), and many studies have shown a complicated relationship between employee emotions and behavioural responses to change (for example, Avey *et al* 2008). Positive employee emotions can be useful to drive change forward and increase trust, but by the same token, negative emotions can lead to fear, resistance to change and mistrust. Traditional approaches to OD assume that employees will fit in and respond to the required change and adapt to new practices, which ultimately become part of the overriding organisational culture (that is, frozen). Does such a view take account of the role of emotions during change? It can be argued that emotions are tied up with how employees adapt to or cope with change. How emotions evolve and develop during the change process must also be considered, and this is likely to vary from employee to employee. Moreover, change does not usually happen as a neatly isolated one-off event. It is more likely to encompass messy, multiple changes, which have the potential to further complicate the relationship between emotion and change. It therefore seems reasonable to surmise that in order to achieve successful, sustainable change, employee emotions should not be ignored.

REFLECTIVE ACTIVITY

Think about an ongoing or recent change that you have experienced.

1   How did you feel about this change?

2   What impact do you think your emotions had on the way you reacted to the change?

ORGANISATIONAL LEARNING

Organisational learning refers to the way in which the organisation as a whole adapts and responds to change as a result of internal and external influences. Many models have been developed to explain this process, one of the most popular being Argyris and Schön's (1978) theory of single-loop and **double-loop learning**. Single-loop learning is concerned with detecting and correcting errors within governing variables (that is, existing practices, procedures and processes), whereas double-loop learning questions the governing variables themselves (see Figure 2.5).

Figure 2.5 Single-loop and double-loop learning

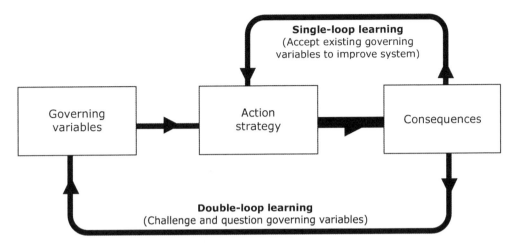

Source: Adapted from Argyris and Schön (1978)

Another influential writer in the field of organisational learning is Peter Senge. Senge (1990) proposed the concept of the **'learning organisation'**. According to Senge (1990, p3), learning organisations are:

organisations where people continually expand their capacity to create the results they truly desire, where new and expansive patterns of thinking are nurtured, where collective aspiration is set free, and where people are continually learning to see the whole together.

Senge's theory uses systems thinking as a means of solving problems and focuses on five key disciplines, namely: personal mastery, which involves developing a personal vision; mental models, which involves developing awareness and reflection; shared vision with a focus on mutual purpose; team learning, which involves collective thought and discussion; and finally systems thinking, which brings the other dimensions together. However, many writers have challenged the assumptions put forward by Senge and there is ongoing debate around definitions, scope and what it actually is to be a learning organisation. One particular criticism of the model is the apparent lack of real-life organisational examples.

RESISTANCE, CONFLICT, DIVERSITY AND MULTICULTURALISM

The power of employee resistance should not be overlooked as a potential barrier to change. The CIPD (2011) defines resistance as: 'an individual or group engaging in acts to block or disrupt an attempt to introduce change'. The Institute identifies two main types of change: resistance to the *content* of change – in other words, *what* the change actually is, such as in the introduction of a new process or procedure – and resistance to the *process* of change – in other words, *how* the change is introduced and managed, rather than the focus of the change. Such resistance may be manifested in behaviours such as refusing to co-operate, withholding information, working to rule and strike action. A key factor here should be identifying the root cause of any resistance (other than the instigation of the change itself). Such causes could include lack of information, poor communication, fear, shock, perceived loss of control, threat to status, job uncertainty, and so on. Any successful change management programme has to address these causes in order to ameliorate or remove them. The CIPD (2011) suggests that it is essential that two-way communication is encouraged and active employee participation and involvement is used as a strategy for overcoming potential conflict and resistance to change.

OD initiatives should also take account of the multicultural and diverse nature of contemporary organisations and the wider national and international context within which many of them operate. Employers need to move away from **Eurocentric** and **ethnocentric** approaches towards developing an awareness of issues specific to wider multicultural and minority groups within the workplace. Strategies that actively encourage employee voice and inclusion have a part to play here. Diversity should be valued as an asset to the business and as a positive force for change.

CASE STUDY

Managing an ageing workforce: how employers are adapting to an older labour market

A survey published in 2010 by the CIPD and the Chartered Management Institute (CMI) examined the attitudes of HR professionals and managers to older workers, how equipped organisations are to cope with an ageing workforce, and the impact on HR policies and practices.

Findings from the survey suggested that employers acknowledge the invaluable contributions made by older employees and revealed that negative perceptions about older workers are generally declining. Nevertheless, the report concluded that there is a worrying lack of preparedness for an ageing workforce and recommended that senior teams must become strategically involved in promoting the age agenda.

(Full details of the survey can be accessed from: www.cipd.co.uk/ binaries/ Managing_Ageing_Workforce.pdf)

THE ROLE AND PURPOSE OF OD INTERVENTIONS

As stated earlier, the main purpose of any OD intervention is to introduce and develop processes designed to enable organisations to adapt to their changing environments. OD focuses on developing the organisations with the aim of improving overall performance. The purpose of OD is for sustainability and adaptability, with the utilisation of people to achieve this.

French and Bell's (1999, pp25–6) perspective of OD as a 'long-term effort, led and supported by top management [...] through an ongoing, collaborative management of organisation culture of intact work teams and other team configurations' highlights the importance of taking a longer-term focus in order to influence and impact upon organisation culture. It is argued that the values espoused by OD (those of employee empowerment, the creation of openness and awareness and shared ownership of change) can most positively impact upon organisational effectiveness if OD is able to permeate across the whole organisation, promoting a culture of collaboration and continuous learning. It is suggested that for any OD process to be successful it must be linked with business objectives and incorporated within **performance management** and measurement strategies.

An OD process can be introduced to address a specific organisational need within a part of the organisation or integrated throughout the organisation's processes and systems. The incorporation of OD processes as stand-alone initiatives could, for example, be effective as a pilot, before rolling out the process organisation-wide. This could cause less disruption to the organisation as a whole and take much less time, effort and resources. However, one of the potential difficulties with using OD in this way is that it risks misalignment with other activities and initiatives within the organisation.

A possible alternative would be to introduce a number of similarly focused OD interventions across the organisation. If this approach is adopted, care should be taken to ensure alignment across these interventions, so as to eliminate the potential for conflicting priorities and outcomes.

Another alternative would be to incorporate one overarching OD intervention that encompasses the organisation as a whole. The benefit of using this approach is that the OD process would be transparent and recognisable to all employees. However, the difficulty associated with this approach could be that if an organisation's functions are highly differentiated (different from one another), the approach might not be entirely suitable for each and every division.

MEASURING THE IMPACT OF OD

Arguably, one of the most important aspects of any OD intervention is to be able to ascertain how and when the organisation will know if the intervention has been successful and what impact it has made upon organisational effectiveness. It is therefore crucial to set and agree realistic and identifiable performance measures from the outset, as noted earlier. Important questions to be posed from the outset include:

- What is it that we want to be doing, and how do we know this? (Establish targets to meet organisational missions, visions and strategic objectives.)
- Who should be involved in these decisions? (This will make an impact on the level of buy-in or resistance demonstrated by organisation members, as discussed above under the heading *Entry and contracting*.)
- How will we know when we are heading in the right direction? (A combination of short-, medium- and long-term measures must be in place in order to identify the extent to which the organisation development intervention is on track and meeting its objectives.)

The three forms of organisational change outcomes OD should aim for, according to Golembiewski *et al* (1976), include *alpha*, identifying the difference between before and after measures (for example, enabling customer service quality improvement to be highlighted as a result of an OD intervention); *beta*, the identification of a shift in perspectives in assessment of the measure (for example, customer service quality might not have shown any dramatic improvements, but there is a greater awareness from those involved in the process of the need for customer service quality improvement); and *gamma*, a comprehensive reconceptualisation of the issue (for example, the focus may not be on before-and-after differentials, or on the greater awareness by employees of the need for customer service quality improvement; following the intervention, those involved in the process might conclude that changes are required in communications, roles and responsibilities, if organisation-wide improvements are to be realised). This outcome is concerned with more general organisational improvement.

A crucial aspect of OD is that it seeks to positively impact upon the organisation's flexibility to change and consequently its adaptability to future challenges. It is argued, therefore, that all three of these organisational change outcomes will contribute to the organisation's continued focus on process improvement and renewal.

QUANTITATIVE AND QUALITATIVE PERFORMANCE MEASURES

In monitoring effectiveness Carnall (2007) suggests that organisations should concentrate on the following four areas: the extent to which the organisation is achieving its objectives; the organisation's utilisation of its resources; how its internal system is maintained; and its adaptability to its changing environment. A range of measures can be utilised to identify these outcomes. Quantitative performance measures are those concerned with numerical analysis and measurement that help us establish past performance (for example, costs, productivity, wastage and turnover) in an attempt to make future predictions. However, solely relying on quantitative measures could mean that past experiences, judgement and intuition are missed. Qualitative performance measures are considered to delve more deeply into individual behaviours and perspectives, gaining insights into employee satisfaction, management style and development, corporate culture, etc. Even though the aims of these two approaches to measurement are very different, they can and arguably should be utilised in conjunction with each other to enable a comprehensive understanding of the extent to which performance outcomes have been achieved. Failure to do this could result in a narrow approach to measurement that misses key issues which have an impact on effectiveness. Table 2.1 lists some of the methods that are associated with each of these approaches to measurement.

Table 2.1 Quantitative and qualitative performance measurement methods

Measurement	Possible quantitative methods	Possible qualitative methods
Sickness absence	Analysis of absence figures to identify frequencies and trends	Return-to-work interviews identifying personal issues or gauging perspectives relating to absence Occupational health report analysis
Customer service	Number of complaints Frequency of product returns Customer feedback survey/ questionnaire involving closed questions	In-depth customer feedback via interview or survey/questionnaire including open questions Observations
Employee satisfaction	Employee survey/ questionnaire involving closed questions to gauge frequencies and inform trend analysis	Employee survey/questionnaire involving open questions Employee interviews or focus groups to gain an in-depth insight into employee attitudes and uncover the issues behind problem areas
Employee performance	Productivity rates Measurable performance target-setting and analysis	Employee interviews to gain an in-depth insight into employee attitudes and uncover the issues behind problem areas Performance review including the in-depth investigation of attitudes and behaviours Observation

Care must also be taken to ensure that a common language and common frameworks are used so that measurement structures can be transparent, easily understood and aligned throughout the organisation.

THE BALANCED SCORECARD

One method that incorporates a range of these OD measurement methods and is utilised by many organisations is the balanced scorecard (Kaplan and Norton 1996). The term 'balanced' is used because it places equal emphasis upon financial and non-financial measures. The four main perspectives of the balanced scorecard are:

- financial – the financial targets to be achieved
- internal processes – the processes that must be in place for the organisation to excel
- customers – how the organisation plans to provide value for its customers
- innovation, growth and learning – the ways in which the organisation can continue to learn and improve.

The measures selected to be used within the balanced scorecard then link these four areas with the organisation's business vision and strategy as a means of striving for continuous organisational improvement. This is usually achieved through the organisation's performance management processes.

SUMMARY

This chapter has provided a detailed overview of the origins, process, practices and measurement of OD. The history of the development of OD highlights human needs and group interaction as those areas that can hold the key to improvements in innovation, productivity and development. Accordingly, optimising transparency and employee engagement within the development of OD interventions is considered to be of utmost importance. Theoretical perspectives and models all place heavy emphasis upon the behaviours of the OD practitioners and organisational leaders as being crucial to the success of an OD intervention. In the evaluation of OD, considerations of combining both quantitative and qualitative performance measures offer the potential for analytical discipline to be supported by intuition in order to gain a holistic understanding of performance issues.

CASE STUDY

Organisational analysis and organisational development

Professor Les Worrall, Professor of Strategic Analysis, Coventry Business School, Coventry University

The context

Whether they are in the private, public or voluntary sectors, organisations exist in increasingly dynamic and unstable operating environments. Increasing instability requires organisations to be able to re-engineer business processes, restructure, re-skill, learn from change and redefine their own cultures. Organisations will need to become increasingly 'dynamically capable' if they are to succeed: this will have major implications for the leadership styles, behaviours and skills that senior managers will have to develop.

Managing strategic change is difficult because senior managers need to be able to trade off the pressures coming from outside the organisation against pressures coming from inside the organisation. While senior managers may see that competitive pressures in the private sector or budget reductions in the public sector are going to make the future problematic, it is difficult for them to respond to these pressures without causing significant negative effects on their workforce, especially if those changes require cost reductions, redundancy or organisational restructuring.

This case study describes an eight-year programme of organisational development in a local authority that had been created from the merger of two pre-existing organisations. The study shows how a succession of biennial employee surveys was used to develop the organisational development initiatives needed to build a new organisation, and how the implementation of these policies was evaluated over time.

The need for information and intelligence to inform the organisational development process

The organisation's senior management understood that building a new unified and cohesive organisation out of two pre-existing organisations was a long-term process that required a sophisticated approach to change management. To achieve this aim, the council appointed a long-term, independent, academic partner to advise them. The council also appointed a head of organisational development to work closely with the academic partner to design an employee attitude survey and to design and implement a communications process for feeding the results of the research process back to the entire organisation. At the outset, a transparent communications strategy and an open and honest approach to dealing with the results of the survey were seen as paramount.

The design of the questionnaire and the wider research process

The council encouraged a high level of transparency in the conduct of the survey. All key stakeholders (for example, councillors, trade unions and specific employee groups – for example, black and minority ethnic employees) were kept fully informed and involved. The head of organisational development facilitated several workshops to give employee groups the opportunity to raise issues that they wanted the questionnaire to cover.

After a long process of discussion, a questionnaire was developed which focused on the following:

To what extent do employees identify with the council?

How does the council treat its employees?

How do employees perceive the prevailing management and leadership styles in the organisation?

How good are employees' relationships with their immediate line managers?

How do employees feel about the work they do, the design of their jobs and the council as a place to work?

What are co-worker relationships like in business units/teams?

How satisfied are employees with their jobs and with facets of their job?

How effective is training, and how well is the personal and performance development process working?

Is there evidence of bullying, harassment or poor management behaviour?

Communicating the results

After each survey, feedback sessions were held for each department, with the academic adviser being given a relatively free rein to develop the presentations and deliver them. Occasionally, there were difficult messages to be communicated but on more than one occasion the chief executive expressed a wish to 'tell it like it is'. On occasions, senior managers had to listen to feedback that was not flattering to them or their management styles.

Experience revealed that a transparent communications strategy is essential if you are going to ensure that employees see surveys as worthwhile and honest. Employees are not stupid; they experience organisational life on a daily basis and they know when they are being lied to and when difficult issues are being glossed over. It became very clear that the managers who most tried to censor the feedback were perceived as having the worst leadership and management styles – it was their departments that were characterised by low reciprocal trust, managerial invisibility and inaccessibility, and poor upward and downward communications.

The survey revealed that the most potent driver of job satisfaction in the organisation was the quality of the working relationship that employees had with their immediate line manager. This finding encouraged the council to look hard at the management behaviours and leadership styles that it wanted to develop in the 125 people that had significant managerial and leadership responsibilities in the council.

What were the key issues that the surveys exposed, and how did the council react to them?

The research exposed and charted trends in a number of important issues. One of the key findings was that employees' experiences varied considerably within the organisation and, consequently, the survey was used to identify those areas where employee perceptions were at their worst. The data for these areas could then be analysed to develop an understanding of what was driving dissatisfaction and negative attitudes in these areas.

It was also possible to identify those areas that were performing well but had problems in specific areas – perhaps revealing concerns about how well a particular manager was performing in aspects of their jobs or with aspects of job design. It was also possible to isolate those areas where negative attitudes were most prevalent and link these attitudes to responses about the management and leadership styles of more senior council managers.

The survey had considerable value in helping the council develop actions targeted either on specific parts of the organisation or on specific issues within specific parts of the organisation. As a specific exercise, the chief executive asked the academic adviser to suggest measures and actions that could be included within the annual performance objectives of senior and middle managers. A detailed analysis of the data revealed that many of the issues raised in the surveys could be traced back to individual managers' leadership styles.

Implications for OD

While many organisations have conducted employee attitude surveys, few will have so systematically embedded their surveys into their organisation's wider organisational development process. The surveys were used to identify those parts of the council that were performing well and badly to identify where and how interventions could have the greatest effect. The surveys were used to test how well corporate initiatives on personal development and training were working; to expose patchiness in the take-up of development; and to expose the areas where some managers were being less than assiduous in responding to corporate drives to enhance the quality of all employees' working lives.

The surveys allowed the council to identify hot spots where employees were overloaded, where jobs were badly designed, where teams were not functioning well and where managers were displaying leadership styles and management behaviours which did not conform with how the council expected their managers to behave. The surveys also allowed the council to see which factors were reducing individual or collective job satisfaction.

Throughout the eight-year process, the council became far more adept at learning how to use the information the surveys provided. Initially, managers at all levels were fearful about what the surveys would reveal, but the more effective managers used the information to develop insights about how issues could be addressed and to learn about how they were being perceived as leaders and managers. These proved to be highly valuable insights.

Questions:

1   What were the main aims of adopting this approach to organisational analysis?

2   In what ways did this method support the organisation's OD process?

3   What were the main outcomes for the organisation of using this approach?

4   How does management behaviour contribute to the way OD

interventions are received by employees?

FURTHER READING

BOOKS

CHEUNG-JUDGE, M.-Y. and HOLBECHE, L. (2011) *Organisation Development: A practitioner's guide for OD and HR.* London: Kogan Page. A concise text offering clear guidance and support from a practitioner's perspective using a theoretical foundation.

COOPERRIDER, D. L. and WHITNEY, D. (2005) *Appreciative Inquiry: A positive revolution in change.* San Francisco, CA: Berrett-Koehler. A short, practical text giving insight into the theory of appreciative inquiry and its potential for collaborative change within organisations.

CUMMINGS, T. G. and WORLEY, C. (2008) *Organization Development and Change,* 9th edn. Cincinnati, OH: South-Western Cengage Learning. This book presents an examination of theory, models, practice and research in the field of organisational development and improvement.

ARTICLES

AVEY, J. B., WERNSING, T. S. and LUTHANS, F. (2008) Can positive employees help positive organizational change? *Journal of Applied Behavioral Science.* Vol 44, No 1. 48–70. This article provides an insight into the influence of employee attitudes upon the change process.

RAINEY TOLBERT, M. A. and HANAFIN, J. (2006) Use of self in OD consulting: what matters is presence, in JONES, B. B. and BRAZZEL, M. (eds) *The NTL Handbook of Organisation Development and Change: Principles, practices and perspectives.* 69–82. New York: John Wiley & Sons. This article presents a practical overview of the OD consultant's role in organisational change.

WEBSITES

CIPD (2011) *Change Management [online].* Factsheet. London: Chartered Institute of Personnel and Development. Available at: http://www.cipd.co.uk/hr-resources/factsheets/change-management.aspx. CIPD factsheet offering guidance on the management of change within organisations and the role of HR.

CIPD (2011) *Organisation Development [online].* Factsheet. London: Chartered Institute of Personnel and Development. Available at: http://www.cipd.co.uk/hr-resources/factsheets/organisation-development.aspx. CIPD factsheet giving an overview of OD, providing practical advice on OD initiatives and discussing the relationship between OD and HR.

REFERENCES

ANDERSON, D. L. (2010) *Organization Development – The process of leading organizational change.* Thousand Oaks, CA: Sage Publications.

ARGYRIS, C. and SCHÖN, D. (1978) *Organisational Learning: A theory of action perspective.* Reading, MA: Addison-Wesley.

AVEY, J. B., WERNSING, T. S. and LUTHANS, F. (2008) Can positive employees help positive organizational change? *Journal of Applied Behavioral Science.* Vol 44, No 1. 48–70.

BARTUNEK, J. M., ROUSSEAU, D. M., RUDOLPH, J. W. and DEPALMA, J. A. (2006) On the receiving end: sensemaking, emotion, and assessments of an organizational change initiated by others. *Journal of Applied Behavioral Science.* Vol 42, No 2. 182–206.

BECKHARD, R. (1969) *Organisation Development: Strategies and models.* Reading, MA: Addison-Wesley.

BLAKE, R. and MOUTON, S. (1981) Management by Grid® Principles or Situationalism, *Which? Group Organization Management.* Vol 8, No 4. 439–55.

BLOCK, P. (2011) *Flawless Consulting – A guide to getting your expertise used,* 3rd edn. Austin, TX: Jossey-Bass.

BRADFORD, D. L. and BURKE, W. W. (2005) *Reinventing Organization Development: New approaches to change in organizations.* San Francisco, CA: Pfeiffer.

CARNALL, C. (2007) *Managing Change in Organisations,* 5th edn. Harlow: Prentice Hall.

CHEUNG-JUDGE, M.-Y. and HOLBECHE, L. (2011) *Organisation Development: A practitioner's guide for OD and HR.* London: Kogan Page.

CIPD (2011) *Change Management [online].* Factsheet. London: Chartered Institute of Personnel and Development. Available at: http://www.cipd.co.uk/hr-resources/factsheets/change-management.aspx [accessed 25 April 2012].

COOPERRIDER, D. L. and WHITNEY, D. (2005) *Appreciative Inquiry: A positive revolution in change.* San Francisco, CA: Berrett-Koehler.

CUMMINGS, T. G. (2008) *Handbook of Organization Development.* London: Sage.

CUMMINGS, T. G. and WORLEY, C. (1996) *Organization Development and Change,* 6th edn. Cincinnati, OH: South-Western.

CUMMINGS, T. G. and WORLEY, C. (2005) *Organization Development and Change,* 8th edn. Cincinnati, OH: Thomson South-Western.

CUMMINGS, T. G. and WORLEY, C. (2008) *Organization Development and Change*, 9th edn. Cincinnati, OH: South-Western Cengage Learning.

EASTERBY-SMITH, M., THORPE, R. and JACKSON, P. (2008) *Management Research*, 3rd edn. London: Sage.

FRENCH, W. L. and BELL, C. (1999) *Organization Development: Behavioral science interventions for organization improvement*. New Jersey: Prentice Hall.

GALLOS, J. V. (2006) *Organization Development*. San Francisco, CA: Jossey-Bass Reader.

GOLEMBIEWSKI, R., BILLINGSLEY, K. and YEAGER, S. (1976) Measuring change and persistence in human affairs: types of change generated by OD designs. *Journal of Applied Behavioural Science*. Vol 12, 133–57.

KANTER, R. M. (1983) *The Change Masters: Innovation and entrepreneurship in the American corporation*. New York: Simon & Schuster.

KAPLAN, R. S. and NORTON, D. P. (1996) *The Balanced Scorecard: Turning strategy into action*. Boston, MA: Harvard Business School Press.

KOGAN, J. (1972) Motives and development. *Journal of Personality and Social Psychology*. Vol 22. 51–66.

KOLB, D. and FROHMAN, A. (1970) An organisational development approach to consulting. *Sloan Management Review*, Vol 12. 51–65

KOTTER, J. P. (1996) *Leading Change*. Boston, MA: Harvard Business School Press.

KUNDA, G. (1992) *Engineering Culture*. Philadelphia, PA: Temple University Press.

LEWIN, K. (1951) *Field Theory in Social Science*. New York: Harper & Row.

LIPPITT, G. and LIPPITT, R. (1975) *The Consulting Process in Action: Examining the dynamics of the client-consultant working relationship*. Washington, DC: Development Publications.

LIPPITT, R., WATSON, J. and WESTLEY, B. (1958) *The Dynamics of Planned Change*. New York: Harcourt, Brace & World.

MARGULIES, N. (1978) Perspectives on the marginality of the consultant's role, in BURKE, W. W. (ed.) *The Cutting Edge: Current theory and practice in organisation development*. La Jolla, CA: University Associates.

MASLOW, A. (1954) *Motivation and Personality*. New York: Harper & Row.

MCGREGOR, D. C. (1960) *The Human Side of Enterprise*. New York: McGraw-Hill.

MULLINS, L. J. (2005) *Management and Organisational Behaviour*, 7th edn. Harlow: Pearson Education.

NEUMANN, J. E., KELLNER, K. and DAWSON-SHEPHERD, A. (1997) *Developing Organisational Consultancy*. London: Routledge.

PETERS, T. and WATERMAN, R. (1982) *In Search of Excellence*. New York: Harper & Row.

RAINEY TOLBERT, M. A. and HANAFIN, J. (2006) Use of self in OD consulting: what matters is presence. In: JONES, B. B. and BRAZZEL, M. (eds) *The NTL Handbook of Organisation Development and Change: Principles, practices and perspectives*, 69–82. New York: John Wiley & Sons.

RAUSCHENBERGER, J., SCHMITT, N. and HUNTER, J. E. (1980) A test of the need hierarchy concept by a Markov model of change in need strength. *Administrative Science Quarterly*. Vol 25. 654–70.

SALANCIK, G. R. and PFEFFER, J. (1977) An examination of need satisfaction models of job attitudes. *Administrative Science Quarterly*. Vol 22. 427–56.

SCHEIN, E. H. (1988) *Organisational Psychology*, 3rd edn. London: Prentice Hall.

SCHEIN, E. H. (1999) *Process Consultation Revisited – Building the helping relationship*. Boston, MA: Addison-Wesley.

SENGE, P. M. (1990) *The Fifth Discipline: The art and practice of the learning organization*. New York: Doubleday Currency.

SENIOR, B. and SWAILES, S. (2010) *Organizational Change*, 4th edn. Harlow: FT/Prentice Hall.

TAYLOR, F. (1947) *Scientific Management*. New York: Harper & Row.

WAHBA, M. A. and BRIDWELL, L. G. (1976) Maslow reconsidered: a review of research on the need hierarchy theory. *Organizational Behaviour and Human Performance*. Vol 15. 212–40.

WHETTEN, D. A. and CAMERON, K. S. (2005) *Developing Management Skills*, 6th edn. Upper Saddle River, NJ: Prentice Hall.

CHAPTER 3

Developing Coaching and Mentoring

Jill Ashley-Jones, Terrence Wendell Brathwaite and Rosalind Maxwell-Harrison

CHAPTER CONTENTS

- Introduction
- Coaching and mentoring definitions
- Coaching and mentoring in a global context
- Coaching skills for managers
- Coaching models, philosophies and practice
- Some ethical considerations
- The Manager as coach or mentor
- Evaluating return on investment
- Summary

KEY LEARNING OUTCOMES

By the end of this chapter, you will be able to:

- Recognise, differentiate, analyse and evaluate coaching and mentoring in organisations in terms of efficacy and effectiveness.
- Understand the line management role and contribution to the coaching and mentoring agenda and acknowledge how they can support those processes in order to develop organisation talent.
- Make a personal contribution to the coaching and mentoring agenda within organisations.

INTRODUCTION

In this chapter we explore coaching and **mentoring** as similar evidence-based activities which seek to bridge the gap between the traditional aspirations of an organisation such as stability and security, and the more current methods of nurturing a culture of learning, innovation and reciprocity between employer and employee. By providing an introduction to the practice of coaching and mentoring our aim is to engage and heighten your interest in the crucial realm of HRD where the effective integration of the employee into the organisational culture is now a key requirement of employers both nationally and on the global stage (Rosinski 2010).

Signposts to interesting supporting materials that will further your learning and understanding of this emergent subject area are provided, including a link to the CIPD Career framework. In addition and in recognition of the increasingly multicultural business landscape that human resource practitioners (HRPs) may find themselves operating within, we offer an example of a cross-cultural coaching and mentoring model known by the name 'Sankofa'. Originally developed from West African traditions, it is now also being effectively implemented within some North American organisations.

We begin by exploring some definitions of coaching and mentoring, before moving into explanations of the background and development of this area of individual and organisational development.

COACHING AND MENTORING DEFINITIONS

Coach, from the Hungarian *kocsi szekér*, wagon of Kocs – a village where coaches were first made (Collins 2011).

In the 1830s the term 'coach' was used as a slang definition for tutors at Oxford University who were said to 'carry their students around'. Use of the word 'coach' at this time conveyed with it an expectation therefore that the person undertaking this coaching activity was an expert, with the knowledge to understand the task to be completed – in this instance, the passing of examinations. Consideration of an apprenticeship model offers some insight into how this may have worked in practice.

Traditionally, the apprentice watches the master until the master deems them to have enough knowledge to practise the task themselves. Only then would the master allow the apprentice (under close supervision) to attempt the task, although it might be many months before the apprentice was considered competent to work alone. This is a markedly different approach from the 'non-directive' style adopted by most modern coaching practitioners who are unlikely to have any actual knowledge of the coachees' tasks but instead operate as experts with skills in the application of the coaching process.

This process, when used appropriately and with consistency, allows the coachees to draw upon their internal resources and, through a process of building their personal insight and awareness, the coachees are enabled to make substantive and sustained change to the way they do things. In this modern coaching model the people being coached 'carry' themselves – which is very different from the original connotations of the term.

It may be helpful for readers to understand what it is to be a coach. In addition, if our role as HR specialists requires us to support the implementation of a **coaching culture** within employing organisations, some form of definition about what is meant by coaching and mentoring may also be helpful. Research undertaken by the CIPD (2008a) revealed that '71% of UK organisations use coaching methodologies' and that this area of practice 'has become a widely used and valuable learning tool'. Price (2011, p240) notes that many organisations have found that 'coaching was an important way of reducing leakage [of employees' learning] from training courses and therefore improved their effectiveness'. This suggests that the rather more intangible HRD technique of coaching can, if used in conjunction with training courses, provide a two-pronged approach to capitalising on investment in learning by providing demonstrable outcomes for the organisation.

Tables 3.1 and 3.2 below offer some widely accepted definitions of coaching and mentoring, as set out in Hawkins (2008).

Table 3.1 Definitions of coaching

Author	Definition
Parsloe	'Coaching is a process that enables learning and development to occur and thus performance to improve'
Clutterbuck	'Primarily a short-term intervention aimed at performance improvement or developing a particular competence'
Downey	'The art of facilitating the performance, learning and development of another'

Table 3.2 Definitions of mentoring

Author	Definition
Price	'Mentors are established managers who provide support, help and advice to more junior members of staff – ideally not a direct line manager'
CIPD	'Mentoring is the long-term passing on of support, guidance and advice'
Clutterbuck	'A mixture of parent and peer, the primary function is to be a transformational figure in an individual's development'

Interestingly, the term 'mentor' has a strong androgynous root, arising as it does from the ancient Greek legend of Odysseus. Before taking his leave to fight in the Trojan Wars Odysseus entrusted his son Telemachus to the virgin goddess of wisdom, craft and war, Pallas Athene, who then transformed herself into human form as (the masculine) Mentor, Telemachus's wise counsellor and helper during his father's absence.

It is clear from the definitions in the above tables that our understanding of the concept of coaching has shifted since the 1830s Oxford interpretation. However, we suggest that perhaps the current use of the term 'mentor' is more closely aligned to that original definition of a coach.

REFLECTIVE ACTIVITY

1   How do these definitions accord with your own current understanding or experience of coaching and mentoring?

2   Are there any definitions that attract you more than others? How do you account for this?

3   Are there any definitions that you disagree with? On what basis?

HOW HELPFUL ARE DEFINITIONS?

Professional coaching bodies – for example, the European Mentoring and Coaching Council (EMCC) – do not provide a single definition of coaching and instead offer a map to measure aspiring coaches' skills against categories of competence. These are listed below. We may deduce from this that the EMCC is of the view that any definition would be best applied to the coach.

EMCC categories:

- understanding self
- commitment to self-development
- managing the [coaching] contract
- building the [coaching] relationship
- enabling insight and learning
- outcome and action orientation
- use of models and techniques
- evaluation.

The CIPD (2011) Factsheet acknowledges that there is still considerable debate amongst coaching practitioners in relation to definitions, but suggests that coaching:

> 'targets high performance and improvement at work and usually focuses on specific skills and goals, although it may have an impact on an individual's personal attributes (such as social interaction or confidence).'

Similarly to the EMCC's, the CIPD's guidance offers a selection of characteristics found in good coaching practice, thus:

- It is essentially a non-directive form of development, though this is not a hard and fast rule.
- It focuses on improving performance and developing individuals' skills.
- Personal issues may be discussed but the emphasis is on performance at work.
- Coaching activities have both organisational and individual goals.
- It provides people with feedback on both their strengths and their weaknesses.
- It is a skilled activity, which should be delivered by people who are trained to do so.

This CIPD definition also recognises that although most coaching interventions occur within the construct of a work environment, we do not shake off our personal and family background when we enter the world of work. We can argue that we are creatures of many parts belonging to many communities – e.g. our families, social groups and religious groups in addition to work teams and the wider work organisation. We also need to recognise that it is inevitable that these parts of our lives impact on how we grow our careers. Coaches therefore need to be skilled at recognising when the non-work elements of a person's life bubble through during a coaching session, and to manage the contractual and ethical boundaries so that coachees may explore these sometimes conflicting elements of their lives safely and within a non-judgemental environment.

Coaching might therefore be classed as a 'helping' strategy. We thus need to consider how it is different from other helping strategies such as counselling or therapy. Figure 3.1 below offers some answers.

Figure 3.1 Similarities and differences between coaching, mentoring and counselling

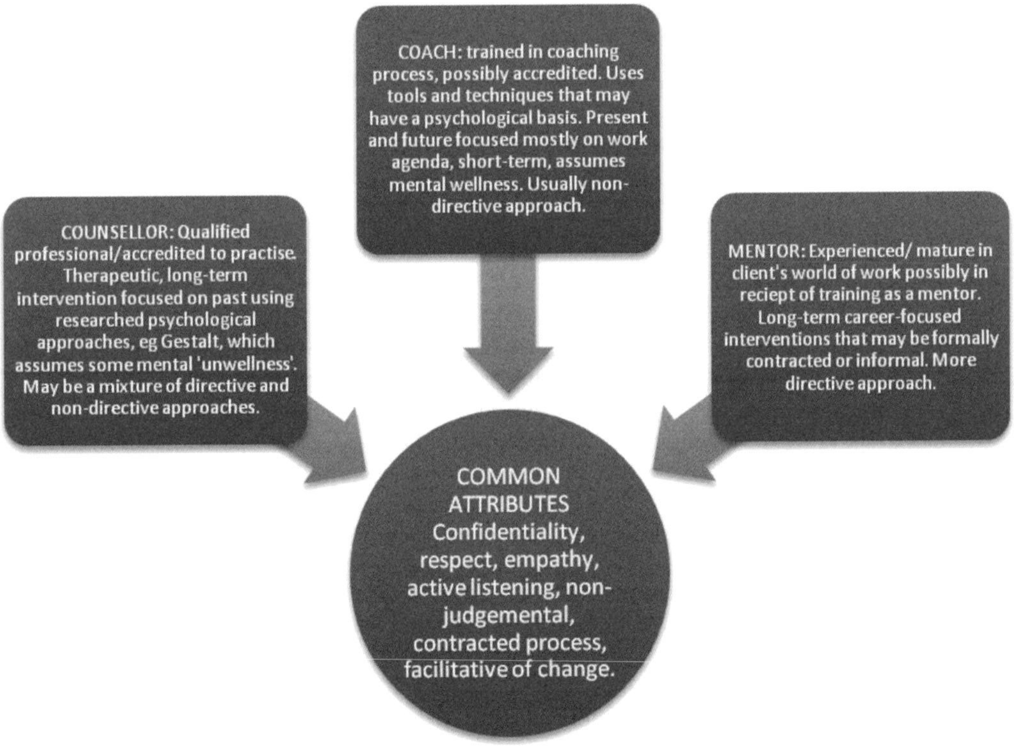

COACH: trained in coaching process, possibly accredited. Uses tools and techniques that may have a psychological basis. Present and future focused mostly on work agenda, short-term, assumes mental wellness. Usually non-directive approach.

COUNSELLOR: Qualified professional/accredited to practise. Therapeutic, long-term intervention focused on past using researched psychological approaches, eg Gestalt, which assumes some mental 'unwellness'. May be a mixture of directive and non-directive approaches.

MENTOR: Experienced/ mature in client's world of work possibly in reciept of training as a mentor. Long-term career-focused interventions that may be formally contracted or informal. More directive approach.

COMMON ATTRIBUTES Confidentiality, respect, empathy, active listening, non-judgemental, contracted process, facilitative of change.

The differing types and styles of coaching available and their backgrounds are considered below and in Table 3.3.

Given that research appears to underline the importance of building and maintaining developmental relationships (if an individual is to enhance his or her career opportunities) and the challenges that these new styles of working may have brought to older, more constricted interpersonal work relationships, we question whether this could have contributed to the growth in coaching within organisations as suggested by Erik de Haan (2008). If it has, should our search for a definition of coaching focus instead upon some way of defining the relationship between the coach and the coachee?

Cox *et al* (2010) propose an alternative approach, in which the question asked is, 'What is the purpose of the [coaching] activity?' Many earlier definitions of coaching – for example, 'Coaching is for the mentally healthy' (Grant 2000, as cited by Cox *et al* 2010, p3) – could nowadays been seen as both inaccurate and discriminatory. This is because evidence suggests that many people access coaching services during periods of change. It could therefore be argued that the resulting levels of anxiety attached to such events (even if the change process has been sought as an element of progressing one's career) can impact on any individual's sense of mental well-being, if only for a short time.

WHERE DOES MENTORING FIT?

Mentoring may appear to be slightly less problematical to define than coaching. Studies undertaken in the1990s recognised that developmental relationships can strengthen the employee–employer psychological contract and create a greater sense of commitment to the organisation. Central to these studies' definition of mentoring is the recognition of the importance within the process for assessment, challenge and support – much like coaching. However, others argue that it is in fact more difficult to define, due to the width and breadth of its application, as well as to the 'mental bandwidth' of the mentors, who can only be effective if they are able to challenge a mentee's expectations while sharing their own thinking and offering much-needed support and encouragement.

A tried and tested definition, originally provided by the Chartered Management Institute, is that mentoring is a powerful scheme for making progress, which depends on the positive partnership of two people: a junior partner, the mentee or protégé who wants to climb the ladder, and a senior partner, the mentor – someone who is already ahead, who wants to help the junior learn to play the game of life. This interpretation, we suggest, still resonates today.

Mentoring as an activity for developing and engaging individuals could be said to have been imported from the US corporate landscape in the late 1980s and since then has become intricately linked with the move to competency-based qualifications in the UK. Essentially, mentoring is one step beyond the traditional training and instruction programmes used to enhance employee performance, shifting the orientation to acquiring and applying skills supported by a protocol of integrated advice and career counselling. However, we would suggest that like coaching, the most effective (in terms of performance outcome by the mentee and satisfaction for the mentor) mentoring programmes are ones that are contracted formally with a clear definition of expected outcomes.

Illustration of practice

'Having a formal framework in place meant I really enjoyed my mentoring role. We both knew how we were going to work together: 'what was in and what was not'. Best of all for me, as a busy executive director, was the fact that I felt it was OK to take time with my mentee, that the organisation really did embrace this approach and that my chief executive valued the learning I could offer to those coming behind me.'

(Mrs Kim Elliott, Assistant Director of Commissioning reflecting upon the experience of being part of the NHS West Midlands Aspiring Director mentoring programme.)

We suggest that mentoring – because of its perceived ability to deliver career progression and its traditional links to the 'training model' of development – makes the process easier to define and be understood by all stakeholders.

Returning to coaching, Crawford (2010) observes that in some mature and established organisations, coaching is seen as service that is provided for individuals who are weak in their performance and, as such, coaching as both a concept and a process has a negative connotation. Interestingly, though, executive coaching – often embraced by those perceived to be at the top of their game, such as chief executives and their executive teams – is an area where coaching is seen to provide a positive and indeed highly prized development route.

So how may we conclude this discussion on definitions? We have seen that from its somewhat uninspiring roots coaching has grown into a key component of many organisations' HRD strategies, preventing good people from 'leaking' either themselves or their expertise out of the organisation by reinforcing more formal learning programmes. In addition, and via the building of interpersonal relationships, coaching interventions have not only enhanced the performance of individuals but also, we would argue, have compensated (in some situations) for loss of accepted psychological contract boundaries.

Defining coaching acceptably for all stakeholders remains challenging, and the question remains whether it should be to the coach that any definition is applied. This could provide greater clarity about the coach's model or philosophy of practice and help the purchasers of services to have greater understanding about exactly what outcomes they could expect. However, those accessing or purchasing coaching services are then required to have a greater knowledge of what those types and styles of coaching models, philosophy and practice are in order to decide on the right fit to the organisation's requirements.

We embrace the definition of coaching developed by Cox *et al* (2010, p1) because it provides a degree of clarity without any presupposition of knowledge on the part of the purchaser:

Coaching could be seen as a human development process that involves structured, focused interaction and the use of appropriate strategies, tools and techniques to promote desirable and sustainable change for the benefit of the coachee and potentially for other stakeholders.

REFLECTIVE ACTIVITY

1 Do you find the suggested definition by Cox *et al* (2010) workable for you? Does it afford you a way of both explaining to senior staff the idea of coaching practice and identifying/ securing coaching services?

2 What are the differences and similarities between mentoring and coaching, and how could both be utilised either together or separately to support HRD programmes?

3 Are there any definitions of coaching and mentoring that you disagree with? How have you made that decision?

COACHING AND MENTORING IN A GLOBAL CONTEXT

In this section we explore a model of coaching and mentoring that has developed from West African traditions to provide a global context to our earlier discussion. For further information on global coaching ideas and models see Malunga and Banda (2012) and Rosinski (2010) listed in the books recommended for further reading at the end of the chapter.

SANKOFA CONTEXT OF COACHING AND MENTORING

Today's globalised business landscape abounds in anomalies, including the situation whereby many people possess a lot of knowledge but never do anything very innovative with their learning. The ancient Greek philosopher Heraclitus said, 'Knowing many things doesn't teach insight,' and suggested to his peers that the key to being more resourceful is to know themselves well so that they can draw on their inner knowledge – and then use it skilfully – in order to deal with challenges successfully (Von Oech 2002). This principle of 'self-knowledge and global wisdom' actually pre-dates Heraclitus and harks back to the temples and tombs of ancient Egypt (*c.*1550 BC), which have since been visited by many Western scholars of medicine and counselling from Hippocrates (see Highfield 2007 and Gadalla 1999, 2008) to Carl Jung, who made extended expeditions to study diverse cultures and to learn 'elemental psychology' from the indigenous societies of Africa, which he subsequently translated into his analytical psychology (see Burleson 2005).

An appropriate analogy which accentuates Heraclitus's notion of being creative with 'self-knowledge and global wisdom' is that our knowledge is a lot like cooking. Imagine that several cooks from different cultural backgrounds have been assigned the task of preparing an interesting dish with the following ingredients: chicken, prawns, smoked sausage, crab, okra, onions, celery, long-grain rice and peppers. Some cooks may make a stew, some soup, and others an authentic New Orleans gumbo. Some dishes might be very tasty, whereas others may not. So, with the same resources, attaining a gratifying result depends on how the cooks work and play with their self-knowledge and global wisdom. This also applies to the HR manager. There are several modern derivatives of the ancient principle 'Know thyself' that are employed as coaching and mentoring mottoes around the world. However, there are also early trans-generational variations on this theme, which are proving quite effective in the field of HR today.

For example, in Ghana there is a very ancient healing symbol, Sankofa, which is acknowledged and shared by the Akan people of West Africa. It is linguistically explained in the Akan language as *san* ('to return') + *ko* ('to go') + *fa* ('to look, to seek and take'), which is then loosely interpreted as, 'It is perfectly acceptable to go back and search for something you've left behind.' Sankofa is one of the oldest underpinning constructs of coaching and mentoring in the world, since it inherently validated a cross-cultural approach to equipping the Akan community with both the traditional skills of reflection (i.e. 'searching within oneself'), along with the trans-generational capacity to enable and empower themselves to contribute more fully and productively to their livelihood, based on an ancestral memory bank of karmic insights gained from consulting their own collective experiences and intuition (see Bynum 1999 and Sheldrake 1988).

Visually, Sankofa is depicted as a mythical bird that flies forward whilst looking backward over its shoulder with an egg – signifying the future – in its mouth (see Figure 3.2). Although not promoted as a 'one-size-fits-all' model, the profundity of the proverb – *You must never forget where you come from. Before you look forward, remember to learn from past experience* – transcends time and space as a truth about life that supplies a common thread to all coaching and mentoring philosophies (Malunga and Banda 2012).

Figure 3.2 The Sankofa bird (traditional design)

With the fast global pace of political, economic, social, technological, legal and environmental development, organisational development is playing an increasingly critical role in helping transcultural corporations to manage the immediate conditions of their existence. Coaching and mentoring as prevailing organisational development strategies are premised on the assertion that 'searching within ourselves' for our own creative characteristics is a wonderful way to gain insight, while changing the relationship between cosmopolitan HR managers (a term often used interchangeably with 'global HR managers', but in this context also denoting an inclusive, multidimensional global vision of the business arena rather than one in which the elements of the HR role are exclusively framed) and employees.

Coaching and mentoring within the context of Sankofa implies that to initiate a progressive organisational culture, cosmopolitan HR managers must equip employees with the tools, knowledge and opportunities required to delve deep inside themselves and find their own creative tendencies. Thus, with a cyclical review, renewal and refinement of their ideas, attitudes and commitment, they will be able to contribute more effectively to the mission of the organisation, in a mode that is relevant to both the present and the future.

In the ongoing EMCC-driven debate on the dissimilarities between coaching and mentoring, there has emerged an acceptance of a number of similarities within identifiable contexts. Koortzen and Oosthuizen (2010) assert that coaching and mentoring may:

- be relatively directive or non-directive
- require and draw upon the helper's experience
- be of long or short duration
- involve giving advice
- work with goals set by the learner or for the learner
- deal with significant transitions the learner wishes to make
- address eclectic personal growth ambitions.

Brathwaite (2005; 2009) reveals further congruences, via a philosophical inquiry into the creative conditions which allow for efficacy and productivity, by using the deep unity between the triad of *language* (the 'power of the word'), *action learning* and *accomplishment*, within a contextualised approach to coaching and mentoring. According to the CIPD, the basic philosophy of action learning is that the most efficient learning takes place when learners are faced with a real problem to solve and thus proceed to 'search within themselves', so as to study their own actions and experience in order to improve performance. As an educational process, action learning is quintessentially a perfect modern manifestation of the Sankofa proverb: 'the palm-oil with which words [and their power] are eaten' (Achebe 1994, p13).

Accordingly, Brathwaite's *raison d'être* for exercising the 'power of the word' in the contextual approach to coaching and mentoring has its key theoretical springboard in the purpose and practice of social (participatory) theatre, which allows actors and audience to interact and confront the interpretatively complex and current dilemmas of life and work. Also grounded in the tradition of Sankofa, social (participatory) theatre methods are underpinned by the postulate that what one considers to be reality is invented through communicated language and understanding, as a matter of interpretative construction on the part of the person experiencing that 'reality' (Brathwaite 2009). That is to say, a person has the capacity to change an unhappy situation via the 'caterpillar-cum-butterfly' transformational law of:

Thought + Word + Deed = 'Reality'.

Coaches and mentors who have searched within themselves and managed their innate technical, interpersonal, intrapersonal and communicative competences to become successful demonstrate the Sankofa principles of integrating communicated language (the 'power of the word'), action learning and achievement (see Figure 3.3). They view challenges as a privilege rather than as a problem, and are empowered by them. Such challenges allow them to achieve the goals they have committed themselves to accomplishing. Moreover, as further illustrated in Figure 3.3, these individuals are not averse to shifting their creative paradigms to employ empowering language that is more appropriate for their journey from *vision* to *attention* to *intention* to *commitment* to *effective action* (see also Ramsden 1993).

Figure 3.3 The Sankofa context of coaching and mentoring

Parsloe (1995) contends that the key methods of coaching and mentoring within this context are fourfold:

- 'hands-on' when engaged with inexpert clients
- 'hands-off' when nurturing optimum performance with seasoned clients
- 'supporter' when facilitating clients in the employment of a flexible learning package process
- 'qualifier' when facilitating a client to develop a specific prerequisite for a competence-based or professional qualification.

These strategic techniques can be applied according to the training needs and aspirations of the clients.

Nevertheless, as a general rule, and in keeping with the old adage 'Once is an instance, twice is a coincidence, three or more times make a pattern,' there are a number of turbulent 'patterns' related to the execution of coaching and mentoring interventions on the job. McLean *et al* (2005) have identified some of these patterns (or 'issues'), which include:

- the fear of losing authority and influence over employees
- the altering or varying of roles between managers and employees, especially when the former choose to maintain an inflexible attitude with regard to their managerial prerogative

- gender demarcations, which reinforce the prevailing attitudes and trends that affect leaders' behaviours
- conflicting roles, wherein managers who function as coaches or mentors also find it difficult to differentiate between competing role expectations and role strain
- the effect of the manager as coach or mentor on the psychosocial behaviour of the employees. For example, managers who were more discerning, offered more endorsements and less sneering criticisms, experienced a very positive relationship with their coachees or mentees, who in turn demonstrated a higher level of work enjoyment, loyalty and self-esteem on the job
- the number of people to be coached or mentored, and the time constraints in providing the coaching and mentoring required by all concerned, since managers with fewer coachees or mentees are more prolific in their coaching skills and behaviours.

To proactively address the root of these patterns or issues, the cosmopolitan HR manager as coach or mentor has to 'search within' (intrapersonal competence) to determine his or her own mental locks and establish his or her own creative tendencies – then, based on such self-reconciliation, communicate (interpersonal competence) to the employee(s) a sense of personal vision and career development mission, which focuses on self-empowerment or taking greater charge of one's self and life. Hobson and Scally (1991) note that to function in a self-empowered mode, we must be able to:

- believe that, and act in the belief that, we are receptive to and able to change
- have the competence to change some aspects of ourselves and the worldview with which we live
- use our convictions to appreciate where there is an incongruity between the way things are and the way we would like them to be
- identify desired outcomes and the action steps required to achieve them
- act – to instigate our action plans
- live each day being aware of our power to assess, review, influence and self-direct (in keeping with the Sankofa spirit of review, renewal and refinement)
- help others to become more self-powered.

Accordingly, the coach or mentor's vision must be checked and goals identified at various levels, and must foster a sense of commitment to these goals which can only be realised through meaningful and coherent communication based on action and deeds. Furthermore, for the coachee or mentee to have trust in and be committed to their manager's advocacy for self-determination, they must be provided with very clear targets and know that their achievements will be given due appreciation. It is only in such a climate that cosmopolitan HR managers as coaches or mentors can expect staff to be truly self-empowered. That is because the integration of the overall company objectives with that of the coachee or mentee's moral values/ethics, personal and professional goals, beliefs, information about self and multiple skills, safely establishes the organisation as a supportive or facilitating function, constructing an environment and a corporate culture within which valuable contributions can be provided by both employer and employee.

This is the crux of the ancient Sankofa proverb in the modern-day context of coaching and mentoring. One-time European Touring Car Division 2 motor racing champion Sir John Whitmore (1996) aptly described this as an 'inner game of tennis', where the focus is on developing a deep sense of self-awareness and self-coaching. By 'searching within oneself', he acknowledges that the adversary in one's head is often more intimidating than a challenger on the other side of the net (Parsloe 1995; see also Rosinski 2010). Therefore, as an organisational development strategy, Sankofa can form a vital part of the transcultural organisational reorientation for employee development in its widest sense.

It can thus be argued that coaching and mentoring with its four dimensions (i.e. open communication, team traditions, valuing people and acceptance of turbulence) in today's global industries represent a shift in the pragmatics of traditional personnel management. The modification is from that of an 'odd job' to being a strategic contribution which focuses not only on obtaining and cultivating skilled healthy people who are in short supply, but on making the best use of the employees' reserve potential in the mental, psychological and physical spheres of their occupational activity, for the purpose of increasing instruction levels, working capacity and creative longevity (Brathwaite 2005). In this way the cosmopolitan HR manager's input into this contextual approach can be consolidated through checking that the vision is shared.

REFLECTIVE ACTIVITY

1   Considering the suggestion put forward in this section that there are patterns to the issues and challenges faced by HR practitioners undertaking coaching and/or mentoring activities within a global context, can you make a connection within your own experience?

2   What might these patterns and issues look, feel or sound like?

3   Have you experienced coincidences in your working life that have suggested to you the existence of a larger pattern or issue?

4   Having explored the Sankofa model, do you think it might be a useful tool in your learning about the application of coaching and mentoring as a key element of HRD strategies within organisations? What leads you to that view?

REFLECTIVE ACTIVITY

From vision to effective action – based on the Sankofa model

Diagnose the present state of your chosen trajectory to effective action and achievement, as you perceive it.

		Strongly agree				Strongly disagree
1	There is a clear understanding that effective understanding and achievement begins with vision	1	2	3	4	5
2	I know what is important to me in life	1	2	3	4	5
3	I know what I want to do with my life	1	2	3	4	5
4	I know what beliefs will help me to achieve what I want	1	2	3	4	5
5	I know what information I need about myself and the cultural world I inhabit	1	2	3	4	5
6	I know what competencies will help me to achieve what I want	1	2	3	4	5
7	I know clearly the needs of the clients that I hope to engage with	1	2	3	4	5
8	I know what particular values and principles I intend to communicate to my clients	1	2	3	4	5
9	I know that between its start and outcome, turbulence most often occurs as obstacles along the journey	1	2	3	4	5
10	I know that initially, something in our organised cultural inheritance invites resignation	1	2	3	4	5
11	Yet I know that if I persist in the face of turbulence, I will be sure to have the opportunity to draw upon my inner excellence	1	2	3	4	5
12	I know that my inner excellence is not just a matter of competence and effort, but rather understand that I am a reflection of my 'word' in real outcomes	1	2	3	4	5
13	I have dealt with and stated the activities and temptations that I will avoid	1	2	3	4	5
14	In general, I know what distinguishes me as unique or special to the clients I serve	1	2	3	4	5

COACHING SKILLS FOR MANAGERS

Chief executives and managing directors are no longer focusing on employee relations, but turning their thoughts to employee engagement. The 2011 GfK Group Employee Engagement Survey (http://www.youtube.com/watch?v=w3fOK-gQGiY&feature=related) supports this view, noting that as an average of results from 29 countries, only 21% of younger workers are highly engaged with their employer, compared to 31% of those in their sixties. In the UK, only

12% of young employees are highly engaged with their employer. These findings, coupled with the increasing need for organisations to be agile and creative in their search for continuing growth, clearly indicate an opportunity for the introduction of new managerial styles and skills. A coaching style of management and the development of a coaching/mentoring culture lends itself to the requirements of both the organisation and the employees, meeting the expectations of Generation Y while attracting and retaining talent. Managers will also feel more confident about embracing a coaching style of management if they are furnished with a 'toolkit' of techniques to call upon as and when required instead of relying on a single approach. Further, by the undertaking of this additional learning the managers' own self-awareness will be enhanced.

Traditionally, many managers were promoted on the basis of their technical ability. Following the career pattern of apprentice, journeyman, craftsman and master craftsman, they may well have developed some important skills in passing on techniques to their teams that enabled them too to become proficient. However, they may not have been trained in management, and may therefore have been limited in their leadership skills.

Illustration of practice

'As a qualified nurse and midwife, I vividly remember my first general management position. After three or four weeks, I went to my boss and said "I have got no time to get on with my own work; I spend all my time looking after my team." My director replied "That's what your job is now!"'

(Jill Ashley-Jones, Former NHS Director of Organisational Development and Strategic HRM)

Although most executive and leadership coaching is currently undertaken by professional coaches external to the organisation, CIPD research shows that there is an increasing expectation on managers to deliver coaching in the workplace. It is possible that individual managers may be qualified as a coach or mentor and undertake more formal coaching or mentoring activities within the company. It is not easy, however, to balance the roles of manager, leader and coach. After all, a manager has to ensure that things get done, and is responsible for the regular appraisal of a team. Above all, time constraints (real or perceived) may not allow the manager and the coachee to fully enter into the espoused spirit of this developmental relationship. The ethical considerations for the manager as coach or mentor is discussed later in this chapter.

COACHING MODELS, PHILOSOPHIES AND PRACTICE

We have explored the background of coaching and mentoring from a Western perspective and considered the global application of the Sankofa model, which grew from a West African tradition. We now consider the view put forward by Jackson (2005) and by Bachkirova (2008) that rather than attempting to define coaching as a singular service, it might be more appropriate to define it with reference to the coaches that practise it and the type and styles of coaching interventions they can offer. We would suggest that in order to align the needs of the organisation and those individuals within it organisations must understand the breadth of coaching models and philosophies of practice available. Olivero *et al* (1997) suggest that coaching and mentoring 'can substantially increase staff productivity (increasing outputs relative to inputs) helping staff to ensure that skills acquired during training develops into skills that are applied at work'.

This briefing also recognises that not everyone tasked with providing coaching will have the necessary skills or knowledge to ensure that this staff development activity occurs, and that there is a need for support, continuous professional development and supervision, as recommended by the CIPD (2009). This briefing and others (CIPD 2008b; Price 2011) are supportive of the benefits that coaching can afford an organisation. However, those who are involved in contracting coaching services or developing internal coaching capacity need to ensure that they achieve the best fit for their own organisation.

FINDING A BEST FIT IN COACHING PROVISION

The art and practice of coaching is an emergent one developing from many disciplines, and it is thus beyond the scope of this work to explore in detail the many models and approaches currently available. For those who wish to investigate further, a list of recommended additional reading is provided at the end of the chapter.

Figure 3.4 Example organisation model of coaching and mentoring interventions

Figure 3.4 offers a suggested model of coaching interventions that could be used to create a framework for an organisation. We do not assume that all organisations will either require or choose to adopt all these areas of practice; it is intended merely as a starting point.

Hardingham (2004) cited in Connor and Pokora (2009, p184) defines 'coaching culture' as 'a culture where people coach each other all the time as a natural part of meetings, reviews and one-to-one discussions of all kinds'.

Clutterbuck and Megginson (2005) cited in Connor and Pokora (2009, p215) assert that a model for creating and sustaining a coaching culture should address the following six areas:

1   *Coaching is linked to business drivers.* A clear connection between organisational strategy and workforce development must be created and owned by all.

2   *Being a coachee is encouraged and supported.* HRPs not only have a role in ensuring that policy infrastructure supports the development of a coaching culture, but may also need to offer advice on recognition (for trained internal coaches) and remuneration packages (for internal and external coaching provision).

3   *Coach training is provided.* Although some HRPs may have coaching qualifications, we suggest that their main contribution to this area of work should be to source, contract, advise on programmes and, with senior managers, determine/undertake evaluation processes.

4   *Coaching is rewarded and recognised.* HRPs have a vital role in 'walking the talk' and using every opportunity to promote the organisational benefits of the creation of a coaching culture.

5   *There is a systemic perspective.* Within an organisation with an active and positive coaching culture, people are deemed to be competent and do their best. Instead of saying, 'You've done it all wrong,' managers should instead ask, 'So how can we make that even better?' – an approach taken from appreciative inquiry models.

6   *The move to coaching is managed.* This involves senior staff 'living' coaching behaviours and not disregarding them when the going gets choppy; this change of culture is integrated throughout the organisation and line managers are supported by their executives and HRPs in this.

This example model for coaching delivery within an organisation displays similarities with the coaching culture model developed by Clutterbuck and Megginson (2005): both assume that the organisation recognises the benefits that a coaching style of management and organisational culture can bring in these times of challenge.

The HRP is likely to be asked for advice on what should be included within any coaching development initiative. We offer the view that the organisation benefits when given exposure to a variety of theories, styles and models. This best fit approach will support the organisation's aspiration to develop a coaching culture.

Table 3.3 outlines our attempt to create a simple framework of reference in which to explore the many varied models of coaching currently being used. It draws upon the work of Cox *et al* (2010, p10) whose matrix model demonstrates the genres and contexts of coaching.

Table 3.3 The manager as a coach: coaching skills for managers

Coaching model	Background and key tools	Benefits for manager as coach
Cognitive-behavioural	• Development began in the 1990s • Works upon our critical 'inner voices' • Encourages different thinking in coachee • May be combined with relaxation techniques and/or assertiveness development • Can explore tolerances to stress/frustration *Key tools:* • SMART goal-setting • PRACTICE (Problem identification, Realisable goals, Alternative solutions, Consequence consideration, Target, Implementation, Evaluation) • SPACE (Social context, Physical, Actions, Cognitions, Emotions)	• Supports development of 'virtuous circle' of performance • Increases self-awareness and impact of negative thinking • Increases skills in managing, upwards and sideways • Personal stress reduction and ability to spot risk of stress in subordinates • Use of motivational interviewing skills may provide a return on investment in terms of sickness absence
Solution-focused	• Therapeutic roots, but does not focus on the problem • Coachee is believed capable of developing own solution if afforded time and space • Works on identifying what state is required to achieve the solution in terms of behaviours and activities *Key tools:* • Miracle question • Scaling (OSKAR/Well Formed Outcome) • Reframing	• Ideal technique for micro-coaching • Works well with GROW model in situations of coachee 'stuckness'

Coaching model	Background and key tools	Benefits for manager as coach
Gestalt	• Therapeutic roots – people do their best in the situation they find themselves in; empathetic style. • Underpins many coaching tools and models, but is possible used in its purist sense by 'expert' coaches *Key tools:* • Use of 'self' as an instrument of change • Cycle of experience – to identify how we satisfy (or don't) our needs, effectively close situations and move forward	• Many in corporate world see using all the senses including 'gut feelings' and working with them in managing situations as too 'flaky'. Understanding how to use these sensations can, however, greatly enhance the management of challenging situations, and assist the reduction of their occurrence
Transactional analysis	• Therapeutic roots – using simple language and effective contracting on three levels • Known as the 'I'm OK, you're OK, and they're OK' model *Key tools:* • Contracting • Working with ego states • Use of stories • Drama triangle	• The drama triangle alone is worthy of managers' understanding; it explores how they may be shifting unconsciously between being a rescuer, a persecutor or a victim and /or allowing others to put them into those roles – a very powerful tool for creating awareness and addressing issues
NLP approach	• Seen as a model rather than a constantly evolving theory, underpinned by 'presuppossistions' • Acknowledges Gestalt/ hypnotherapy roots *Key tools:* • Meta modelling • Reframing of behavioural patterns • Anchoring/de-anchoring	• Specialist training required to use *all* NLP approaches effectively • Understanding that our personal views of the world are just that –'ours' and not the way everyone sees a situation • Using language to create effective rapport quickly

It is beyond the remit of this work to discuss in detail the type, style or model of coaching that may be of benefit to the cohorts of organisational employees. We anticipate that these categories of staff – e.g. those on **talent management** or development programmes and senior team/organisational leaders – will find their coaching needs met by external 'professional' coaches, but this may change as internal coaching cultures mature. HRPs may be asked to source an external coaching provider for these individuals, and so in order to support those explorations we offer Table 3.4 which identifies some of the models currently perceived to add value to a coaching interventions at this level.

Table 3.4 Developmental versus executive coaching

Developmental coaching	Executive coaching
As for manager as coach, plus: • psychodynamic approaches • person-centred approaches • narrative coaching • cognitive developmental approaches • positive psychology approaches.	As developmental, plus • transpersonal approach • neuro-leadership coaching • mindfulness coaching.

SOME ETHICAL CONSIDERATIONS

Moving on to the ethical issues that arise for coaches and organisations which commission and support coaching, we do not present a complete or extensive exploration but rather a few examples that will stimulate thinking and discussion. Peltier (2010) clearly identifies a cultural problem for the practising coach who has to navigate between the client's interests (which may be intensely personal) and the business culture, where the profit motive may rule. Although we have focused on the coaching element for our discussion, it is worth remembering that many of these issues may also arise and require consideration within a formal mentoring programme.

For whatever reason organisational coaching is used, the HRP will be called upon to advise and/or organise the activities, so he or she must understand and keep watch over whatever code of ethical conduct is agreed on. Hawkins and Smith (2006, p248) offer the following definition of professional practice:

A professional is one who professes; one who can go and stand in the market square and publicly declare what they believe and stand for. To practise ethically is to attest to the standards you wish to be judged by and to provide a mechanism whereby you can be held accountable for living up to those standards.

Practising ethically is not always an easy path, and certainly not for those whose ambition is to be liked. Ethical practice maintains respect for all parties while working with integrity to formulate a moral course of action.

Perhaps the most difficult ethical dilemma that the HRP may face when practising or overseeing coaching activities is to keep the balance between the goals and needs of the organisation, the individual who is to be coached, and the practitioners who deliver the coaching service. Individual values, beliefs and loyalties may be significantly challenged in such a situation.

THE COACHING CONTRACT

An ethical framework has to feel fair and meet the needs of all parties. Defining fairness is complicated, and any definition is open to interpretation and influenced by the cultural environment in which coaching and mentoring are practised. In coaching and mentoring there is not only a written contract but also a psychological contract that may be interpreted differently by all stakeholders. It is therefore important to be as transparent as possible when undertaking this work in order to prevent assumptions and uninformed expectations from arising. The contracts between each of the stakeholders are multiple (see Figure 3.5), with each party engaged in at least three separate relationships. All of these relationships, of course, exist in the wider context of society and community.

Figure 3.5 Stakeholders and relationships with the wider environment

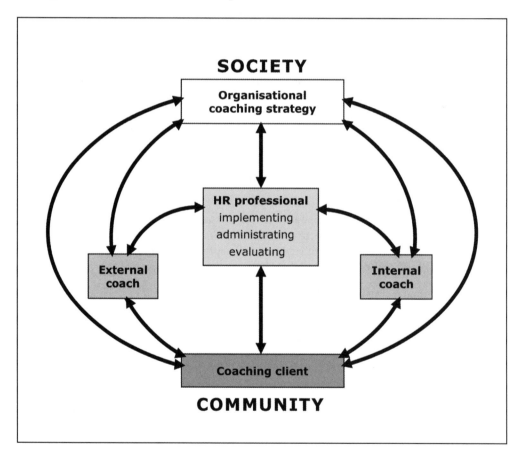

THE INTERNAL COACH PERSPECTIVE

It is now common for organisations to develop their own internal coaching capacity in an effort to promote a coaching culture and reduce the cost of external coaching. This involves commissioning robust training programmes, delivered to a cohort of employees who show the aptitude and desire to develop coaching skills, who are then subsequently authorised to deliver formal coaching in their organisations. Such initiatives underpin a coaching ethos of helping individuals to achieve their own solutions and to increase their own and the organisation's performance.

Although there is a business objective driving organisational coaching, the coach may face some personal ethical dilemmas relating to his or her knowledge of the organisation. If a piece of information is shared within the confidentiality of the coaching scenario about which the coach has some personal knowledge, and which may potentially adversely affect the coachee, others and/or the organisation, what course of action should the coach take? It is therefore important to have in place a code of ethical conduct that the coach and organisation must sign up to. The question is not, 'What do I do with this information?' but rather, 'Where does my duty of care lie in this situation?' The coach and coachee have entered into an agreement of confidentiality that must be respected. It is essential, therefore, that the initial contracting phase of the coaching relationship is robustly undertaken and includes an explicit statement that will allow the coach to challenge a proposed course of action. It may, for example, include a clause which states: 'If I believe you are at risk of harming yourself or others, I reserve the right to break confidentiality in order to prevent harm. However, I would only do this in extreme circumstances and would always try to discuss it with you first, before taking any action.'

THE EXTERNAL COACH PERSPECTIVE

The external coach will also be looking to develop a partnership relationship with the employing organisation and hold a contract with a number of parties, in relation to which some of the same ethical dilemmas may occur. One of the major differences, however, is in the negotiation of the contract between employer and external coach as a *contractor*. We have personally seen many cases where the external party is engaged (in good faith) to undertake developmental coaching, only to find that they have in fact been brought in as 'the grim reaper' tasked with facilitating the individual's exit from the organisation. In this case it is the contract between coach and employer that must be challenged. This can be particularly difficult for the external party because there are implications for both their income and their reputation.

The role of the HRP in selecting and hiring coaches is highlighted in such a scenario. If the coach decides to withdraw from the contract, the HRP may be 'blamed'. If the coach goes ahead despite their ethical misgivings, are they abiding by the professional code of ethics to which the organisation and their professional body subscribe? Meanwhile, who is undertaking the duty of care towards the employee? Many coaches are expert in working with clients in firms that are downsizing or reorganising, and therefore able to undertake the role professionally and ethically as long as the brief is clear and explicit.

THE MANAGER AS COACH OR MENTOR

In this relationship, interpersonal power dynamics inevitably come into play, and are often unspoken. If coaching is to be formalised, the initial contracting stage is of vital importance.

The ground rules must be carefully developed and constantly checked and recontracted.

The degree of honesty and openness in the relationship must be explicit, both from the standpoint of the coach/manager and the coachee.

There must be clarity about what is 'different' in the coaching relationship from the manager–employee relationship.

An agreement that the expectations of each party correspond is necessary.

As the coaching relationship develops, it is vital to recontract regularly in order to prevent assumptions from arising. There may therefore be occasions on which it is inappropriate for the manager to enter into a formal coaching relationship with members of his or her team, and this relationship may not deliver the outcomes that coaching is capable of doing. As yet, there is no consensus on whether the line manager as coach is feasible or desirable (CIPD 2008b) and there is perhaps a gap between the espoused desire to implement a coaching culture in this way and the efficacy of such an action.

A formal mentoring role may be more appropriate. Here, there is an explicit recognition of the power dynamic. The mentee expects the mentor to be more senior and more knowledgeable and to pass on tools and techniques that will further their career prospects. The mentor, however, can also face dilemmas:

What if the mentee does not take the advice and has other ideas on how the job can be done?

Is the mentor prepared to prioritise the development of the mentee's skills over his or her own, potentially enabling the mentee to progress to a more powerful position than him or her?

This again supports our argument that, whether coaching or mentoring, the need for a formal arrangement and effective contracting and training is crucial.

If the formal coaching relationship proves inappropriate, managers can still acquire coaching skills that enable them to support the development of the organisational coaching culture in an informal and opportunist way within their teams. This is known as 'micro-coaching'. Opportunities for micro-coaching occur regularly, and part of the development of the manager as coach must include looking out for these opportunities. Managers need to become smarter rather than work harder; empowering others will save time in the long run.

What is important here is that the manager maintains responsibility for *what* needs to be done but the coachee is responsible for *how* it is done. The advantages are twofold: the employee is engaged and empowered to use his or her own resources, and the organisation reaps the benefit of the creativity and innovation that the employee can offer.

REFLECTIVE ACTIVITY

1   What do you consider to be the advantages to an organisation for training managers to use a coaching management style? (Some suggested benefits are listed in Table 3.4.)

2   What organisational barriers do you perceive for implementing training of this nature for managers?

3   What ethical issues could arise for the manager as coach, and what ongoing support will they need?

QUALITY ASSURANCE

As the coaching profession expands there is a growing agreement amongst professional coaching bodies and purchasers of coaching services that supervision and accreditation is required in order to assure the quality of services and the continuing professional development of coaches. Not all professional coaches adopt this position, however. Many of the organisations that have adopted internal coaching practices are now developing their own supervisors. The clinical professions, from which many of coaching skills have developed, have long been used to regular supervision. If coaching is aligned towards these therapeutic professional norms, supervision will soon become essential. On the other hand, if coaching is aligned to a more business-oriented model – for example, if it became chartered – there is an expectation of continuing professional development. Our view is that supervision is necessary and indeed vital to support the practising coach.

A quality assurance (QA) process must be included in the initial implementation strategy and when hiring external coaches; choices have to be rigorously defensible, taking into account the supervision and accreditation debate above; this alone will not necessarily achieve the best fit for an organisation. Senior members of organisations may already have professional coaching relationships (either with an individual coach or through a coaching company) that they wish to expand. This has the advantage of a known quantity and a tacit expectation that style and engagement is appropriate. The HRP should still be explicitly assured of qualifications, professional-body membership, professional indemnity insurance, references and capacity.

The relationship is important between coach and coachee, and the 'imposition' of a specific coach may be counterproductive. For this reason, many larger organisations create an assessment centre to select a panel of coaches. Alternatively, they may access the services of an established coaching company or support from a professional body. With the establishment of a panel of coaches, the potential coachees maintain an element of choice.

The QA process must be ongoing. Best practice includes a regular contract-review process with supplier(s). This not only ensures that the psychological and physical contracts are securely in place and explicit, but also offers the opportunity (while maintaining the confidentiality codes in place) to map any trends and themes that are emerging, and thus feed back into the underpinning strategy.

So, what are the advantages to the HRP in developing a coaching style? In terms of the HR Profession Map, one of the first capabilities in reaching Band 4 competency is to be a leadership colleague, client confidant(e) and coach. As with all skills – technical or behavioural – they do not develop overnight. We strongly suggest that effort invested in developing the 'manager as coach' skills at an early stage in an HR career will increase client satisfaction, allow HRPs to work in partnership with their clients to facilitate the resolution of issues (after all, the clients are the experts in their area) and build the trust required of such a relationship.

LINKS TO PROFESSIONAL BODIES

For the HRP, significant work has already been undertaken in defining both codes of ethics and codes of professional conduct. The CIPD 2011 code is available through the CIPD website (www.cipd.co.uk). Professional coaching organisations, including the International Coach Federation (ICF) (www.coachfederation.org), the European Mentoring and Coaching Council (EMCC) (www.emcouncil.org), and the Association for Coaching (AC) (www.associationforcoaching.com) publish their codes of ethics for practising coaching and mentoring. Information on supervision can also be found at these sites. Additionally, information on specialist coach supervision training can be found at centres such as the International Centre for Coaching and Mentoring at Oxford Brooks University Business School (www.business.brooks.ac.uk), the Coaching Supervision Academy (www.coachingsupervisionacademy.com). All professional coaching and supervision bodies, including the CIPD, assert that in order to practise coaching professionally and ethically coaches should be in formal and regular supervision with a qualified and experienced coaching supervisor.

EVALUATING RETURN ON INVESTMENT

In approaching the end of this chapter we address the challenge of the financial measurement of a developmental process. There is a cost involved and the organisation will require a return on its investment (ROI) or on its expectation (ROE). Measuring the impact of coaching and mentoring on organisational performance has so far proved to be an elusive quest.

Still the most regularly used method of evaluating HRD interventions and training is the model originally introduced by Kirkpatrick in 1959. This model has been refined continually by the author and his son; the latest iteration can be found in the most recent edition of their book (Kirkpatrick and Kirkpatrick 2006). Although this framework covers many angles, it still does not completely answer the specific question of how ROI for coaching and mentoring can be evaluated in isolation from other HRD activities. Firstly, there must be a baseline from which any shift in the coachee's productivity, efficiency and efficacy can be measured. Various methodologies can be used to establish this baseline, including 360-degree appraisals, a variety of psychometric assessments, one-on-one appraisal with the line manager, and self-assessment. However the baseline is defined, the measurement of success is likely to combine specific goals achieved, self-assessment and line manager feedback. Whereas the first is tangible and quantitative and may be expected to be shared openly, the latter two are necessarily qualitative and subjective measures, and may prove more difficult to gauge due to the variety of responses that may emerge.

This mix may not necessarily appeal to a finance director, but an enlightened organisation will know that a triple bottom line relating to profit, people and planet will achieve the organisational adaptability and flexibility that will grow not only the workforce but also the company.

 REFLECTIVE ACTIVITY

What and how much information does an HRP need to collect and analyse in order to effectively evaluate the ROI on coaching and mentoring?

SUMMARY

Our aim for this chapter has been to provide an introduction to coaching and mentoring and to highlight the learning outcomes. We have offered some practical elements to assist HR specialists who may well find themselves charged with securing and/or developing coaching and mentoring services within organisations. In addition, we have also sought to illustrate how the development of individual skills in this area of practice could assist one's own personal career pathways.

Currently, much of the research into coaching and mentoring is undertaken from a psychological perspective. Increasingly, however, it is within the business world that these researched techniques are being applied, and these can be explored with reference to the *Further reading* section below. The importance of an ethical framework and the risks associated with *not* having one in situ prior to undertaking any form of coaching or mentoring activity has been emphasised.

The global context and the need to recognise how coaching and mentoring have developed from ancient roots and been implemented in other countries and cultures has also been highlighted. We hope this will encourage you to explore other ancient and indigenous teaching modalities/aural traditions that underpin many models of coaching and mentoring.

CASE STUDY

Sally has accepted a new job as HR partner with a medium-sized company. The company is expanding, having secured a contract that will double its current annual turnover. The board has agreed that it will not take on additional permanent core staff to service this contract but will outsource to subcontracting firms. It believes that the current senior managers have the capability to manage the contracts and relationships with the subcontractors, although it is aware that they may not have the necessary experience. The board wants to support its senior managers in their expanded roles. The executive team is keen to try coaching as part of its developmental approach. The HR director has persuaded board members to work with an executive coach who has supported him previously. The board members have deemed coaching provided by this individual positive and believe that they can measure the ROI through the improved working relationships between board members with stakeholders and the company's growth and ability to secure new contracts.

The HR director requires Sally to review the appointment of several external coaches to support the development of the senior managers, and has also asked her to give her suggestions on how the board members can offer themselves as mentors to this group. The HR director advises Sally that the coaching should initially focus on relationship management. (This is an identified skills gap.) Sally must present a paper at the next board meeting offering an approach to implementing coaching and mentoring in the organisation, including suggestions on how the company will

be able to identify the ROI that they are making.

Put yourself in Sally's shoes as the HRP tasked with providing a report and recommendations to the board. Working with a group of fellow students, create a draft report. The questions below are there to prompt your discussion (they are indicative but not exhaustive).

- When Sally is looking for available coaches she should ask them to identify their approach/style and which model(s) of coaching they use. Consider Tables 3.3 and 3.4 above. Which models of coaching do you think might be most appropriate for the senior managers in this company?

- How could Sally (ethically) check out the credentials of coaches that might apply? Which professional coaching bodies might she approach for help?

- Do you think that Sally should investigate mentor training for the board members? What should she ensure was undertaken prior to any actual mentoring taking place in addition to the training for those who are providing mentoring?

- What ethical considerations should Sally take into account when suggesting a matching process for mentors with mentees (remembering that each of the senior managers reports directly to a board member)?

- What quantitative and qualitative outcomes can Sally suggest that will form the basis of identifying the ROI, and what HR metrics should be in place in order to measure them?

FURTHER READING

BOOKS

COX, E., BACHKIROVA, T. and CLUTTERBUCK, D. (2010) *The Complete Handbook of Coaching*. London: Sage. A comprehensive and accessible overview of key approaches to coaching.

HAWKINS, P. and SMITH, N. (2006) *Coaching, Mentoring and Organisational Consultancy, Supervision and Development*. Buckingham: Open University Press. An industry stalwart, opening the dialogue out beyond coaching and mentoring.

ROSINSKI, P. (2010) *Global Coaching*. London: Nicholas Brealey Intercultural Press. A cosmopolitian approach rooted in contextuality.

ARTICLES

Coaching at Work (www.coaching-at-work.com)

Harvard Business Review (www.hbr.org)

People Management (CIPD) (www.peoplemanagement.co.uk)

WEBSITES

CIPD Factsheets (http://www.cipd.co.uk/hr-resources/factsheets/)

CIPD Research (http://www.cipd.co.uk/research/_curprj.htm)

REFERENCES

ACHEBE, C. (1994) *Things Fall Apart*. New York: Anchor Books.

BACHKIROVA, T. (2008) Role of coaching psychology in defining boundaries between counselling and coaching, in PALMER, S. and WHYBROW, A. (eds) *Handbook of Coaching Psychology*. London: Routledge.

BRATHWAITE, T. (2005) Human resource management in sport, in BEECH, J. and CHADWICK, S. *The Business of Sport Management*. Harlow: Pearson Education.

BRATHWAITE, T. (2009) Trinidad's Camboulay street dance-play and the carnivalesque placebo: a neurotheological interface between social theatre and post-traumatic slave syndrome, in JENNINGS, S. *Drama Therapy and Social Theatre: Necessary dialogues*. London: Routledge.

BURLESON, B. (2005) *Jung in Africa*. New York: Continuum International.

BYNUM, E. B. (1999) *The African Unconscious*. New York: Teachers College Press.

CIPD (2008a) *Coaching [online]*. Factsheet. London: CIPD. Available at: www.cipd.co.uk/factsheets.

CIPD (2008b) *Coaching and Buying Coaching Services [online]*. Guide. London: CIPD. Available at: www.cipd.co.uk/guides

CIPD (2009) *Taking the Temperature of Coaching [online]*. Survey report. London: CIPD. Available at: www.cipd.co.uk/surveys

CIPD (2011) *Coaching and Mentoring [online]*. Factsheet. London: CIPD. Available at: www.cipd.co.uk/factsheet.

CLUTTERBUCK, D. and MEGGINSON, D. (2005) *Making Coaching Work: Creating a coaching culture*. London: Chartered Institute of Personnel and Development.

COLLINS, J. (2011) *Great by Choice*. London: Cornerstone Press.

CONNOR, M. and POKORA, P. (2009) *Coaching and Mentoring at Work: Developing effective practice*. Buckingham: Open University Press.

COX, E., BACHKIROVA, T. and CLUTTERBUCK, D. (2010) *The Complete Handbook of Coaching*. London: Sage.

CRAWFORD, C. J. (2010) *Manager's Guide to Mentoring*. Wisconsin: McGraw-Hill.

DE HAAN, E. (2008) *Relational Coaching*. Chichester: John Wiley & Sons.

GADALLA, M. (2008) *Exiled Egyptians: The heart of Africa*. Charlotte, NC: Tehuti Research Foundation.

GADALLA, M. (1999) *Historical Deception – The untold story of ancient Egypt*. Charlotte, NC: Tehuti Research Foundation.

GfK (2011) *Group Employee Engagement Survey 2011 [online]*: http://www.youtube.com/watch?v=w3fOK-gQGiY&feature=related

HAWKINS, P. (2008) *The Coaching Profession: Some of the key challenges* [online]. Available at: http://www.thecoachingcollaborative.co.uk/wp-content/uploads/coaching_-_some_of_the_key_challenges.pdf [Accessed 12 June 2012].

HAWKINS, P. and SMITH, N. (2006) *Coaching, Mentoring and Organisational Consultancy, Supervision and Development*. Buckingham: Open University Press.

HIGHFIELD, R. (2007) *How Imhotep Gave Us Medicine [online]*: http://www.telegraph.co.uk/science/science-news/3293164/How-Imhotep-gave-us-medicine.html

HOBSON, B. and SCALLY, M. (1991) *Build Your Own Rainbow*. London: Mercury Books.

JACKSON, P. (2005) How do we describe coaching? An exploratory development of a typology of coaching based on the accounts of UK-based practitioners. *International Journal of Evidence-Based Coaching and Mentoring*. Vol 3, No 2. 45.

KIRKPATRICK, D. L. and KIRKPATRICK, J. D.(2006) *Evaluating Training Programmes: The four levels*, 3rd edn. San Francisco, CA: Berrett-Koehler.

KOORTZEN, P. and OOSTHUIZEN, R. (2010). A competence executive coaching model. *SA Journal of Industrial Psychology/SA Tydskrif vir Bedryfsielkunde*. Vol 36, No 1.

MALUNGA, C. and BANDA, C. (2012) *Understanding Organizational Sustainability Through African Proverbs: Insights for leaders and facilitators*. Washington: Pact Publications.

MCLEAN, G., YANG, B., MIN-HSUN, C., TOLBERT, A. and LARKIN, C. (2005) Development and initial validation of an instrument measuring managerial coaching skill. *Human Resource Development Quarterly*. Vol 16, No 2. 157–78.

OLIVERO, G., BANE, K. D. and KOPELMAN, R. E. (1997) Executive coaching as a transfer of training tool: effects on productivity in a public agency. *Public Personnel Management*. Vol 26, No 4 461–9.

PARSLOE, E. (1995) *Coaching, Mentoring and Assessing*. London: Kogan Page.

PARSLOE, E. (1999) *The manager as coach and mentor*. London: CIPD.

PELTIER, B. (2010) *The Psychology of Executive Coaching*. New York: Routledge.

PRICE, A. (2011) *Human Resource Management in a Business Context*, 4th edn. London: Thomson Learning.

RAMSDEN, R. (1993) *Action Profiling: Generating competitive edge through realizing management potential*. London: Gower.

ROSINSKI, P. (2010) *Global Coaching*. London: Nicholas Brealey Intercultural Press.

SHELDRAKE, R. (1988) *The Presence of the Past: Morphic resonance and the habits of nature*. Rochester, VT: Park Street Press.

VON OECH, R. (2002) *Expect the Unexpected Or You Won't Find it: A creativity tool based on the ancient wisdom of Heraclitus*. San Francisco, CA: Berrett-Koehler.

WHITMORE, J. (1996) *Coaching for Performance*, 2nd edn. London: Nicholas Brealey.

CHAPTER 4

Meeting Organisational Development Needs

Jim Stewart and Dalbir Sidhu

CHAPTER CONTENTS

- Introduction
- Establishing learning needs and learning activities
- General approaches to meeting development needs
- Roles and responsibilities of learning
- Evaluating learning outcomes
- Summary

KEY LEARNING OUTCOMES

By the end of this chapter, you will be able to:

- Discuss and assess key requirements in the design and development of inclusive learning activities.
- Assess the use and application of a range of methods to meet learning needs.
- Compare the roles and responsibilities of different individuals in meeting L&D needs.
- Design and apply appropriate methods of evaluating the outcomes of learning interventions.

INTRODUCTION

Organisations need to develop employees to ensure that performance can be sustained and improved. This requires learning needs to be identified, decisions to be made on the methods to meet those needs, and the establishment of the benefits or otherwise of investments in learning interventions. Various individuals have different roles in ensuring that organisation development needs are met. This chapter explores those activities and roles and provides an overview of this critical organisational function.

ESTABLISHING LEARNING NEEDS AND LEARNING ACTIVITIES

Over the years the learning and development agenda has increasingly grown and gained prominence within organisations. One of the reasons for this is the continually expanding and competitive industry and marketplace within which organisations operate (Roffe 1999). The development of employees' knowledge, skills and abilities (KSA) is essential in ensuring that organisations have a sustainable competitive advantage, because this supports the ability to learn effectively and stay ahead of the competition (Morey and Frangioso 1998).

- Although the traditional approach to learning is often seen as classroom-based training activity away from the work environment, it is important to understand that learning takes place everywhere and can be a planned activity or take place through cognitive insight (Boydell and Leary 1996). There are several methods and approaches to learning, both formal and informal, some of which are discussed later in this chapter.
- One of the most common methods of learning is through the delivery of formal training interventions. Although this method of training can be considered an expense to an organisation, if designed and conducted effectively it can be a worthy investment which will support the organisation's overall business strategy (Denby 2010). By supporting the business strategy, learning needs align with the performance goals, thus allowing the organisation to clearly identify the performance gaps and establish the necessary KSA to address these.
- Valuing and developing people capability will ultimately impact upon organisational performance, and it can therefore be argued that investing time and resources to accurately identify learning and development (L&D) needs will in the long term prove a valuable return on investment. However, the process must be aligned with the organisation and not become a tick-box exercise (CIPD 2012).
- Furthermore, the identification of learning needs cannot be completed in isolation from the business and requires an integrated approach, with input and data collection from various sources. There are a number of significant factors that have to be considered when identifying learning needs, along with a clear and coherent strategy and approach. Some approaches to identifying learning needs, and the impact these have upon individuals and organisations, are discussed in this chapter.

WHAT IS A LEARNING NEEDS ANALYSIS?

Firstly, it is useful to explore the purpose of a learning needs analysis (LNA). Gibb (2003) views LNA as the gathering of systematic information to ascertain the skills, knowledge and abilities of employees which will enable the organisation to identify current and future performance gaps and how to address these. An LNA is sometimes known as a training needs analysis (TNA) or training and learning needs analysis (TLNA), and although the terminology may differ, the output of such activities remains the same (CIPD 2012). The gathering of information to explore learning needs can include both quantitative and qualitative data obtained via:

- skills matrices

- **key performance indicators** (KPIs)
- workplace observations
- outputs from performance appraisals
- recruitment and retention data
- research interviews with subject matter experts and managers.

The quality of this information provides a valuable insight to the learning needed at an individual, team or organisational level (CIPD 2012). Conducting an LNA enables an organisation to identify areas of development (weaknesses) and how these may lead to business threats which can have a significant impact on performance, as well as surfacing areas of strengths which can be utilised to sustain business performance.

There are various approaches to conducting an LNA; the principles of any approach should underpin the outputs of the LNA with the current and future goals of the business. The LNA should therefore remain a continuous process, aligned to organisational performance goals and vision, and not be seen as a one-off event (Denby 2010). However, many organisations fail to recognise the value of an LNA, often spending little time identifying learning needs and more commonly focusing on the design and delivery stage (Denby 2010). This can prove costly to the organisation if the learning outcomes fail to match the operational requirements that support sustained business performance. In this case, learning is not conducive and holds little value.

Furthermore, organisation success and HRD's credibility is at stake if learning interventions have low impact and do not support required learning. While exploring the impact of a poorly conducted LNA, or in the absence of one, it must be acknowledged that an effective LNA can deliver significant benefits for the organisation and its employees, which can outweigh the investment in the LNA, firstly by supporting the development of a high-performance culture and demonstrating how it embraces learning and the role it plays to support performance; and secondly by empowering and engaging employees through effectively designed performance-focused learning and development interventions that extend beyond developing employees' current capabilities to achieve their performance goals. These benefits impact positively on the retention and recruitment of employees and support wider HRD policies.

 REFLECTIVE ACTIVITY

Consider the benefits of identifying learning needs from an organisational perspective and from an employee perspective.

Discuss this with a group of colleagues.

APPROACHES TO LNA

An LNA usually takes place at beginning of the learning cycle, which is often referred to as the ADDE model: Analyse, Design, Deliver, Evaluate (Dick and

Carey 1996). It is crucial to invest time in the 'analyse' stage because the outputs will drive and impact significantly on the stages that follow. For instance, without understanding the purpose of the learning and what it is intended to achieve and how success can be measured, it will be difficult to design and deliver an appropriate and value-adding learning intervention. Each stage must be fully explored before moving to the next. This model demonstrates a systematic formal approach to conducting an LNA and can be used to identify needs at a wider organisational level as well as team and individual needs.

The RAM approach (Relevance, Alignment, Measurement), developed by the CIPD and based on research from Portsmouth University on the value of learning, supports the LNA by focusing on organisational outcomes, as defined below (CIPD 2012):

- Relevance – ensuring that existing or planned training will meet new opportunities and challenges for the organisation.
- Alignment – ensuring that all organisational learning interventions are integrated and support the overall business strategy.
- Measurement – ensuring that all learning interventions can be measured and linked to success criteria, notably the expected change of behaviour and improved KPIs.

GATHERING DATA ON LEARNING NEEDS

As mentioned above, there are various methods of data gathering and the method employed will depend on the nature of the analysis required. For instance, interviews with key stakeholders and line managers provide valuable data on KSA needs to meet business plans and specific business requirements. Other methods, such as workplace observations, one-to-one appraisal meetings, employee surveys and measuring KPIs, are additional useful methods of gathering data.

LEVELS OF LNA

The culture and climate of an organisation influence the extent of the value it places and invests in a LNA and the way in which it approaches undertaking one (Conner and Clawson 2004). The size of the organisation and the extent to which HRD has a strategic role in the organisation, therefore aligning and influencing the organisation strategy, will also have a fundamental impact on the role of a LNA, which is commonly conducted at three levels:

- organisational
- team
- individual.

Although each of the three levels interlinks with and supports the others, as shown in Figure 4.1, the learning requirements arising from each level may differ, and these are discussed below.

Figure 4.1 The alignment of learning needs

Organisational level-
Strategic needs

Team level-
Operational level
needs

Individual level-
personal
development needs

Organisational level

At organisational level, the LNA focuses on identifying learning needs which support the overarching organisation strategy, goals and vision (Clarke 2003). At this level the LNA determines the performance gaps, skills, knowledge and competencies required to support and achieve the overall organisational goals, and usually involves alignment to the business planning cycle, KPIs and future priorities.

It has two primary purposes: identifying current levels of performance requirements and establishing future performance goals (Stewart and Rigg 2011). The outputs from the LNA seek to address 'common' needs across the business, and this level of LNA is usually undertaken as part of organisational change programmes, where cultural change, new KSA, new behaviours and competencies are required to support the change in the business direction. Similarly, this level of LNA supports HRD policies and implementation of training that an organisation is legally required to undertake, such as compliance, accreditation and health and safety training. This strategic, formal approach to LNA requires input from senior managers and key stakeholders who identify and influence the organisation's business direction and goals, and data is usually gathered through focus groups and interviews.

Team level

At team level, the focus of the LNA is on the operational requirements of a department or function. Here the LNA seeks to determine the KSA required to achieve the operational performance goals of a particular function or job. Several approaches such as a comprehensive analysis, key task analysis and problem-centred analysis can be adopted to understand the KSA required for a job or function, and commonly these are together described as a job training analysis (Stewart 1999). At the team level, the key sources of data include workplace observation, reviewing business plans, KPIs and job specifications.

Individual level

At individual level, the LNA supports the personal development of employees, usually arising from development plans that stem from the **performance appraisal** process which outlines the performance goals required for an employee (Harrison 2011). Individual needs can also be captured at the organisation and group level; however, any specific needs are usually revealed as a result of individual performance problems. The focus of the LNA is to establish the extent to which the required performance in terms of KSA compares to the actual performance. The LNA here would be tailored through an informal process, usually via the line manager as part of the performance management system (Amaratunga and Baldry 2002). Interviews, personal development plans that individuals are encouraged to pursue, employee development surveys and **360-degree feedback** are common sources for collecting data at an individual level. Although 360-degree feedback provides both the individual and the organisation with multiple-source feedback from all those with whom they interact, it will only be effective in an environment where open and honest feedback is encouraged and accepted (McCarthy and Garavan 2001).

REFLECTIVE ACTIVITY

Consider the approach to identifying learning needs within a specific organisation at an organisational, group and individual level.

1   How effective are the approaches?

2   How could they be improved?

Discuss with colleagues.

RESULTS OF THE LNA

As mentioned above, the LNA's primary focus is to inform the design and delivery of learning interventions as the next stages in the learning cycle. Commonly presented as a report to form and shape the L&D strategy, the results of the LNA should present clear and measurable learning outcomes prioritising the learning needs of the organisation and aligning these to organisational performance goals (CIPD 2012). An important element for consideration is the different way in which people learn, taking account of their learning style and how this affects the design and method of learning (Coffield *et al* 2004). These learning needs form the basis of an L&D plan, which will influence the design and method of delivering the learning through a combination of methods. We discuss this stage in the cycle below.

GENERAL APPROACHES TO MEETING DEVELOPMENT NEEDS

Every L&D professional is faced with wide array of options when it comes to selecting appropriate methods to facilitate learning. A number of significant factors help to assess methods and make judgements on which is the most effective in any given situation (Glaister *et al* 2010). Some of those factors are listed and discussed below. It is, however, important to understand that the factors cannot influence a decision in any automatic way; the decision will inevitably require professional judgement.

SOME SIGNIFICANT FACTORS

A key factor is always the *organisation context*. This does in fact encompass a number of related factors. Size and structure will influence the possibilities and limitations of methods. Related to this are the resources available, which will include physical, people and skills, as well as finance. For example, a small company with no dedicated L&D function may well lack the necessary expertise for direct provision. It may also lack the finance for more expensive methods. Resources available reflect the additional organisation context factor of management and cultural support for learning activities. Senior management will allocate more or fewer resources depending on their view of the value of learning interventions. They will also influence levels of support provided for learners by colleagues and line managers – i.e. the cultural state of the organisation in relation to learning.

Two additional factors are the *learners* themselves and the specific *learning needs* being addressed (Glaister *et al* 2010). In the former case, different job categories are likely to demand different methods. For example, those holding senior positions will not respond the same to methods used for those at entry level. Biographical and demographic differences between learners also have to be taken into account; age and educational level attained, for example. Attention also has to be paid to individual circumstances such as care responsibilities outside of work, since blanket approaches cannot be assumed to be appropriate to everyone in a particular job. Specific learning needs will demand particular approaches. Examples of this include whether the need is to develop knowledge or skills; each will require different methods to be effective. Skills also vary – for example, between cognitive, physical and social/interpersonal. While there may be some commonality in methods – e.g. all skill development can be said to require practice – specific methods adopted will differ according to the nature of the skill.

REFLECTIVE ACTIVITY

1   Consider how individual biographical and demographic factors can influence learning interventions.

2   Consider how this might relate to varying job categories and, taken together,

influence decisions on the methods adopted in learning interventions.

3   Discuss your conclusions with a group of work or student colleagues.

APPROACHES

The approach adopted is also influenced by the level of need being met. An organisational-level need usually implies that significant numbers are to be developed. Conversely, an individual-level need will be limited to that one person. So it would make little sense to adopt the same approach in both cases. For example, significant numbers may justify designing and delivering a specific formal course, perhaps delivered by an external partner. Designing a such a course would not, though, be justified for a single individual. In that case, the person may attend an established external course if a formal approach is decided upon. These examples illustrate that there are some general approaches which help to make decisions to fit particular circumstances.

The first choice relates to whether formal or informal methods are to be adopted. Methods do vary according to degrees of formality – i.e. how much planning and design is involved in providing the learning (Tansley *et al* 2007). Courses are considered more formal than coaching, for example. A related choice is whether the learning is to be provided off- or on-the-job. Off-the-job is considered to be usually more formal than on-the-job. To help decision-making and to take account of some of the significant factors above, there are some general guidelines that can be applied:

• More formal approaches are generally more expensive.
• Off-the-job approaches are generally more expensive.
• On-the-job methods are more effective in an organisation with a culture supportive of learning.
• The further away from the job that learning occurs, the less effective it will be.

The last point applies because of the **'transfer of learning'** problem. Research has shown that learners who receive development away from work can experience problems applying their learning once they are back at work doing their jobs. Research effort has also been applied to discover ways of overcoming this problem (Baldwin and Ford 1988; Holton *et al* 2007). The simple solution to the problem may be thought to have all learning interventions on the job so that there is no need for research into overcoming the problem. But such research is worthwhile because learning interventions away from work have other advantages that mean they will always be used. And so, researching how to overcome the transfer-of-learning problem will help to make those types of intervention more effective. This is discussed in more detail in the next main section.

SOME SPECIFIC LEARNING METHODS

There is not space in this single chapter to examine all the available methods in detail. This section instead discusses two common methods that can and do have application in meeting a range of learning needs at all levels and most circumstances.

Action learning

Action learning (AL) is commonly associated with facilitating L&D for managers; in other words, it is perceived as a management development method. While that was the context of its invention by Reg Revans in the latter half of the twentieth century, it has since been used successfully in a range of other contexts (Rigg and Richards 2007). These contexts include those of professions such as accountancy, teaching, nursing and HR management (see Kellie *et al* 2010, for one example). At least two business schools in the UK utilise AL in their Doctorate in Business Administration programmes, which are delivered to consultants, professionals and academics as well as senior managers. Some of the professions mentioned can also be considered at 'technical' levels in organisation hierarchies, and so AL may be said to be relevant to technical as well as professional and managerial jobs. It does therefore offer a possible method for meeting a wide range of needs. In addition, it is also suited for use as an internal method with groups of employees perhaps drawn from different departments, levels and functions within a single employer. But AL is also commonly used in interventions with participants drawn from different employers.

The basic design elements of AL (see Pedler *et al* 2005 for a full discussion of AL principles) are first a small group of between four and eight individuals forming what is known as an AL set – a set simply being the group of people. AL can be used for any number of people so long as each individual is allocated to one of any number of AL sets. Criteria for allocating individuals to sets are not universal and may vary depending on the learning need being addressed. Common criteria that are often used include gender, age, job role, functional specialty and hierarchical level.

The second element is that each individual attempts to solve a real organisational problem during his or her participation in the AL programme and AL set, and this forms the basis of the individual's AL project. This has to be a problem that matters to the individual himself or herself and to others in the organisation. Revans distinguished between what he called 'puzzles' (a question with a single correct answer) and 'problems' (a question with a range of possible answers which are not all initially knowable and which also vary in their effectiveness). AL projects have to address problems, not puzzles. They also have to include 'action' in the organisation as a basis of L&D.

A third element of AL is the use of reflection as a learning method. This is helped through membership of an AL set and the regular set meetings. Sets meet typically for half a day and, depending on the length of the overall programme, usually at weekly or monthly intervals. Individuals are allocated time in each set meeting to report their ideas, plans and progress on their projects and to outline actions to be taken before the next set meeting. They receive questions and questioning from other set members. So each member of what Revans called 'comrades in adversity' has, usually, an equal amount of time in each set meeting for them and their project. Being questioned by others supports each individual in reflecting on what and how they are learning.

The final feature of AL is the use of a set facilitator. This role is commonly carried out by an L&D professional who uses skills of observation and understanding of group processes to facilitate the work and development of the set.

AL sets can be seen as one form of what is called more widely 'communities of practice'. This idea rests on learning being seen as a social rather than an individual process whereby knowledge, understanding and skills are constructed within, by and through social groups (see Wenger 1998 for more details). Designing and implementing an AL programme would be one way of encouraging and facilitating the flourishing of communities of practice within an organisation. This in turn would help to develop a culture supportive of learning, make continuous learning more likely and support the L&D necessary for sustained organisation performance.

 REFLECTIVE ACTIVITY

1   Decide on a particular organisation as a focus.

2   Identify the range and types of occupations/jobs employed.

3   Evaluate the pros and cons of utilising AL for three different occupations/jobs in the organisation.

Coaching

Coaching forms part of the focus of Chapter 3 in this book and so will only be briefly summarised here. The first point to note is the popularity of the method with employers in the UK (CIPD 2011). Second is that it can be used to address and meet needs at all levels. Managers and supervisors can employ the method to develop their subordinates, both individually and in team contexts. In this case, the coaches are internal to the organisation. As with AL, the method is commonly used for managers at all levels and for professional staff, especially those identified as **knowledge workers**. When used for managers, coaching can be applied as a development method for all managers at a particular level, or can be used for just some managers or even one single individual. In those circumstances the coach is usually an external coach/consultant (CIPD 2011). Such coaching activity is commonly referred to as executive coaching (Peltier 2010).

There is in theory no job, role or occupation which cannot be a target for coaching as a development method. Individuals occupying the archetypical example low-level job of cleaner can potentially benefit from coaching provided by their line manager or perhaps by a colleague. 'Doing' coaching clearly demands some skills; what is referred to as 'performance coaching' needs the coach to be skilled at observation, questioning and providing feedback. These are skills which themselves can be developed and improved in supervisors and managers so that they can coach their staff to improve performance. As an approach to managing, a coaching style is argued to build a coaching culture supportive of continuous improvement (Whitmore 2009). Such a style obviously reflects and also develops a learning culture and so is associated with gaining competitive advantage through continuous development and improvement.

Coaching does, though, extend beyond organisations. Executive coaching is to some extent sought and funded by individuals themselves, perhaps to help further their career. Roles with titles such as personal coach, career coach and life coach suggest demand from individuals rather than organisations. This also reflects the claim that skilled coaches can support development in any area and with any focus, even those in which the coach has no personal knowledge, experience or expertise. Whatever the validity of that claim, it is clearly the case that coaching is one of the most widely used methods of development in the UK for both organisations and individuals.

REFLECTIVE ACTIVITY

As with the previous activity, decide on a particular organisation as a focus and identify the range and types of occupations/jobs employed.

1 Evaluate the pros and cons of utilising coaching for three different occupations/ jobs in the organisation.

2 Assess whether AL or coaching is likely to be the most cost-effective method of developing staff and improving performance in each of the occupations/ jobs.

3 Discuss your conclusions with a group of work or student colleagues.

The fact that coaching is used by individuals on their own behalf raises the question of roles and responsibilities in meeting learning needs. We now turn to that question.

ROLES AND RESPONSIBILITIES OF LEARNING

Everyone has a responsibility for their own L&D. Taking ownership for one's development and taking time to invest in opportunities to develop KSA is essential for personal development and building capability. Learning is therefore valuable and enhances performance and competitive advantage. However, it requires commitment and dedication from everyone, especially those who specialise in the field of L&D and those responsible for managing people. This section focuses on the role of the L&D professional and line managers to examine how both can support, encourage and facilitate an effective process of learning.

DEVELOPING A LEARNING CULTURE

Conner and Clawson (2004) suggest that a learning culture supports an organisation's sustainable competitive advantage. Developing a culture where everyone is committed and engaged in learning to enhance their capability will ultimately impact upon an organisation's performance and also how it is viewed as an employer. There are therefore many benefits for organisations in encouraging learning and creating an inclusive environment in which learning is valued, aligned to the business needs, promoted by management and accessible to everyone. A lack of support from management and the inability to invest time and resources for learning are major barriers that inhibit a learning culture (Maccoby 2003).

Although everyone has a responsibility to take ownership for their L&D, there is a greater onus on the L&D professional to offer guidance, support and encourage stakeholders to promote an organisational learning climate and culture.

THE ROLE OF THE L&D FUNCTION AND SPECIALIST

Over the years there has been a wider shift from the notion of 'training' to 'learning' (Hutchinson 2007), which has moved the role of L&D from an 'input'-focused service towards a more outcome-focused service aligned with organisational strategic needs. L&D has a primary focus to support an organisation by responding to organisational development (OD) needs and becoming an enabler of performance to achieve strategic objectives (Cunningham 2008). In order to achieve this, the role of the L&D professional requires flexibility and agility so as to position L&D as a key business partner in the organisation which focuses on the whole organisation's needs rather than exclusively on individual needs. In doing so, the role of L&D operates in a transparent manner, being more visible in the organisation and demonstrating added value.

Making a visible difference and enhancing performance will add to L&D's credibility and therefore raise its profile. However, there are a number of challenges for L&D – firstly, in building trusting and effective relationships with stakeholders to enable it to influence at a strategic level, and secondly by adding value and measuring performance outcomes rather than merely delivering activities (Sheppard and Knight 2011) The latter point regarding adding value is vital to how L&D is seen and positioned in an organisation; L&D must be involved in business issues and discussions from the outset rather than after decisions have been made (Smith 2010). This reflects a shift in the role of L&D, moving from a training service to a strategic consultancy whereby the business becomes the client and L&D works closely in partnership with the business to identify and solve L&D requirements. However, the organisational culture and the value it places on L&D will influence the extent to which L&D is strategic and consultative or remains merely operational.

One of the key roles for L&D is facilitating the process of learning in an environment in which managers take ownership of learning and promote a learning culture within the workplace. To support this, the creation of L&D plans which derive from business needs are a useful tool which focus on real development issues that impact upon organisational performance. Whereas L&D professionals play a key role in creating and delivering the L&D plan, this should not be in isolation from key stakeholders. In fact, L&D planning encourages involvement in the business and influences stakeholders to increase their commitment to, and to invest in, L&D activities. It can be said that the role of the L&D professional is to ignite small fires of L&D activity within the organisation and watch them grow and develop through the involvement of line managers and other key stakeholders.

THE ROLE OF LINE MANAGERS IN FACILITATING LEARNING

With the pressures of meeting organisational targets, L&D is not always a priority for line managers (Smith 2010). L&D must therefore align its business priorities and become a part of those priorities rather than be seen as an obstacle or burden. Amaratunga and Baldry (2002) suggest that the role of performance management is a key contributor to organisational learning and therefore encourages managers to become proactive in seeking L&D opportunities, which support them to meet organisational performance. In addition to this, the line manager's proactive role in conducting performance appraisals and agreeing development plans which support individuals to achieve their performance objectives (as mentioned above) can also support the notion of continuous learning (Hutchinson 2007).

While there may be structured formal L&D interventions available, such as traditional training courses, plus a range of L&D products and *ad hoc* activities, the ability of the line manager to support these interventions by offering informal learning methods such as coaching and mentoring is growing. There is a greater demand and onus on line managers to support pre- and post-learning activities through methods such as coaching and mentoring. However, according to research undertaken by the CIPD, coaching is mainly undertaken to manage poor performance rather than to support the facilitation of learning (Swart 2010).

There is a misconception that learning is primarily the role of L&D professionals. However – and as shown by the 'transfer of learning problem' mentioned above – learning is only as effective as the culture that encourages it back in the work environment. The line managers' role is thus vital to facilitate learning (Hutchinson 2007). Sending individuals on a training course will not necessarily mean that they have achieved or learned anything if there is no learning outcome or measure agreed beforehand. Prior to attending any learning event, the learner and his or her line manager should meet to discuss learning requirements, agree learning outcomes and decide how this learning will be measured – a meeting usually described as constituting 'pre-learning' activity or revealing 'learner readiness' (Leimbach 2010). This is generally aligned to performance outcomes and therefore, as suggested earlier, makes L&D a valued-added resource that directly supports organisational performance. In addition, this process can motivate the learner, address any concerns and manage expectations. Furthermore, time should be invested in 'post-learning' activity whereby the learning outcomes are assessed afterwards and measured against what both the line manager and learner have agreed. Similarly, this activity enables the learner to focus on integrating the learning with his or her work environment (Leimbach 2010). Pre- and post-learning activities manage expectations as well as enabling the line manager to facilitate the process of learning and link it to the effective management of performance and development.

REFLECTIVE ACTIVITY

Decide on a particular organisation as an example.

1   What kind of learning culture exists within the organisation?

2   What is the role of key stakeholders – i.e. line managers and L&D professionals?

3   Discuss and compare your findings with a colleague, and suggest what recommendations, if any, you would make to enhance a learning culture.

MAKING THE LEARNING 'REAL'

Whereas new skills and knowledge are developed during a learning event, the real application of learning happens after the event, usually back in the 'live' environment. There are two fundamental factors that can improve the transfer of learning. Firstly such improvement is dependent on the quality and design of the learning event itself, which should ensure that learner profiles and learning activities are reflective of the real environment and take into consideration individual learning styles (Ford 2009). Secondly, the line manager has a fundamental role to promote the transfer of learning into actual job performance following the learning event. Research conducted by Sak and Belcort (2006) as cited in Leimbach (2010) suggests that only 35% of newly attained skills are in use 12 months after a training event. With the huge investment made in L&D, it can be argued that organisations need to seek opportunities to consolidate the learning and measure the return on investment (see the next main section).

Longenecker suggests that 'to maximise the transfer of learning it is imperative that the manager be an action-oriented learner during the actual education experience' (2004, p5). Although this focuses on managerial learning, the principles are very much the same in that learning and embedding skills and knowledge extends beyond the classroom environment, and every opportunity should be explored to maximise the learning. Activities might include:

- linking the learning to performance objectives and a personal development plan as part of performance appraisals
- feeding back key messages or teaching the learning to other members of the team
- encouraging and making opportunities to apply the learning back in the work environment
- regularly reviewing training materials
- creating AL sets and networking with those who attend the learning event.

Investing time and commitment to facilitating the learning process by promoting the practising of skills in a safe environment will encourage and motivate learners to explore their learning and seek new meaning which they can then apply to their everyday work. This is a minimum requirement for achieving a return from a learning intervention. Assessing such returns is the focus of the next section.

 REFLECTIVE ACTIVITY

Consider other ways in which learning and the retention of skills and knowledge can be maximised back in the work environment following a learning event.

EVALUATING LEARNING OUTCOMES

Usually seen as the final stage in the ADDE model, evaluation is aimed at ensuring that learning interventions remain effective. This is because evaluation is concerned in part with establishing whether intended benefits have been achieved, and also because it triggers the starting stage of a new cycle by identifying new and further learning needs. The potential for linking back into the start of the cycle is only one reason why evaluation should not be an afterthought but instead planned for and applied only when an intervention is complete. As we saw earlier in the chapter, learning interventions are designed to meet learning needs, and those learning needs are, usually, associated with some element of improving performance. So it is arguably more sensible to think about and design evaluation of the intervention right at the start in order to directly link evaluation to the identified needs and expected performance improvements.

THE PURPOSES OF EVALUATION

Establishing the worth of the investment in a learning intervention is not the only purpose of evaluation. Others include *proving, improving, learning* and *controlling* (Easterby-Smith 1994). 'Proving' is the demonstration that the intervention has met the learning needs and achieved the intended/expected improvements in performance: that the intervention was worthwhile. 'Improving' is concerned with learning lessons from the implementation of the intervention so that it can be developed for future iterations. This is common in further and higher education and for formal off-the-job courses. Learning views evaluation as a means of supporting, adding to and reinforcing learning from the intervention. Finally, controlling is to do with quality assurance – i.e. L&D professionals monitoring learning interventions to ensure that they are consistent and of the desired quality.

Deciding on the purpose(s) is a necessary first step in designing an evaluation study. It can be inadvisable to mix too many purposes since they can conflict with each other (Devins and Smith 2010). For example, the purpose of controlling may inhibit learning and shut off opportunities for learners to explore new and different areas. Ideally, only one purpose should be pursued in any single study. Some additional key questions are given below. They are all related to one another and to purpose; the purpose that is decided on will influence answers to the other questions.

- What is to be evaluated?
- When is it to be evaluated?
- Who is to design/manage/carry out the evaluation, and who is to contribute – e.g. whose views will be sought?
- When is the evaluation to take place?
- How is the evaluation to be undertaken?

REFLECTIVE ACTIVITY

1   Consider how the possible purposes may conflict with each other.

2   Consider how each purpose may influence the answers to the other key questions.

3   Discuss your conclusions with a group of work or student colleagues.

One additional possible purpose is *promoting* (Stewart 1999; Gold *et al* 2010). Senior managers, for example, do not necessarily value learning interventions and may need persuading to support them. Evaluation studies can provide the evidence in favour of investing in L&D.

THE PROCESS OF EVALUATION

As with LNA, evaluation studies collect and analyse data and evidence. The nature and sources of that evidence will vary depending on the purpose and on answers to the other questions. Common sources of evidence are learners themselves, learners' colleagues and managers, learners' subordinates if the learners are managers, the facilitators delivering interventions, customers of the learners and/or the organisation and organisation management information systems. Not all of these sources are used in all evaluation studies, but any study will collect data from at least one of them.

Data collection methods vary in the same way as sources, but the source will be a significant influence on the method adopted. Again, as with LNA, common methods include questionnaires, interviews and focus groups for any of the 'human' sources. The most common and basic evaluation process uses questionnaires completed by learners either periodically throughout or at the end of a learning intervention. These usually ask for opinions on whether the learning objectives have been met, on the relevance of the content, on the effectiveness and appropriateness of the methods, on the quality of the facilitators and on organisational factors such as venue, briefing and facilities. Such questionnaires are often referred to as 'happy sheets' (usually pejoratively) or 'reactionnaires', which refers to the fact that the questionnaire collects individual reactions to the intervention from learners. More sophisticated use of questionnaires include 360-degree assessments of learners' performance and effectiveness in their job. This can take place before and/or after the intervention to measure differences as an indicator of learning, change and improvement. An additional common and more sophisticated approach to evaluation utilises pre-intervention interviews with learners and their managers to establish expectations, and then post-intervention interviews with each to assess how well, or not, expectations were met. As noted previously, this also supports transfer of learning back in the job.

Note that all of these processes collect and analyse opinions and not facts; learners and their managers and/or subordinates may report differences in performance and effectiveness, but that is not the same as actual differences. Data from management information systems provide more factual assessments of outcomes. For example, an intervention aimed at improving sales skills will be expected to result in increased sales and monitoring actual sales provides the relevant data. Or a management development intervention will be expected to result in more effective managers. Data that might establish whether this has been achieved could be represented by improved performance in the managers' departments and thus also by whatever performance measures are relevant to those contexts – e.g. increased income, decreased costs, or a reduction in customer complaints. Alternatively, data related to staff satisfaction might be more relevant – e.g. reduced absence, fewer grievances and stability in labour turnover. Which data is relevant depends on the initial learning need and the associated objectives of the learning intervention. In all cases, data pre- and post-the learning intervention should be collected and analysed in order to establish whether the intervention has had the intended effect.

REFLECTIVE ACTIVITY

Select a learning intervention you know well – it could be a course you are currently studying or one at work you have recently experienced.

1   Decide which purpose of evaluation is most appropriate to pursue in an evaluation of the intervention.

2   Decide what data, sources and method of data collection and analysis will best serve your purpose.

3   Report and discuss your conclusions with a group of work or student colleagues.

PROBLEMS OF EVALUATION

The first approach to data collection and analysis can be referred to as qualitative and the second as quantitative. The simple distinction is between data comprising words and data relying on numbers. Quite often, however, words are converted into numbers when, for example, end-of-course questionnaires include rating scales and responses are analysed to provide percentages. Where questionnaires do not use scales and learners can provide free responses, the responses are often interpreted in the analysis stage as expressing satisfaction or dissatisfaction; and then each is counted as such and turned into absolute numbers and then into percentages. So the validity of the data used and reported can render outcomes suspect (see Pawson and Tilley 1997; Holton and Naquin 2005).

There are debates on which types of data provide the most valid and reliable evidence, but this is just one problem in evaluation (Stewart 1999). Another is the veracity of responses – as the television character Dr House is fond of saying, 'There is only one truth: people lie.' This does not necessarily mean that learners or other stakeholders deliberately tell untruths, but rather that people can give what is termed 'socially desired responses' in reply to questions – i.e. they respond either to please the questioner or in a way which they believe will best serve their own interests, and thus their responses might not even be genuine opinions.

A related problem is that questionnaires assume that the respondent understands and shares the *meaning* given to words by the designer of the questionnaire. If a question asks for a rating of the *relevance* of the content, for example, the definition of 'relevance' may vary between respondents and also differ from that of the evaluator. As a result, respondents give truthful responses, but within their own understanding of 'relevance', which cannot be known by the evaluator.

There are at least two additional problems for evaluators (Stewart 1999). The first is to establish cause and effect, the main method of which is to take 'before' and 'after' measures. However, any change in assessment cannot be attributed to the intervention with any certainty: other factors may have caused the change but, as with meaning, this usually cannot be known by the evaluator. The common method of overcoming this problem in scientific studies is to have a control group, although that is rarely possible when evaluating learning interventions in organisations. Two further problems are worth mentioning. First, imagine a questionnaire administered at the end of an intervention that simply asks learners 'Was the intervention successful?' The results show that 50% said yes and 50% said no. What do you conclude? What percentage above 50% is needed to conclude it was successful or that it was unsuccessful? The final problem is related. Imagine that 100% said it was successful. The implication is that everything is fine and nothing needs to change – but the only safe conclusion is that it was successful for those particular learners. The next group of learners will be different in myriad ways and so it cannot be known in advance if their assessment will be the same or different.

AN EVALUATION MODEL

Despite these problems, evaluation is nonetheless important. It is critical that the purpose of evaluation is agreed first: the problems discussed above have varying significance and impact according to the purpose being pursued. The 'holy grail' of evaluation is to establish the return on investment (ROI) of learning interventions (Russ-Eft and Preskill 2005). A simple formula for establishing that is given below.

Financial benefits – costs = ROI

ROI is also the final stage in the most commonly applied model, first developed by Donald Kirkpatrick (Tamkin *et al* 2002). This model consists of four levels which, while appearing to be separate and independent, are all interconnected and represent a form of causal chain:

- Reaction – how learners feel about the intervention
- Learning – what new knowledge and skills learners have developed

- Job behaviour – changes in learners' behaviour and performance at work
- Results – improvements in department and/or organisation performance. The financial benefits should be compared to the costs of the intervention to give the ROI.

Different types, sources and methods of data collection and analysis are used at each level but, broadly, these will fit into the approaches discussed above.

REFLECTIVE ACTIVITY

What data types and sources, and methods of data collection and analysis, are most appropriate for each level of the Kirkpatrick model?

Discuss with a group of work or student colleagues how the problems of evaluation can be overcome, or at least minimised, when using the Kirkpatrick model.

The most recent influential work on evaluation of learning is the RAM approach mentioned early in this chapter. Rather than emphasising ROI and other 'factual' measures, it values interventions based on achieving intentions and expectations, as applicable (Anderson 2007). Intentions and expectations vary from context to context, case to case, and so standardised criteria of success are inappropriate. This approach certainly helps to overcome some of the problems with longer-established approaches to evaluation of learning interventions.

SUMMARY

Meeting organisational needs for development is the core activity of L&D professionals. It is accomplished through the activities encompassed in the ADDE model. Applying ADDE effectively may be encompassed by the more recent RAM model. Organisations rely on their employees to deliver sustainable and sustained performance; identifying and meeting their development needs is therefore crucial. This chapter has summarised the key questions and steps in each stage of meeting organisational development needs. Applying the ideas covered in the chapter will help to ensure high levels of individual, team and organisation performance.

BOOKS

BUCKLEY, R. and CAPLE, J. (2009) *The Theory and Practice of Training*, 6th edn. London: Kogan Page. This is a practice-based book that also covers all elements of L&D.

GOLD, J. *et al* (eds) (2010) *Human Resource Development: Theory and practice*, Basingstoke: Palgrave Macmillan. This is an introductory text for undergraduates that covers all areas of L&D.

FURTHER READING

REFERENCES

AMARATUNGA, D. and BALDRY, D. (2002) Moving from performance measurement to performance management. *Facilities*. Vol. 20, No. 5/6. 217–23.

ANDERSON, V. (2007) *The Value of Learning: From return on investment to return on expectation*. London: Chartered Institute of Personnel and Development.

BALDWIN, T. and FORD, J. K. (1988) Transfer of training: a review and directions for future research. *Personnel Psychology*. Vol. 41, No. 1. 63–105.

BOYDELL, T. and LEARY, M. (1996) *Identifying Training Needs*. London: Institute of Personnel and Development.

CIPD (2005) *Training to Learning*. Change agenda. London: CIPD.

CIPD (2011) *Learning and Talent Development*. Annual survey report. London: CIPD.

CIPD (2012) *Identifying Learning and Talent Development Needs [online]*. Factsheet. London: CIPD. Available at:http://www.cipd.co.uk/hr-resources/factsheets/identifying-learning-talent-development-needs.aspx [Accessed 7 June 2012].

CLARKE, N. (2003) The politics of training needs analysis. *Journal of Workplace Learning*. Vol. 15, No. 4. 141–53.

COFFIELD, F., MOSELEY, D., HALL, E. and ECCLESTONE, K. (2004) *Learning Style and Pedagogy in Post-16 Learning: A systematic and critical review*. London: Learning Skills Research Centre.

CONNER, M. L. and CLAWSON, J. G. (2004) *Creating a Learning Culture: Strategy, technology and practice*. Cambridge: Cambridge University Press.

CUNNINGHAM, I. (2008) The future of learning and development functions: a new era for L&D. *Development and Learning in Organizations.* Vol. 22, No. 6. 5–6.

DENBY, S. (2010) The importance of training needs analysis. *Industrial and Commercial Training.* Vol. 42, No. 3.147–50.

DEVINS, D. and SMITH, J. (2010) Evaluation of HRD, in GOLD, J., HOLDEN, R., ILES, P., STEWART, J. and BEARDWELL, J. (eds) *Human Resource Development: Theory and practice.* Basingstoke: Palgrave Macmillan.

DICK, W. and CAREY, L. (1996) *The Systematic Design of Instruction*, 4th edn. New York: HarperCollins College Publishers.

EASTERBY-SMITH, M. (1994) *Evaluating Management Development, Training and Education*, 2nd edn. Aldershot: Gower.

FORD, L. (2009) Improving training transfer. *Industrial and Commerical Training.* Vol. 41, No. 2. 92–6.

GIBB, S. (2003) Line manager involvement in learning and development: small beer or big deal? *Employee Relations.* Vol. 25, No. 3. 281–93.

GLAISTER, C., HOLDEN, R., GRIGGS, V. and MCCAWLEY, P. (2010) The design and delivery of training, in GOLD, J., HOLDEN, R., ILES, P., STEWART, J. and BEARDWELL, J. (eds) *Human Resource Development: Theory and practice.* Basingstoke: Palgrave Macmillan.

GOLD, J., THORPE, R. and MUMFORD, A. (2010) *Leadership and Management Development*, 5th edn. London: Chartered Institute of Personnel and Development.

HARRISON, P. (2011) Learning culture, line manager and HR professional practice. *Journal of European Industrial Training.* Vol. 35, No. 9. 914–28.

HOLTON, E. F. and NAQUIN, S. (2005) A critical analysis of HRD evaluation models from a decision-making perspective. *Human Resource Development Quarterly.* Vol. 16, No. 2. 257–80.

HOLTON, E. F., BATES, R. A., BOOKTER, A. I. and YAMKOVENKO, V. B. (2007) Convergent and divergent validity of the learning transfer system inventory. *Human Resource Development Quarterly.* Vol. 18, No. 3. 385–419.

HUTCHINSON, S. (2007) *Learning and the line. The role of line managers in training, learning and development.* Change agenda. London: CIPD. Available at http://www.cipd.co.uk/NR/rdonlyres/45B74613-3157-4064-93CD-7EA30AA8A172/0/learnline.pdf.

KELLIE, J., HENDERSON, E. and MILSOM, B. (2010) Leading change in tissue viability best practice: a development programme for link nurse managers. *Action Learning; Research and Practice.* Vol. 7, No. 2. 213–19.

LEIMBACH, M. (2010) Learning transfer model: a research-driven approach to enhancing learning effectiveness. *Industrial and Commerical Training.* Vol. 42, No. 2. 81–6.

LONGENECKER, C. (2004) Feature articles Maximizing transfer of learning from management education programs: best practices for retention and application. *Development and Learning in Organisations.* Vol. 18, No. 4. 4–6.

MACCOBY, M. (2003) The seventh rule: creating a learning culture. *Research Technology Management.* Vol. 43, No. 3. 59–60.

MCCARTHY, A. and GARAVAN, T. N. (2001) 360 feedback processes: performance improvement and employee career development. *Journal of European Industrial Training.* Vol. 25, No.1. 5–32.

MOREY, D. and FRANGIOSO, T. (1998) Aligning an organization for learning – the six principles of effective learning. *Journal of Knowledge Management.* Vol. 1, No. 4. 308–14.

PAWSON, R. and TILLEY, N. (1997) *Realistic Evaluation.* London: Sage.

PEDLER, M., BURGOYNE, J. and BROOK, C. (2005) What has action learning become? *Action Learning; Research and Practice.* Vol. 2, No 1. 49–68.

PELTIER, B. (2010) *The Psychology of Executive Coaching.* New York: Routledge.

RIGG, C. and RICHARDS, C. (2007) *Action Learning, Leadership and organisational development in public services.* London: Routledge.

ROFFE, I. (1999) Strategic planning for the development of a training innovation. *Industrial and Commercial Training.* Vol. 31, No. 5. 163–73.

RUSS-EFT, D. and PRESKILL, H. (2005) In search of the holy grail: return on investment evaluation in human resource development. *Advances in Developing Human Resources.* Vol. 7, No. 1. 71–85.

SHEPPARD, R. and KNIGHT, J. (2011) L&D partnering for success. *The Training Journal.* April. 46–50.

SMITH, J. (2010) From service provider to strategic consultant: how L&D practitioners can improve their internal consultancy skills. *The Training Journal.* March. 34–7.

STEWART, J. (1999) *Employee Development Practice.* London: FT/Pitman Publishing.

STEWART, J. and RIGG, C. (2011) *Learning and Development.* London: Chartered Institute of Personnel and Development.

SWART, T. (2010) The line manager as coach: the pros and cons of getting line managers to coach. *The Training Journal.* July. 67–71.

TANSLEY, C., TURNER, P. A., FOSTER, C., HARRIS, L., STEWART, J., SEMPIK, A. and WILLIAMS, H. (2007) *Talent: Strategy, management, measurement.* London: Chartered Institute of Personnel and Development.

TAMKIN, P., YARNELL, J. and KERRIN, M. (2002) *Kirkpatrick and Beyond: A review of models of training evaluation.* Brighton: Institute of Employment Studies.

WENGER, E. (1998) *Communities of Practice: Learning, meaning and identity.* Cambridge: Cambridge University Press.

WHITMORE, J. (2009) *Coaching for Performance: Growing people, performance and purpose.* London: Nicholas Brealey.

CHAPTER 5

Contemporary Developments in Human Resource Development

Jim Stewart and Sharon McGuire

CHAPTER CONTENTS

- Introduction
- What is HRD?
- Perspectives on HRD
- External trends influencing HRD
- Approaches to HRD
- Summary

KEY LEARNING OUTCOMES

By the end of this chapter, you will be able to:

- Evaluate competing approaches that contextualise contemporary developments in HRD.

- Analyse contemporary external trends and data and the implications of these for HRD practice.

- Describe and explain the role and contribution of HRD practice to developing different categories of employees and organisation functions.

- Discuss and debate contemporary developments in HRD practice.

INTRODUCTION

This chapter examines recent and current academic debates in **Human Resource Development** (HRD) literature and how the influences of these are applied and reflected in practice. It also speculates on how both theory and practice might develop in the future and, based on that, what challenges might be faced by professional practitioners in varying contexts and sites of HRD practice.

The content is organised according to a number of themes: varying perspectives on HRD; external trends and data; and HRD practice related to different occupational groups and organisation functions. It is, however, important to state that the themes are merely a useful organising device and that other devices are possible. The themes overlap and connect in various ways, some of which cannot be identified. For example, perspectives on HRD are influenced by external trends and data and in turn influence how those trends and data are interpreted and given meaning. Both perspectives and external data influence approaches to learning and development for different occupational groups and that development in turn provides data for producing external trends. How all of these examples of influence and connections work and what effects they have cannot be known with any precision or certainty – not, at least, in all respects. So it is important to bear in mind that the structure of the chapter is simply one way of thinking about the content.

WHAT IS HRD?

A useful starting point is to recognise that the term HRD is relatively new and that it has no settled meaning either in theory or practice (Hamlin and Stewart 2011). There are also competing terms – for example, 'learning and development' and 'learning and talent development' seem to be favoured by the CIPD for both qualifications and associated publications (see Stewart and Rigg 2011 for a fuller discussion on this point). Different contexts of practice also seem to favour varying terms: for example, 'workforce development' is a common feature of job titles and programmes of learning in public services, especially the NHS.

So to talk about HRD is in itself to take a particular perspective on one aspect of managing the employment relationship between employers and employees. However, one interesting factor of the term HRD is that it extends the boundaries beyond the learning undertaken by employees. John Walton, for example, argued that HRD encompasses what he referred to as 'non-employee development' (Walton 1999). This might include, for example, agency workers and volunteers in any sector as well as learning provided for the unemployed. Sambrook (2012), among others, has argued that education, and especially higher education (HE), is a site of HRD practice – i.e. that universities and their staff are practising HRD through both undergraduate and postgraduate degree programmes, whatever the subject. Neither the case of non-employees nor that of HE students is based on an employment relationship.

REFLECTIVE ACTIVITY

1 Consider the pros and cons of limiting a definition of HRD to only learning for those in an employment relationship.

2 Discuss and debate your thoughts with a group of work or student colleagues.

3 What similarities and differences of opinion can you identify within the group, and what are the reasons for the differences?

The argument advanced by Sambrook (2012), and that by Walton, reflects in part a definition of HRD offered by Stewart (2007, p66) which states simply that 'HRD is constituted by planned interventions in organisational and individual learning processes.' This definition does not imply any form of relationship between an individual and organisation, employment or otherwise – interventions can be aimed separately at individuals and/or organisations – but it does encompass any situation where such a relationship exists: employer and employee, or university and student, for example. However, the definition offered by Stewart is not the only one available. In their review of the literature on the meaning of HRD, Hamlin and Stewart (2011) found well over 24 different definitions of the term and identified four 'core purposes' of HRD within the definitions they examined in detail. They also noted that 'core purpose' is one of the key factors on which competing definitions vary. We will begin a closer examination of perspectives on HRD with the notion of 'purpose'.

PERSPECTIVES ON HRD

THE PERFORMANCE VERSUS LEARNING DEBATE

McGoldrick *et al* (2002) stated that the purpose of HRD was one of the key differentiators in definitions of HRD. As other authors since have reinforced (e.g. Rigg *et al* 2007), a significant difference is between those theorists who argue that the purpose of HRD is to improve organisational performance through enhancing individual and collective competence and those who argue that the purpose is to enhance individual development, growth and potential through learning. The former focus on performance is generally associated with a traditional or conventional view of HRD and long-established understandings of training and development. The perspective is also associated with a functional analysis of organisation and management, and a positivist view of reality. The latter perspective, which emphasises learning as opposed to performance, is argued to be a more recent development in theorising HRD and a reaction to (against?) the previously prevailing and dominant performance perspective. The learning perspective is associated with a radical and humanist analysis of organisation and management, and with a constructivist view of reality (see Stewart 1999 for a detailed discussion of these terms in the context of HRD).

The debate on performance versus learning as the key purpose of HRD suggests that they are mutually exclusive. This is not necessarily the case: it is possible at least that individual learning is a necessary condition and precursor for improved performance. However, the difference is based on more fundamental principles, related to the ultimate, as opposed to immediate, purpose claimed for HRD. As McGoldrick *et al* (2002) point out, the performance orientation on purpose defines the value and measures the worth of HRD in exclusively economic and financial terms. There is in this perspective no inherent value in individual learning and none exists or is achieved by individual learning unless 'objective' economic and financial gains are realised, usually to a work organisation or to a nation. Measures such as increased efficiency, productivity and effectiveness (indicated, for example, by rises in profit and shareholder value at organisational level or GDP at national level) are customarily used to indicate whether such value has been achieved.

Conversely, in the learning perspective individual development and growth has inherent value and the facilitation of achievement and development of individual potential is worthy in its own right. Social and cultural outcomes are valued in place of, or perhaps as well as, economic and financial criteria and measurement. Measurement of outcomes has a less important place than in the performance perspective, and where measurement *is* used, more subjective criteria such as learner satisfaction or other individually reported benefits are considered valid and significant (McGoldrick *et al* 2002).

REFLECTIVE ACTIVITY

1   Identify five advantages of the performance perspective from the point of view of organisation managers.

2   Identify five advantages of the learning perspective from the point of view of individual employees.

3   Consider if each of the items on your lists could be perceived as an advantage for the other party – i.e. whether an item on the

second list might be seen as an advantage by organisation managers and an item on the first list might be seen as an advantage by individual employees.

4   Consider the implications of your results for the practice of HRD in work organisations.

5   Discuss your conclusions with a group of work or student colleagues.

CRITICAL HRD

The learning perspective is an alternative to conventional views of HRD as being a 'tool' of management justified only in helping to meet managerial goals and objectives. As such, it is sometimes associated with what is termed **'Critical HRD'** (CHRD). CHRD is part of the wider literature of what is termed Critical Management Studies (CMS) (see Alvesson *et al* 2011 for more on CMS). However, many writers on CHRD question how critical the approach actually is. This relies on an analysis of CHRD as resting on four critiques of conventional perspectives of HRD. The first of these critiques, purpose, is discussed above. The other three critiques are examined below, based on the work of Rigg *et al* (2007).

The second critique central to CHRD argues that the learning perspective does not constitute part of CHRD. It challenges the humanist assumptions informing traditional HRD, which are also shared by the learning perspective. These assumptions see the individual in purely instrumental terms, with self-development being both possible and desirable. This notion is central to the learning perspective – e.g. the development of potential being valued as worthy in its own right. However, a more critical analysis of the concept of the individual questions the assumption of a coherent, autonomous and self-directed 'I' which lies at the heart of both traditional and learning perspectives on HRD. Critical analyses of these assumptions question this basic understanding and conceptualisation of the self. Drawing on both psychoanalytical and especially social theory, alternative conceptualisations of the self suggest that it is socially situated and constructed through social relations with 'others'. So identity, as Mary Midgley put it, 'is a continuing, lifelong project, an effort constantly undertaken in the face of endless disintegrating forces' (1996, p23). The 'disintegrating forces' that Midgley refers to include structures such as class and gender which define social identities and which in turn shape personal identity. A conceptualisation of the self as autonomous and self-directing is therefore both limited and limiting as a basis for HRD practice. The learning perspective shares with CHRD a purpose of human emancipation through L&D. But it inherently fails as a means of achieving that objective through its invalid assumptions on the nature of the self and human behaviour (Rigg *et al* 2007).

The third critique within CHRD is that of representational views of organisations within traditional HRD. Such views are in fact central to the vast majority of research, writing and prescriptions for organising and managing, and so are not unique to conventional HRD. Most management and related professional practice texts are predicated on such views. Put simply, representational views see organisations as 'things' – that is, organisations are reified. In other words, organisations are made concrete and attributed characteristics such as structures and hierarchies as if they were real in the same sense that trees are real and have branches and leaves. But organisations are abstractions: to the extent that they are 'real' and 'concrete' they depend on human beings to create them through interactions and individual and collective actions. But not understanding and accepting that we are engaged in creating organisations limits our understanding of and ability to influence and shape them through, among other activities, HRD. CHRD therefore argues for applying a different understanding of organisations as a more valid base for HRD practice. Some examples of where this will make significant differences include HRD contributions to organisational change efforts (Rigg *et al* 2007).

This third critique also rests on application of social theory, and the main arguments cannot be rehearsed here. It is necessary at this point only to understand that the critique is central to the analysis offered by CHRD. The same is true of the fourth critique – critical pedagogy – which is again drawn from both psychoanalytical and social theory. This focuses on the practice of HRD in institutions of education such as schools, colleges and universities, as well as in the context of organisations. It is 'practical' in that it calls for a shift in the power relations between those who teach or train, and those who are taught or trained. It also calls for changes in the content and methods, or pedagogy, of formal L&D programmes. An associated part of the critique is a call for the development and application of 'critical thinking' and of 'critical reflection' by learners to be facilitated by the content and methods of formal programmes of L&D. Within CHRD, critical pedagogy is seen as the primary means through which the aims and aspirations of the other three critiques can best be served and achieved by professional practitioners in all settings and sites of HRD practice. But there are reservations which centre mainly on the ethics of developing critical thinking among individuals who may then become isolated in the organisations in which they work (Rigg *et al* 2007). For example, managers who undertake a management development programme designed on the principles of CHRD may return to work with a very different understanding of their organisation and their role from that of their fellow managers, employees and bosses, and so become alienated in their jobs.

REFLECTIVE ACTIVITY

1   Read an article on CHRD from one of the special issues on the topic in the journals *International Journal of Training and Development* or *Journal of European Industrial Training*.

2   Summarise the arguments in the article and present them to a group of work or student colleagues.

3   Discuss in the group your understanding of CHRD based on the articles presented.

4   Produce a group consensus definition of CHRD.

5   Discuss the implications of your definition for professional practice in HRD.

ADDITIONAL PERSPECTIVES

Two further perspectives currently influence HRD theory and practice. The first is the view that HRD needs to become (more?) strategic. This argument was most ardently supported by John Walton in his 1999 book *Strategic Human Resource Development*, and it is an argument that has continued to be advanced. However, HRD itself was previously defined in part by adopting a strategic approach to organisational and individual development (Stewart and McGoldrick 1996) and that view of HRD is evident in most of the definitions analysed by Hamlin and Stewart (2011). So it is difficult to maintain an argument that there is a meaningful distinction between HRD and **Strategic HRD** (SHRD). Walton did draw attention to the useful distinction between SHRD (or HRD itself depending on your position) and HRD strategies, which is accepted by probably every leading writer on the subject. However, the distinction provides little grounds for theorising a difference between HRD itself and SHRD. Most, if not all, extant definitions of HRD implicitly or explicitly include a strategic focus for HRD and so it remains debatable whether a supportable distinction can be drawn between SHRD and HRD.

Perhaps of more importance is the perspective on HRD implicit in the CIPD Profession Map (see http://www.cipd.co.uk/cipd-hr-profession/hr-profession-map/professional-areas/) and the major research projects undertaken by the Institute on 'Shaping the Future' (see http://www.cipd.co.uk/shapingthefuture). The former uses the preferred language of the CIPD and so the relevant professional area in the map is that of 'Learning and Talent Development'. However, organisational development is defined by most theorists as being a constituent part of the practice of HRD (Hamlin and Stewart 2011) and so that area of professional practice in the CIPD map is also relevant to gaining an understanding of the CIPD perspective on HRD. The 'Shaping the Future' research provides additional insight and focuses on what it identifies as an important need to sustain organisation performance; the final report of the project is entitled 'Sustainable organisation performance: what really makes the difference' (CIPD 2011), which implies a performance orientation. But sustainability is also associated with some aspects of CHRD (Stewart 2007) and was the theme adopted for the major European conference on HRD in 2011. It seems, therefore, that sustainability is a relevant and current perspective on HRD.

REFLECTIVE ACTIVITY

Analyse the perspective taken on HRD in the CIPD Profession Map.

Compare that to the learning and performance debate and determine which of those, if either, most closely fits the CIPD perspective.

EXTERNAL TRENDS INFLUENCING HRD

As well as perspectives, trends and data on a range of features of what is usually referred to as the 'external environment' (Stewart and Rigg 2011) also influence HRD practice. This label covers a number of different but related factors which include the labour market. This in turn includes population trends and the (changing) demographics of populations, and the policies and actions pursued by national governments and their agencies. We will begin an examination of external trends with a brief overview of writing on government policies.

NATIONAL HRD AND VOCATIONAL EDUCATION AND TRAINING

Government action related to HRD is usually referred to as either **Vocational Education and Training** (VET) or **National HRD** (NHRD) (Gold *et al* 2010). The term NHRD is a recent invention and one which has been subject to critique by, among others, Wang (2008). Both country governments and international agencies such as the United Nations (UN) concern themselves with the economic status and health of nations. The term HRD was originally coined in the context of economic research focused on policy measures intended to stimulate economic development. As Wang argues, the actual focus in those studies is more accurately represented by the term 'human development' (HD) since the research was concerned with the effects of investment in human capital; in the form of education and training; in improving national economic performance and alleviating poverty in less developed countries. Wang further argues that NHRD should be renamed 'HRD national policy studies'. Interestingly, the term 'national policy' was used in curriculum specifications of professional qualifications for HRD practitioners in the 1980s and 1990s, and so Wang may have a point. While there may be debate about the accuracy or appropriateness of the terms used, it is clear that what the majority of researchers refer to as VET or NHRD is concerned with government and other agencies' attempts to stimulate economic development within countries through direct investment, and through stimulating indirect investment by employers and individuals in human capital through the provision and supply of education and training.

An additional and potentially complicating notion is that of **International HRD** (IHRD). As with the other terms, there is debate on the meaning and scope of IHRD. Studies in IHRD began in response to the need to understand HRD practice in multinational and transnational companies (Hamlin and Stewart 2011). However, the term has been expanded to encompass what is also covered by VET and NHRD. This is clear from the definition of IHRD offered by Metcalfe and Rees (2005, p455):

A broad term that concerns process that addresses the formulation and practice of HRD systems, practices, and policies at the global, societal, and organisational level. It can concern itself with how governments and international organisations develop and nurture international managers and how they develop global HRD systems; it can incorporate comparative analyses of HRD approaches across nations and also how societies develop national HRD policies.

It is clear from this that for Metcalfe and Rees at least, IHRD encompasses studies of national policies. The inclusion of comparative studies in the definition is useful because it is a common feature of VET and NHRD research (see, for example, Gold *et al* 2010), not least because national governments and international agencies seem keen to learn lessons about what works to inform their own policy development.

There are of course problems and limitations with comparative analyses. These arise mainly from differences in national culture and economic circumstances (see Hamlin and Stewart 2011). Another difficulty arises because VET/NHRD policies are used to pursue various policy objectives in different countries and in the same country at different points in time. As an example of the latter, national policies in the UK are influenced by the state of the economy and especially levels of unemployment, and so policy objectives might in one period be aimed at alleviating and reducing unemployment while in more prosperous times they might be aimed at pursuing 'lifelong learning' and the development of high-level skills (see Stewart and Rigg 2011 for a brief review of the history of VET policy in the UK). National policy in some countries sometimes also pursues what may be defined as 'non-employment' and so non-economic objectives to do with health, safety and community issues, for example (Hamlin and Stewart 2011). However, this is a somewhat weak argument because health and safety indicators are used as measures of economic well-being as well as measures of human development, which is itself both a measure of stimulating and of assessing economic development and progress. In addition, and as was argued in the *Perspectives on HRD* section above, economic rationales are favoured by governments to justify investment in HRD at national level. So in summary, it does seem to be the case that VET/NHRD is concerned with the use of HRD to stimulate economic development and growth.

REFLECTIVE ACTIVITY

Undertake some wider reading based on the sources referred to in this subsection.

1   Consider the terms VET, NHRD and IHRD. What do you see as the major differences in meaning, if any, between these terms?

2   Discuss your conclusions with a group of work or student colleagues.

There have been some attempts to produce overarching classifications of approaches to VET/NHRD, although these do tend to generate additional new terms. A common approach is to assess the extent of government intervention. Based on this, any particular nation's approach to VET/NHRD can be classified on a scale between 'interventionism' to **'voluntarism'** (Gold *et al* 2010). Interventionism at one end of the scale indicates a high amount of government influence or control. Voluntarism at the other end of the scale indicates a low amount of government influence or control. The term 'voluntarism' seems to be peculiarly UK in origin and use, for the term 'non-interventionism' is more often used elsewhere. An alternative term for interventionism is **'corporatism'**, which can have a slightly different meaning in that it indicates co-operation and collaboration between government, employers (usually bodies such as the Confederation of British Industry), employee representatives (usually trade unions and their bodies such as the Trades Union Congress) and, often, bodies representing suppliers of VET such as education institutions. Compulsory education is usually (but not always, and especially if the focus is HD rather than HRD) excluded from the scope of VET/NHRD and so educational interests in corporatist approaches imply, in the UK context at least, colleges and universities. It can be safely said that in the UK both interventionism and voluntarism have been tried by governments at different points in time, although neither in pure nor extreme form. The UK has tended to span the middle of that continuum with shifts in approach being small movements in one direction towards one extreme or the other (Stewart and Rigg 2011).

In his analysis undertaken in the late 1990s, Hamlin (1999) utilised a classification of three approaches for VET/NHRD aimed at young people. The first of these is what is known as the Dual System, which is best illustrated by the VET/NHRD system in Germany where it originated and is still practised. Similar approaches have been adopted in Austria, Switzerland and Denmark. The Dual System reflects three possible applications of 'duality'. The first of these is the dual focus on general education and vocational education/training and the associated skills of both. So young people (following compulsory education) spend time in colleges which provide both kinds of education and training. The second 'duality' is that the young people are at the same time apprenticed for a specific occupation/job with an employer and also receive planned work-based training alongside their college studies, creating duality in the structured and integrated off-the-job and on-the-job learning and development. The third aspect of duality is in the shared responsibility for organising and managing the system between employers (both as single entities and in their collective bodies) and social partners. Social partners are in effect trade unions. The role of the state – in Germany, at both national and regional levels – is to oversee the system rather than to actively participate in its operation.

The second approach in Hamlin's classification is what he terms 'state-led'. This has two subforms – one labelled 'Broad occupational VET' and one labelled 'General education'. The basic defining features of the approach are government responsibility for and direct provision of post-compulsory education and training. The basic distinguishing feature of the two subforms is the nature of the education provided. In the former, it is overtly vocational and technical, and directly linked to employment. In the latter, there is less overt focus on particular occupations and jobs and the main focus is on knowledge and skills with general applicability and value in the labour market. Hamlin (1999) includes Sweden and Belgium as examples of countries adopting the first subform, and the USA and Japan as examples of countries adopting the second.

According to Hamlin, the UK (along with Australia) adopts an approach consistent with his third approach, which he labels the 'mixed' approach This perhaps reflects the point made earlier that the UK occupies the middle ground between the extremes of interventionism and voluntarism. The basic components of the mixed approach are elements of the Dual System, such as apprenticeships managed by employers and trade unions, together with state-led systems of vocational and academic education. One of the problems with the mixed approach, in the UK at least, is the difference in prestige and desirability between academic and vocational education post-18.

Hamlin (1999) offers a different classification of approaches to VET/NHRD for adults. Making this distinction is not universal in the literature, but it does have some validity because governments and agencies do tend to adopt different policies for the two broad groups of young people/school leavers and adults. There are four categories in Hamlin's classification of approaches for adults: state intervention, state-led employer co-operation, employer-led co-operation, and market-based systems. In the first of these, governments directly fund and/or provide, perhaps through their own agencies, education and training for adults. Provision may be through third parties such as colleges and training providers. In the second category, governments encourage and facilitate employers to work together to ensure a sufficient supply of education and training related to their skills needs. This may involve tax and other forms of financial incentive. The third category covers countries such as Germany where strong employer links and co-operation already exist and so there is little need for state involvement. An additional feature of employer-led co-operation suggests that the term is a slight misnomer because such approaches also usually rely on strong employee representation through trade unions and a tradition of employer–union co-operation. The final category, market-based systems, uses a name which is also sometimes used as a synonym for 'voluntarism'. The forces of supply and demand are left to operate unfettered by state intervention in this system. So individual employers and citizens determine how much and what kind of VET is demanded, and suppliers satisfy that demand. Hamlin (1999) cites the UK and the USA as countries in which this approach is adopted.

REFLECTIVE ACTIVITY

Based on your wider reading and on the above, identify five potential advantages and five potential disadvantages for the UK in adopting each of the approaches to adult VET in Hamlin's classification.

Research current UK policy and assess which of Hamlin's categories it would fit best. You might find the following websites useful:

● http://www.apprenticeships.org.uk/

● http://www.bis.gov.uk/
● http://www.direct.gov.uk/en/index.htm
● http://www.dwp.gov.uk/
● http://www.ukces.org.uk/

Assess how far you think current NHRD/VET in the UK is realising the potential advantages and minimising the potential disadvantages of the category you assessed it best fits.

As discussed above, one potential use of classifications such as those offered by Hamlin (1999) and Gold *et al* (2010) is in comparing the approaches of different countries to evaluate the effectiveness and appropriateness of a current approach in a given country. A crude way of doing this would be to compare national economic performance in two or more countries on the assumption that the better-performing countries have more effective approaches to NHRD/VET. At the very least, and without accepting direct causal relationships, approaches adopted in other countries can be a source of insight, ideas and creativity in policy development. For example, the creation of Training and Enterprise Councils in the 1980s in the UK was modelled on an initiative in Boston, USA. In 2008 the author along with colleagues produced a research report entitled *World Class Comparisons* for the then Learning and Skills Council. The report compares VET/NHRD in the UK with that in five other countries (see Gold *et al* 2010 for a summary). There is not the space here to go into detail on other countries' approaches but information can be found in various sources including the 'International briefings' which appear regularly in the *International Journal of Training and Development* and in journal articles providing country studies of NHRD authored by Gary McLean and his colleagues. We now move on to consider the other significant external factor of population and labour market trends.

CASE STUDY

Work experience skills to count towards university degree

Universities are developing different models and modes of delivery to ensure that their graduates can provide employers with practical evidence of the skills they possess. For example,

University of Leicester students can earn credits for managing a workshop or giving a presentation, Durham University is also considering awarding course credits for valuable work experience, while University College London's career unit is devising a system of employment credits. There is a clear trend towards ensuring that every course offers the opportunity for work experience, not just the traditional vocational subjects such as engineering.

Paul Jackson, director for student support and development at University of Leicester informed the *Telegraph* newspaper that the university was 'looking closely at how to embed corporate skills into the curriculum at the undergraduate stage'. Increasing employment skills within undergraduate courses was further supported by the CBI. Jackson commented that, 'There is no difference

between academic skills and employment skills. We are looking for students who can apply things in a new context.'

This has fuelled debate from James Ladyman, Professor of Philosophy at Bristol University, who predicts that awarding credits for employment skills could shift the focus too far towards the employer's requirements in the short term. The long-term focus should be to provide education which will be instilled in students for life. This in turn will provide a valuable course for international students rather than focusing on employment skills.

Source: adapted from Churchard (2011)

POPULATION AND LABOUR MARKET TRENDS

One significant and important trend is the size of population. While there has been concern for a number of years over an increasing world population, more recent trends suggest a clear decline in the rate of increase, as well as a reversal of growth in some countries. However, the numbers entering the labour market continue to rise and present a challenge in respect of the availability of employment opportunities, despite a declining birth rate in, for example, the EU as a whole (Stewart and Rigg 2011). The size of the population in a particular country is a function of factors other than birth rates. These include mortality rates and life expectancy, and net emigration/immigration – i.e. the difference between the two. Both of these factors are significant in the UK, with life expectancy now at over 75 years for men and nearly 80 years for women. Net immigration in the UK also contributes more to population increases in the UK than natural replacement. So the population of the UK continues to be increasingly diverse in terms of ethnic and cultural origin. The three most significant factors of the UK population therefore are providing jobs for those of working age, an ageing population and increasing ethnic and cultural diversity. Action by the UK Government on abolishing compulsory retirement and on state and public sector pensions is a response to the ageing population, but this also has consequences for those of working age who are seeking employment opportunities.

It is not only population that impacts upon the labour market. Although it affects labour supply, the demand for labour is also significant – for example, the global change in distribution of demand such as the general and broad shift in manufacturing from Western, developed countries to less developed countries where labour costs are lower. This affects the type of labour demanded in the

West. Related to this is the general rise in demand in countries like the UK for labour in service- and knowledge-based industries, which tend to demand better educated and higher-skilled labour. This can be characterised as a shift from physical or manual labour to intellectual and what is termed 'emotional' labour (see Stewart and Tansley 2002; Stewart and Rigg 2011).

These general trends are based on regular surveys undertaken by international bodies such as the UN, the European Commission and the UK Government. Key sources for the UK are the quarterly 'Labour Force Survey' (see http://www.esds.ac.uk/government/lfs) and the CIPD 'Labour Market Outlook' (LMO) surveys (see http://www.cipd.co.uk/research/_labour-market-outlook). The autumn 2011 LMO reflects the general trend of reducing employment in manufacturing and shifts to demand for higher skills. It also indicates continuing problems for employers in securing all of those skills and intentions to recruit migrant workers as one means of dealing with those problems. This is of course in the current context of declining demand for labour and rising unemployment in the UK. But whatever the overall demand for labour, it seems clear that jobs requiring intellectual and emotional labour will continue to feature more than those that require physical labour in the demand side of the labour market, and immigration will continue to be a significant feature in the supply side.

REFLECTIVE ACTIVITY

Access the four most recent issues of the CIPD's 'Labour Market Outlook'.

1   Analyse the data on skills in those publications.

2   Consider the trends revealed by your analysis and the implications they may

have for HRD practice in work organisations.

3   Discuss your conclusions with a group of work or student colleagues.

APPROACHES TO HRD

This section considers developments in practice and how they might influence approaches to HRD for different categories of employees and functions in organisations. A useful starting point is to look at broad approaches to HRD practice and their current application.

SOME BROAD CATEGORIES

There are a number of ways to classify approaches to developing people. One is simply differentiating between those that occur at work ('on-the-job') and those that occur away from the direct workplace ('off-the-job'). A related differentiation is between formal and informal methods: off-the-job methods tend to be more formal and on-the-job more informal in nature. However, another classification, which differentiates education, training and development, may disrupt this generalisation. The meaning of these terms are themselves debatable (see Stewart 1999 for a discussion), but differences between them – such as education being associated with qualifications and transferable skills, and training being associated with organisation-based jobs and job-specific skills – are well recognised. However, National Vocational Qualifications (NVQs) are for many occupations awarded following on-the-job training and can often be very job- if not organisation-specific. This specificity is becoming increasingly less well demarcated, with employers now being able to award qualifications and large employers such as McDonalds taking advantage of the opportunity. In addition, while the assessment may be very formal, the learning and development leading up to assessment is often quite informal. The upshot is that previously widely applied and accepted classifications such as on- or off-job, formal versus informal, and education and training, are becoming outdated and no longer either valid or useful.

An additional factor causing confusion in established classifications is developments in professional and management development. This is in part associated with NVQs as they are also used at these levels. More significant, though, is the growth in university involvement and partnerships with employers in relation to delivery of higher-education qualifications. This applies at both undergraduate and postgraduate levels, especially in business and management, with first degrees and Masters in Business Administration (MBA) now commonly delivered 'in-company' by UK business schools for specific employers. Similarly, employer involvement in design and delivery of foundation degrees is required and the qualifications are often approved and awarded by universities, even if delivered by colleges of further education. Employer–university partnerships are the focus of considerable research in the HRD literature, which has shown that it is not without problems for all parties, including individual employees (see for example the special issue of *Journal of European Industrial Training* edited by Weir and O'Donoghue (2005); Kellie 2007; Stansfield and Stewart 2007; Stewart and Rigg 2011). A related factor is the growth of what are termed 'corporate universities'. These are arrangements for HRD within, owned and controlled by work organisations which may or may not have links with a formally constituted university (one of the oldest and best known is the McDonalds Hamburger University; see http://www.aboutmcdonalds.com/mcd/ corporate_careers/training_and_development/hamburger_university.html). The meaning of the term **'corporate university'** is debatable and may, in some cases at least, be simply a renaming of an existing central HRD department and function (Walton 2005). However, the term is also illustrative of the changing nature of HRD practice and the changes since the terms 'on-the-job' and 'off-the-job' used to cover all possibilities. There has, then, been a clear need for alternative classifications.

Stewart and Rigg (2011) offer an alternative classification that resolves to some extent the confusions of older typologies. Here, a simple framework of three methods is used: away from work, at work and through work. Some specific approaches and methods can combine more than one type. For example Stewart and Rigg place e-learning (see next section) in both 'away from work' and 'at work'. This recognises that e-learning programmes are designed to be undertaken in either context – e.g. at a work station or on a mobile phone while travelling – and that some programmes are designed with elements to be undertaken in both contexts. So it is entirely possible that because of the unique elements of particular programmes, specific approaches and methods do not to fit neatly into one. However, the classification offered by Stewart and Rigg does reflect developments in both theory and practice. These include much more emphasis in HRD on learning 'through work', which is based in significant part on developments in learning theory such as situated learning and the associated idea of 'communities of practice'.

SOME SPECIFIC METHODS

There are too many specific methods of HRD to consider them all in this chapter. Instead, we will examine a small number that have wide application for broad job categories, beginning with management and professional development.

Managers and professionals are much more likely to be developed through formal, off-the-job and education-based approaches and methods, and so 'away from work' (see CIPD annual 'Learning and Talent Development' reports for data). This is in some cases because of legal requirements: for example, professional (usually university-delivered) qualifications are essential in law and accountancy, which require a licence to practice. Other professions, such as IT, marketing and HR, do not require a legal licence to practice but are sufficiently recognised as being professions to have professional bodies which heavily inform professional development within the field. So employers routinely support employees seeking professional recognition and membership through qualifications, and view that as the most appropriate method of training and developing individuals in functions such as marketing and HR.

However, there is not a professional body for managers that has gained the same status as even those for marketing and HR. Anyone can manage – or at least, that is how it seems. Certainly, anyone is allowed to manage. There have long been qualifications for managers, some associated with professional bodies, and NVQs in management have been available for around 20 years. The MBA degree is probably the most widely used and recognised qualification for management, but that has been subject to heavy criticism (e.g. Mintzberg 2004). More recently, there has been an increasing focus on leaders and leadership development. However, the distinction between a manager and a leader is debatable and certainly blurred since leadership development is commonly reserved for those who are currently in or being prepared for managerial positions. Many leadership development programmes do, however, counter the criticism of MBAs levelled by Mintzberg and others that the 'soft' side and associated skills of managing need to be emphasised more in developing managers.

One development method that has a long and successful history in HRD practice for both management and professional development is action learning (Rigg and Richards 2007). This method was originally developed for managers by Reg Revans in the late 1940s/early 1950s, but has since been applied in a wide variety of contexts. According to the classification offered by Stewart and Rigg, the method is an example of L&D 'through work'. There are three key features in action learning programmes:

- A work-based problem that an individual seeks to resolve through an action-based project.
- A small group of individuals, referred to as a set, each conducting their own action learning project, who meet regularly to review progress and to receive challenging questioning and feedback from their peers.
- No specified curriculum or content and no use, unless requested by a set, of expert tutors or academics.

Action learning continues to be popular in leadership development programmes and it can be argued that it has stood the test of time.

REFLECTIVE ACTIVITY

1   Identify five advantages of 'through work' methods over 'away from work' methods from the perspective of an employer.

2   Do the same from the perspective of an employee.

3   Discuss your conclusions with a group of work or student colleagues.

Additional methods that also seem to stand the test of time – especially for management, leadership and professional development – include coaching, mentoring, secondments, work shadowing and special projects (see Stewart and Rigg 2011). Most of these also fit the category of 'through work', at least in some respect. Two other broader approaches also fit that category and, while certainly used for management and professional development, they are becoming more widely expected of employees in many occupations and functions. These are self-development and continuous professional development (CPD). The latter is often a condition of continuing membership of professional bodies, but the principle is now more widely applied. There is also clear overlap in the methods as CPD is self-managed by individuals. It might be argued that the term CPD is used to cover self-development for professionals and 'self-development' applies to non-professional occupations and roles. Whatever the case, they are similar enough to be treated here as a single method and so we use the acronym CPD to include both self-development and continuous professional development in the following paragraphs.

It is a slight misnomer to describe CPD as a 'method' because any of the methods mentioned above can be utilised by individuals for CPD purposes. Gold and Smith (2010) list the following methods as recommended by a variety of professional institutes, and any could be also used by members of other occupational groups:

- focused discussions with colleagues
- online research
- reading

- researching a specific issue related to a particular work/role
- researching legislation related to a particular work/role
- work shadowing
- mentoring and coaching
- the preparation and delivery of training courses
- distance learning and the use of audio-visual materials.

The last of these includes online podcasts and videos on YouTube as well as those on more specialist sites such as www.ted.com. Gold and Smith (2010) argue that the increasing emphasis on CPD is associated with the need to promote lifelong learning, itself a response to a fast-changing world economy. They also present a model of CPD which has five stages: appraise/assess needs; prepare a personal development plan; development; review learning; monitor implementation. Given its cyclical structure and the nature of the five stages, it is not dissimilar to the systematic training cycle, and so it is arguable that CPD is in fact applying HRD practice as it is commonly done in organisations. But the distinguishing factor is that the application of CPD is the responsibility of individual employees. This is also consistent with the increasing use of personal development plans (PDPs) in organisational HRD practice. These too devolve to some extent responsibility for development to employees. This devolution of responsibility away from the professional function is also a feature of another current development in HRD, in which line managers are increasingly being held responsible for the development of their staff. In the case of CPD, however, line managers are more likely to be a resource available to support rather than be responsible for its application. In summary, CPD utilises all possible forms of HRD: work-based; education-based; formal and informal; at work; away from work; and through work. The key differentiator is that CPD is controlled by individuals although in some cases, such as accountancy and law, it may be monitored and have some parameters prescribed by professional institutes. This may also be the key differentiator between CPD and self-development.

Two final contexts of HRD practice are based on particular approaches. The first is team development. This can occur both within and across occupational groups and organisation functions. For example, a group of IT specialists all working together on a daily basis in the same department could be the focus, or it could be a group of managers from the same hierarchical level but across different functions and who collectively constitute the 'middle management team' without working with each other directly. A third common possibility is a project team composed of individuals from various functions and perhaps different hierarchical levels who have been brought together for a defined length of time to carry out a specific task – e.g. planning, preparing and implementing a new store opening in a supermarket business. There are some general approaches that apply to team development whatever the composition of the team. According to Iles *et al* (2010) these include examining and improving goal-setting, clarity on goals, group dynamics and processes, relationships, and roles within the team. A range of methods are also available, including use of the outdoors and 'challenge' activities such as sailing, or personality-based analyses such as those developed by Belbin to match individual members to team roles (Iles *et al* 2010).

The second of the two final contexts is graduate development. Many methods are utilised in graduate development programmes but, as the name implies, access and entry to them is restricted to newly recruited university graduates. In fact, recruitment and selection of graduates is commonly defined as the first stage in a graduate development programme. According to Holden and his colleagues (Holden *et al* 2010), current developments in graduate development include three key changes. The first is the rising number of graduates over the last 10 years or so – a rise of over 50% between 1995 and 2007. The second and related factor is the changing nature of graduate jobs and careers. Put simply, as the supply of graduates has increased, new jobs have emerged, defined as suitable for graduates. And some jobs have been redefined as being at graduate level – nursing, for example. The latter change has had the reverse effect of increasing the numbers of graduates because entry into the occupation did not previously require a first degree: the change to graduate entry meant new university programmes and a whole new set of graduates. The third factor is an increasing emphasis in all first degree programmes on 'employability' and the development of generic, transferable skills relevant to employment. These include literacy, numeracy, communication, information and communication technology, and teamworking skills. Graduates in all disciplines and subjects are therefore expected to be able to demonstrate similar skills of value to employers. It is not yet known what consequences recent rises in tuition fees will have on the graduate labour market and thus on graduate development programmes. One widely anticipated consequence is a reduction in participation in higher education and consequent reductions in the number of graduates, even if only temporarily while the market adjusts to the new fees. This in turn will increase competition among graduate recruiters who will have a smaller pool to draw from. A related consequence may well be that graduate development programmes will become even more of a critical 'selling point' used by employers to attract the 'best' graduates. This will present opportunities for HRD professionals to make a valued contribution in some work organisations.

SUMMARY

This chapter has considered and discussed a wide range of issues and concepts related to contemporary HRD theory and practice. In relation to theory, the varying perspectives influence understandings and meanings attached to the term HRD. This in turn influences approaches to and methods of practising HRD through the design and delivery of interventions for varying roles, functions and categories of employees. As well as perspectives, changing external conditions and especially those in populations and local labour markets also affect practice as the mix of employees becomes increasingly diverse. So both theory and practice have to respond to the changing nature of employees in work organisations. This can be helped in part by understanding brought to practice by a study of cross-cultural HRD and diversity management. New technologies also present opportunities for dealing with these challenges as they open up new ways of delivering HRD interventions. But new concepts such as talent management will continue to emerge and exert new influences. The key requirement seems to be that an ability to identify and analyse changes and developments as they emerge is essential for successful HRD practice.

 Developing a corporate university

CASE STUDY

A large corporate oil company in South Africa decided to raise the talent of the whole organisation, using the ethos of an 'inclusive' approach to managing talent. Its strategy was to share knowledge within the organisation and to align this knowledge with its business strategy. The three-year plan was to ensure that all employees possessed a university degree. The five-year plan was to ensure that the entry criterion for working in the organisation was a postgraduate qualification. In the long term, this would raise the reputation and quality of the employees, ensuring that they were performing at the highest levels

Ivan Dias was the President of Training and Public Policy within this organisation. He had extensive experience of working in collaboration with different training providers, partnerships with different universities within the local area and throughout the world. He strove to push through as many employees as possible onto university courses, but it was often quite difficult for the organisation to release staff for long periods at a time. Ivan's plan had to incorporate many different methods of training and development, including distance learning, training the trainer, e-learning, and using different modes of delivery – for example, in-house delivery, semesterisation and blended learning.

Towards the end of the first six months of the business strategy, Ivan decided that it would be beneficial to build a corporate university (CU) to guarantee the targets for the five-year business plan. The CU would not only be a training place but would also offer

postgraduate qualifications through partnership links with established universities. The CU would enable the company to build up its own training and development facility to ensure the transferability of knowledge into the workplace and, more importantly, within its counterpart international country, which should also simulate the organisation's strategy. One of the ultimate objectives was to amalgamate teaching of theoretical knowledge with organisational expertise.

The CU was built in the following six months at HQ in Johannesburg. Its sole purpose was to focus on internal employees although it would sometimes support the external environment too. The CU was staffed by the organisation's own professional staff and forged partnerships with traditional universities all over the world. The CU also had 200 bedrooms for international employees engaged in long-term stays. Ivan found that it was quite a balancing act to ensure that employees had equal access to opportunities at the CU.

Three years into the plan it was apparent that the organisation was achieving its targets, but the overheads were becoming quite costly – e.g. maintenance, estates, catering and housekeeping. This impacted upon on the quality of care and standards that employees were expecting. Simultaneously, the worldwide economic recession was also putting strain on the organisation.

Ivan was now under increased pressure to devise both a short-term and long-term plan for the future of the CU.

Questions:

1   Provide a training and development plan appropriate for the organisation to ensure long-term success. What would you hope to accomplish through such an effort?

2   Is the training programme for HRD necessary for everyone in the organisation?

3   Assume that Ivan Dias has asked you for advice. What would you tell him?

Reflective commentary

The case study above highlights the necessity to use an inclusive approach in developing everyone in the organisation and the importance of reviewing and evaluating the business strategy both in the short term and the long term.

FURTHER READING

BOOKS

GOLD, J., STEWART, J. and ILES, P. (2010) National HRD policies and practice, in GOLD, J., STEWART, J. and ILES, P. (eds) Human Resource Development: Theory and practice. Basingstoke: Palgrave Macmillan. A distinctive and detailed book strengthened considerably by the eclectic inclusion of materials.

RIGG, C., STEWART, J. and TREHAN, K. (2007) *Critical Human Resource Development: Beyond orthodoxy.* Harlow: FT/Prentice Hall. This concise text provides critical extensive coverage offering clear guidance and theoretical support.

ARTICLES

BALL, M. (2011) Learning, labour and union learning representatives: promoting workplace learning. *Studies in the Education of Adults.* Vol. 43, No. 1. 50–60. This article provides an insight into the influence of workplace learning.

DOORNBOS, A. J., SIMONS, R. and DENESSEN, E. (2008) Relations between characteristics of workplace practices and types of informal work-related learning: a survey study among Dutch police. *Human Resource Development Quarterly.* Vol. 19, No. 2. 129–51. This article presents a survey of the relations between characteristics of workplace practices and informal learning.

HAMEED, A. and WAHEED, A. (2011) Employee development and its effect on employee performance: a conceptual framework. *International Journal of Business and Social Science.* Vol. 2, No. 13. 224–9. This article provides a conceptual framework in understanding employee development and how this affects employee performance.

LOHMAN, M. C. (2009) A survey of factors influencing the engagement of information technology professionals in informal learning activities. *Information Technology, Learning and Performance Journal.* Vol. 25, No. 1. 43–53. This article presents a survey of the factors influencing the engagement of IT professionals in learning activities.

RIDDELL, S., AHLGREN, L. and WEEDON, E. (2009) Equity and lifelong learning: lessons from workplace learning in Scottish SMEs. *International Journal of Lifelong Education.* Vol. 28, No. 6. 777–95. This article provides an insight into the lessons learned from workplace learning.

WOLFE, G. A. (2005) Corporate universities: transforming learning, accelerating results. *Chief Learning Officer.* Vol. 4, No. 2. 20–5. This article reviews different aspects of learning in CUs.

ZAHRANI, A. A. L. (2012) Psychological empowerment and workplace learning: an empirical study of a Saudi telecom company. *Advances in Management.* Vol. 5, Issue 2, 37–46. This article presents a practical case study overview of psychological empowerment and workplace learning.

WEBSITES

CIPD (2011) Learning and Talent Development Survey 2011 *[online].* http://www.cipd.co.uk/hr-resources/survey-reports/learning-talent-development-2011.aspx

National Occupational Standards (2010) National Occupational Standards For Learning and Development 2011 *[online].* http://dera.ioe.ac.uk/1040/1/

NOS_learn_and_dev_add.pdf

National Training Awards *[online]*: http://
nationaltrainingawards.apprenticeships.org.uk/

REFERENCES

ALVESSON, M., BRIDGMAN, T. and WILLMOTT, H. (eds) (2011) *The Oxford Handbook of Critical Management Studies*. Oxford: Oxford University Press.

CHURCHARD, C. (2011) Work experience skills to count towards university degree. *People Management*. January.

CIPD (2011) Learning and Talent Development Survey 2011 *[online]*: http://www.cipd.co.uk/hr-resources/survey-reports/learning-talent-development-2011.aspx.

GOLD, J. and SMITH, J. (2010) Continuing Professional Development and lifelong learning, in GOLD, J., HOLDEN, R., ILES, P., STEWART, J. and BEARDWELL, J. (eds) *Human Resource Development: Theory and practice*. Basingstoke: Palgrave Macmillan. 379–404.

GOLD, J., STEWART, J. and ILES, P. (2010) National HRD policies and practice, in GOLD, J., HOLDEN, R., ILES, P., STEWART, J. and BEARDWELL, J. (eds) *Human Resource Development: Theory and practice*. Basingstoke: Palgrave Macmillan.

HAMLIN, R. (1999) The national context, in STEWART, J. *Employee Development Practice*. London: FT/Pitman.

HAMLIN, R. G. and STEWART, J. (2011) What is HRD? A definitional review and synthesis of the HRD domain. *Journal of European Industrial Training*. Vol. 35, No. 3. 199–220.

ILES, P., MEETOO, C. and GOLD, J. (2010) Leadership development, in GOLD, J., HOLDEN, R., ILES, P., STEWART, J. and BEARDWELL, J. (eds) *Human Resource Development: Theory and practice*. Basingstoke: Palgrave Macmillan.

KELLIE, J. (2007) Shifting boundaries in work and learning: HRD and the case of corporate education, in RIGG, C., STEWART, J. and TREHAN, K. (eds) *Critical HRD: Beyond orthodoxy*. Harlow: FT/Prentice Hall. 129–44.

MCGOLDRICK, J., STEWART, J. and WATSON, S. (2002) Theorising human resource development. *Human Resource Development International*. Vol 4, No. 5. 343–56.

METCALFE, B. D. and REES, C. J. (2005) Theorizing advances in international HRD. *Human Resource Development International*. Vol. 8, No. 4. 449–65.

MIDGLEY, M. (1996) *The Ethical Primate: Humans, freedom and morality*. London: Routledge.

MINTZBERG, H. (2004) *Managers Not MBAs*. San Francisco, CA: Berrett-Koehler.

RIGG, C. and RICHARDS, S. (eds) (2007) *Action Learning, Leadership and Organizational Development in Public Services*. Abingdon: Routledge.

RIGG, C., STEWART, J. and TREHAN, K. (2007) *Critical Human Resource Development: Beyond orthodoxy*. Harlow: FT/Prentice Hall.

SAMBROOK, S. (2012) What's so critical about human resource development?, in LEE, M. (ed.) *Human Resource Development as We Know It: Speeches that have shaped the field*. Abingdon: Routledge.

STANSFIELD, L. M. and STEWART, J. (2007) A stakeholder approach to the study of management education, in HILL, R. and STEWART, J. (eds) *Management Development: Perspectives from research and practice*. Abingdon: Routledge.

STEWART, J. (1999) *Employee Development Practice*. London: FT/Pitman.

STEWART, J. (2007) The ethics of HRD, in RIGG, C., STEWART, J. and TREHAN, K. (eds) *Critical Human Resource Development: Beyond orthodoxy'*. Harlow: FT/Prentice Hall.

STEWART, J. and MCGOLDRICK, J. (eds) (1996) *HRD: Perspectives, strategies and practice*. London: Pitman.

STEWART, J. and RIGG, C. (2011) *Learning and Talent Development*. London: Chartered Institute of Personnel and Development.

STEWART, J. and TANSLEY, C. (2002) *Training in the Knowledge Economy*. London: Chartered Institute of Personnel and Development.

WALTON, J. (1999) *Strategic Human Resource Development*. Harlow: Pearson Education.

WALTON, J. (2005) Would the real corporate university please stand up? *Journal of European Industrial Training*, Vol. 29, No. 1. 7–15.

WANG, G. G. (2008) National HRD: a new paradigm or the reinvention of the wheel? *European Journal of Industrial Training*. Vol. 31, No. 4. 303–16.

WEIR, D. and O'DONOGHUE, J. (2005) Enhancing the university–industry interface. *Journal of European Industrial Training*. Vol. 29, No. 6. 425–522.

CHAPTER 6

Knowledge Management

Carol Woodhams and Graham Perkins

CHAPTER CONTENTS

- Introduction
- What is knowledge?
- Tacit and explicit knowledge
- Perspectives on knowledge
- Single- and double-loop learning
- Defining organisational learning
- The learning organisation
- Approaches to knowledge management
- Barriers to knowledge management
- Summary

KEY LEARNING OUTCOMES

By the end of this chapter, you will be able to:

- Analyse the nature of knowledge in an organisational context and distinguish it from data and information.

- Critically discuss the key differences between tacit and explicit knowledge and objectivist and practice-based knowledge perspectives.

- Analyse the concepts of single- and double-loop learning, understanding how both may be beneficial in organisations.

- Critically discuss the term 'organisational learning' and distinguish it from 'the learning organisation'.

- Evaluate the various approaches to knowledge management and discern where particular approaches may be most successful in organisations.

INTRODUCTION

Over the last century or so, Western economies, including the UK, have shifted their reliance from manufacturing to the service sector for an increasing proportion of output. As Sewell (2005, p685–6) states:

> the physical toil of manufacturing is being replaced by a world where we work more with our heads than our hands.

Of course this shift in emphasis means that managers in organisations must now focus on different priorities. Today, managers are less concerned with controlling manual tasks and far more interested in managing the information contained within the minds of their employees. This is why the field of knowledge management is growing in importance and why it is increasingly referred to in both academic and practical circles.

This chapter explores the territory of 'knowledge management' in detail. It begins by evaluating the term 'knowledge' and distinguishing it from 'data' and 'information' before exploring the different types of knowledge and perspectives that individuals can have about knowledge. Attention then turns to the concepts of single- and double-loop learning before various approaches to knowledge management are evaluated. Different approaches to knowledge management are explored, along with their applicability in different organisational contexts and settings. The chapter closes with an exploration of the term 'organisational learning' and provides an overview of the concept of 'the learning organisation'.

WHAT IS KNOWLEDGE?

In order to manage knowledge effectively, practitioners must understand what it is and how it differs from information and data. Beazley *et al* (2002) define knowledge as:

> information organised into a framework, model, worldview, concept, principle, theory, hypothesis or other basis of action that increases the understanding of a situation, improves problem-solving and decision-making.

This definition is certainly interesting, but what does it really mean in practical terms? It implies that knowledge is derived from information – information that has been organised or processed in some way. Beazley *et al* argue that processing leads to information that is useful in helping individuals better understand the world around them. Ward and Peppard (2002) provide another useful definition of knowledge. They suggest that knowledge is:

> information combined with experience, context, interpretation and reflection and which sees knowledge as part of a continuum.

Again, it can be seen that knowledge is information 'plus something else'. The key point here is that knowledge is part of a continuum rather than something that exists on its own. Let's explore this continuum to understand where knowledge exists and how it differs from information and data.

Figure 6.1 The information continuum

DATA   **INFORMATION**   **KNOWLEDGE**

The model depicted in Figure 6.1 clearly shows where knowledge sits in the information continuum. Knowledge itself is situated on the far right of the system and directional arrows demonstrate that it interacts directly with information, which is immediately to the left of it. Whereas knowledge itself is derived from information, information is derived from data. It is very important to understand the difference between these two concepts. As discussed above, knowledge is information which has gone through some form of processing or has been organised in some way. Knowledge is information plus something else.

Examples of data might include today's date or measurements taken on a production line. Examples of information could be a bank statement, a telephone directory or a sales forecast. Finally, an example of knowledge might be how a manager responds to a sales forecast, applying his sales skills to boost his department's takings. Perhaps the key point to remember here is that there is a clear progression through the system. Data is a simple fact or measurement which is then combined with other facts or measurements to become information. When this information is processed, the end result is knowledge.

 REFLECTIVE ACTIVITY

Can you think of examples of data, information and knowledge from your own organisation or personal experience?

It is, however, too simple to state that knowledge is information that has gone through some form of processing or has been organised in some way. There can be different types of knowledge inside organisations and employees interact with these forms in different ways. Below we examine the idea that knowledge can be either 'tacit' or 'explicit', and seek to explain the differences between these basic forms of knowledge.

TACIT AND EXPLICIT KNOWLEDGE

Ikujiro Nonaka and Hirotaka Takeuchi are two well-known authors within the field of knowledge management who first split the concept of knowledge into what they term 'tacit' and 'explicit' components. **Explicit knowledge** is knowledge which can be found written down in official documents – for example, manuals, procedures and guides. By contrast, **tacit knowledge** can roughly be described as the intangible knowledge which is typically intuitive and is to be found within our heads.

Generally, explicit knowledge is said to be 'know *what*' and tacit knowledge is said to be 'know *how*'.

Explicit knowledge is easy to recognise in the external environment. Company procedures, how-to documents and the laws of the land all contain explicit knowledge – in other words, knowledge which has been written down for other individuals to read and understand. By contrast, tacit knowledge is unique and personal to different individuals. Tacit knowledge arises from the experience of actually doing something such as a job or interacting with different managers, peers and customers. It combines tangible elements such as technical skills and information with intangible elements such as intuition and judgement. For this reason tacit knowledge cannot be written down in a document and is therefore not something that can learned from reading information alone.

CASE STUDY

 ### Socialisation at work within the Matsushita Electric Industrial Company

The Matsushita Electric Industrial Company was a designer and manufacturer of electrical goods based in Osaka, Japan. In the late 1980s the company was developing an automatic home bread-making machine when it came across a major problem surrounding how the dough-kneading process could be automated. No matter what they tried, the bread came out 'not quite right' and no one within the organisation knew why this was. Dough kneaded by the machine was examined under X-rays and compared with dough that was kneaded by a master baker, but no meaningful insights were obtained. Ikuko Tanaka, head of software development, knew that the area's best bread came from the Osaka International Hotel.

To capture the tacit knowledge of the kneading skill, she and several

engineers volunteered to apprentice themselves to the hotel's head baker. Making the same delicious bread as the head baker's was not easy, and no one could explain why. One day, however, she noticed that the baker was not only stretching the dough but also twisting it – which turned out to be the secret for making tasty bread. Thus she socialised the head baker's tacit knowledge through observation, imitation and practice and was then able to convert this into explicit knowledge which she could share with her colleagues.

Source: Nonaka and Takeuchi (1995, pp 63–4)

Often, in organisations, employees are shown one particular way of completing a process or task during their induction meetings only to be told by their colleagues or co-workers 'Yes, but we all do it like this.' This is tacit knowledge in action and demonstrates a key way in which tacit knowledge is spread – i.e. through conversations and interactions. The key differences between tacit and explicit knowledge are set out in Table 6.1.

Table 6.1 Differences between tacit and explicit knowledge

Tacit knowledge	Explicit knowledge
Knowledge of experience (body)	Knowledge of rationality (mind)
Simultaneous knowledge (here and now)	Sequential knowledge (there and then)
Analogue knowledge (practice)	Digital knowledge (theory)

Table 6.1 demonstrates that tacit and explicit knowledge are different from one another. Whereas tacit knowledge is that which individuals gain from experience and practice, explicit knowledge refers to rationality and personal theories which can be captured and stored for later reference.

It is also important to recognise that there are different perspectives within the field. The 'objectivist' and 'practice-based' perspectives on knowledge are introduced below. It should come as no surprise that individuals can have different ideas about what knowledge is and what is to be accepted as 'knowledge' in organisational settings.

PERSPECTIVES ON KNOWLEDGE

The 'objectivist' and 'practice-based' perspectives have been discussed in detail by many theorists and writers, including Donald Hislop (2009).

THE OBJECTIVIST PERSPECTIVE

In basic terms the objectivist perspective sees knowledge as an entity or a commodity – something that can exist outside of an individual. In other words, objectivists think that knowledge can be captured in databases or operating manuals and can then be distributed to where it is needed in organisations. These individuals view knowledge as:

- an entity or object
- objective 'facts'
- something that is derived from an intellectual process – i.e. it can be taught or learned.

This school of thought places more stock in explicit than in tacit knowledge. It affirms that knowledge itself can exist in many different forms such as CDs, reference manuals, web pages, etc. It also views knowledge as a statement of fact. Objectivists believe that there can be no debate about whether knowledge exists and that it must be accepted as it is. They therefore prize explicit knowledge more highly than tacit knowledge.

THE PRACTICE-BASED PERSPECTIVE

The practice-based perspective critiques the objectivist perspective and sees knowledge as something that is embedded within, and inseparable from, work activities or practices. The practice-based approach is founded on the following tenets:

- Knowledge is embedded in practice.
- Tacit and explicit knowledge are inseparable.
- Knowledge is embodied in people.
- Knowledge is socially constructed.
- Knowledge is culturally embedded.
- Knowledge is contestable.

The list above clearly sets out the key differences between the two schools of thought. Perhaps the most important aspect of the practice-based view is that knowledge is seen as personal and contestable. Under this perspective, knowledge is constructed in a social arena – this is very different from the structured ideas of the objectivist perspective.

This leads to a key question about how knowledge actually comes into existence in organisations. The following discussion highlights two different forms of learning: single-loop and double-loop.

SINGLE- AND DOUBLE-LOOP LEARNING

According to Armstrong (2006), learning in organisations can be characterised as an intricate three-step process consisting of knowledge acquisition (i.e. gathering), dissemination (i.e. sharing) and implementation. Argyris (1992) extends the concept of learning, making a distinction between what he terms 'single-loop' and 'double-loop' learning. Argyris does not state that double-loop learning is 'correct' while single-loop learning is 'wrong'; he simply states that they are very different forms of learning which are applicable in different situations.

Single-loop learning is a very straightforward concept. It occurs where individuals take action to achieve a particular goal or purpose, monitor their progress and then take corrective action if and when needed. In an HR context an HR professional implements this process when working through a performance management problem with an employee. The HR professional might take action by setting specific objectives, monitoring the employee's progress and then taking more action depending on the situation. If the employee's performance improves, the HR professional may cease the formal performance management process; if it does not, he or she may apply specific disciplinary sanctions. Double-loop learning is very different from this.

Within double-loop learning systems, individuals take action as they would have in single-loop learning systems, but when they are monitoring their situation they think deeply about their initial expectations as well as the ongoing actions that are occurring. Keeping with the performance management example above, the HR professional, while monitoring the situation, might discover that the employee's job description is incorrect or that their manager was creating a hostile working environment. The HR professional might then be able to see the initial problem in a new light – and in this way double-loop learning has occurred: the HR professional has 'redefined expectations'. Figure 6.2 highlights the key differences between single- and double-loop learning.

With reference to Figure 6.2, it can certainly be argued that single-loop learning is likely to be appropriate for routine, repetitive tasks whereas double-loop learning is applicable in complex situations where perhaps a greater level of thought and reflection is needed. For single-loop learning it can be seen that action is taken, a situation monitored and then further action taken as necessary, whereas double loop learning occurs when underlying assumptions are questioned.

Figure 6.2 Single- and double-loop learning

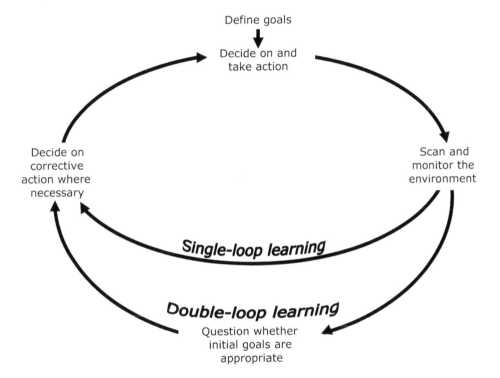

Examples of single- and double-loop learning can be found everywhere. Consider the following, well-known, example which looks at a central heating system:

- The goal of the central heating system is to keep the room temperature at 17°C.
- The function of a thermostat is to detect error (i.e. any gap between the actual temperature in the house and the desired temperature of 17°C).
- The action is that the heating is turned on or off automatically to raise or lower the temperature in the house to 17°C.

This is definitely a single-loop learning system. An expectation is defined (the temperature of the room), monitored, and action is taken if there is any deviation from the specified requirement. Now, what would happen in a double-loop system? The question might arise as to whether maintaining 17°C is the appropriate way to deal with the discontinuity, and alternatives may be explored.

These alternatives might be the occupants' wearing thicker clothes, redesigning the house or not living in the house during some part of the year. Within double-loop learning individuals question the underlying assumptions within various systems rather than simply dealing with a surface-level problem.

REFLECTIVE ACTIVITY

Can you think of examples of single- and double-loop learning which occur within either your personal or your professional life?

It is very important to understand that single-loop learning can cause rigidities to form in an organisation, and this can limit the organisation's ability to be creative. As the business world rapidly changes, organisations that are too rigid may well find themselves pushed out of business. The case of General Motors is a classic example of this. The organisation did not change; it did not question its underlying assumptions, and as a result began making unsustainable losses as the economic crisis of 2008 to 2010 took hold.

Alongside double-loop learning a further key way in which knowledge is generated in organisations is through organisational learning. The following section of the chapter explores this concept in detail.

DEFINING ORGANISATIONAL LEARNING

As with many other areas of HR, there are several different definitions of organisational learning. So that a considered opinion of the term can be built, it is important that different definitions are explored and the differences and similarities between them are considered. The first definition reproduced below comes from Armstrong (2006, p540):

> [Organisational learning is] an efficient procedure to process, interpret and respond to both internal and external information of a predominantly explicit nature.

Argyris and Schön (1978), on the other hand, argue that organisational learning is:

> when individuals, acting from their own images and mental maps, detect a match or mismatch of outcomes to expectation which confirms or disconfirms organisational theory-in-use.

There are fundamental differences between these definitions. Armstrong (2006) is looking at organisational learning almost as a management process whereas Argyris and Schön highlight the human side of the concept more clearly. Arguably, the reality of the situation sits somewhere between the two definitions – i.e. that organisational learning occurs when individuals process, interpret and respond to information.

This begins to tell us how organisational learning can produce knowledge which can then be managed inside organisations. By processing pieces of data and information, employees produce understandings and documents which contain new knowledge. It is the resultant knowledge which we then must manage, if our firms are to gain competitive advantage in the marketplace. The following case study illustrates just this point.

Unipart – a learning organisation?

CASE STUDY

The transformation of motor components firm Unipart, led by its high-profile chief executive John Neill, is one of the UK's best-known business stories of the 1990s.

The company started life as British Leyland's components arm. Since its management buy-out from British Leyland in 1987, the Unipart Group of Companies (UGC) has become highly profitable and is now expanding beyond the automotive industry into communications, healthcare logistics and a variety of other businesses.

Unipart U is the company's in-house university. It has played a central role in implementing and supporting many of these initiatives. Unipart U is designed to be the organisation's core learning function. It serves all employees and an increasing number of other stakeholders.

One of its key tasks is that of disseminating knowledge across the company. For example, the manufacturing expertise gained through joint ventures with Toyota and Honda is channelled through the university to other manufacturing centres within the company.

Both managers and employees take on the roles of teachers and learners. The university is also the mechanism for sharing learning with other stakeholders, and for linking learning processes within the organisation to improvements in performance. It is not surprising, then, that Unipart managers believe they have developed effective

methods of linking continuous workplace learning to their business needs, and think they are justified in calling their company a learning organisation. But are they?

The University Forum for Human Resource Development, a network of HRD academics, set up a one-day workshop at the company's site in Cowley, near Oxford, to investigate whether Unipart U could be considered a learning organisation.

Delegates were split into five discussion groups, each with a separate topic to explore. The topics were entitled 'linking learning and business strategy', 'Unipart U', 'use of information systems', 'learning from critical incidents' and 'knowledge management'. Each group was given a set of questions to guide their inquiry, and six Unipart employees acted as tour guides around the site, answering questions and relating their experiences. People were observed at work and making use of Unipart U, and several of them talked about the learning opportunities the company provided.

At the final plenary session, each group commented on what had been learned and was asked to conclude whether or not Unipart is a learning organisation. The clear consensus was that it is one. Of course, not everyone agrees on the definition of the term, or even on its usefulness. One of the visiting academics, Kevin Morrell, said: 'People learn – not organisations. So I still don't

> think there's such a thing as a learning company. But this is as close to a systematic approach to a learning organisation as I've seen.'

Source: adapted from Miller and Stewart (1999)

A term which is linked to organisational learning is 'the learning organisation', which was coined by Senge (1990). Senge (2006, p3) argues that a learning organisation is:

> an organisation where people continually expand their capacity to create the results they truly desire, where new and expansive patterns of thinking are nurtured, where collective aspiration is set free, and where people are continually learning how to learn together.

Other theorists and researchers, including Pedler *et al* (1991), have defined the learning organisation differently, but the definitions all have commonalities. A key fact to keep in mind is that the definitions of the learning organisation are all aspirational and depict both new learning and increased capability. These characteristics can be seen in the definition above in Senge's (1990) use of words such as 'desire', 'free' and 'expansive'. In fact, it has been suggested that the learning organisation as a concept is nothing more than an aspiration. It has often been noted that there is little information about how companies can actually turn themselves into learning organisations. The following section provides a little more information on the characteristics of learning organisations.

THE LEARNING ORGANISATION

Peter Senge suggests that there are five distinct disciplines which make up the vision of the learning organisation. These disciplines cannot be simply acquired by individuals; rather, they develop over time in an organisation. Senge (1990) argues that an organisation can spend a lifetime mastering the five disciplines, and that 'as one learns more, one becomes more aware of one's ignorance'.

The implication of these statements is that the learning organisation should not be seen as a destination in itself, but rather a state of 'being' which continuously unfolds within an organisation and the individuals within it. The five disciplines which Senge links to the learning organisation concept are:

- *Personal mastery*: the ability to continually clarify and deepen personal vision.
- *Mental models*: unearthing internal pictures of the world and opening them to others.
- *Shared vision*: developing a shared picture of the future and fostering genuine commitment to this.
- *Team learning*: attaining the capacity to 'think together' and make synergies that work.
- *Systems thinking*: the (fifth) discipline that integrates the four others into a coherent body of theory and practice.

Although the concept of the learning organisation is enticing, it is important to recognise that it is not without its flaws. Sadler-Smith (2006) argues that the concept has two fundamental flaws. The first of these flaws (which, as noted earlier, is common to other theories in this field) is that it neglects the issues of organisational power. The second is that it presents a restricted view of learning and work.

With respect to the second point, Sadler-Smith argues that the view of work (and learning) as being conducted in teams within the learning organisation is not true of all, or even most, workplaces. For instance, work can be conducted on an individual or an inter-organisational level. Senge's theory also assumes that learning takes place through discussion and reflection, but this approach ignores a wider account of the range of approaches. Classroom learning or one-to-one mentoring, for example, certainly have their benefits but do not appear to fit well with the concept of the learning organisation.

A final point to keep in mind is that the concept of the learning organisation is 'visionary': the learning organisation is a state to which people aspire, not something that can just be arrived at. Furthermore, in some respects the theory of the learning organisation is not clearly articulated. There is little discussion in the literature of implementation strategies – rather, the focus is on the concept as a whole and the benefits of being a 'learning organisation'. Sloman (1999), for instance, asserts that the learning organisation theorists often fail to recognise that learning is a continuous process and not a set of discrete training activities. This is a key point which is worth keeping in mind.

APPROACHES TO KNOWLEDGE MANAGEMENT

This section focuses on some of the basic approaches organisations can adopt when attempting to manage their knowledge. In this context an 'approach' to knowledge management is a conceptual framework of the different ways in which organisations might attempt to capture and use knowledge. Bee and Bee (2005) suggest that there are five basic approaches to knowledge management:

- knowledge communities
- intranet-/Internet-based knowledge centres
- knowledge continuity management
- expert systems
- communities of practice.

Each of these approaches is discussed in turn below.

KNOWLEDGE COMMUNITIES

Finneran (2004) as cited in Bee and Bee (2005, p99) defines knowledge communities as:

> Communities of interest that come together to share knowledge that affects performance. Knowledge communities operate independently of traditional organisation structures to find common ground for their category of

interest. They are virtual, global communities that are boundary-less and are not hindered by organisational or physical barriers.

This definition is certainly thought-provoking, and two key aspects of it require further discussion. The first of these is that the sharing of knowledge affects performance: competitiveness in a knowledge-driven environment comes from individuals and groups willingly sharing what they know because this leads to increased creativity and innovation. The second is that knowledge communities are said to cut across traditional boundaries. What does that mean in practice?

An interesting example of a knowledge community is Nokia, which has set up 150 'virtual companies' with its largest suppliers. These virtual organisations work together on shared problems and regularly meet to discuss new ideas and ways in which they can improve their working relationships. In effect the organisations are loosely networked and tied to Nokia via working groups or teams. Figure 6.3 demonstrates the relationships within the Nokia virtual community more clearly.

Figure 6.3 Knowledge communities at Nokia

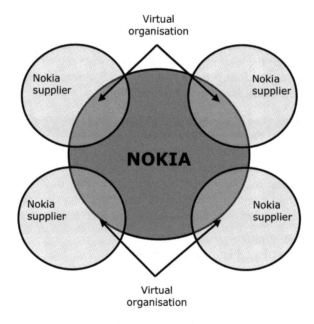

Figure 6.3 clearly shows the close relationships which Nokia has developed with supplying organisations (depicted by the overlapping bubbles). The 'virtual' organisation model has allowed Nokia to draw its suppliers closer, and as a result knowledge flows more freely between them. This arrangement means that problems (such as defective components in a new phone) can be tackled more quickly and innovations can spread more rapidly throughout the chain.

INTRANET-/INTERNET-BASED KNOWLEDGE CENTRES

Many organisations are now tapping into the power of their internal computer networks or the Internet to set up central sources of information. The sorts of information that are often accessed through these systems are telephone directory entries or personal profiles, company news items, links to relevant websites, and even the minutes from board meetings.

It is important to recognise that intranets can be used in many different ways, depending on how they are configured. At a basic level they might contain a telephone directory or list of key contacts in a particular area such as an R&D or production team. A more advanced intranet may contain online forums where messages can be posted and individuals can reply. More generally, the Internet can be used as a powerful research tool when writing HR policies or researching best practice in a particular area, such as appraisals or training. All of these examples should be considered 'knowledge activities' as technology is being used to access sources of expertise or information.

Alongside the setting up of banks of information, organisations must also set up effective search tools. It is vital that individuals can navigate their way through databases and online sources of information; otherwise, they will be reluctant to use them. This is perhaps where a number of knowledge management systems and interventions fall down. Organisations are sometimes more interested in storing knowledge than in actually working out how it can be mobilised and used, which is a key goal of knowledge management.

 REFLECTIVE ACTIVITY

Does your organisation have its own intranet? Do you use it or the Internet to store or access information while you are working?

KNOWLEDGE CONTINUITY MANAGEMENT

A different and altogether more human approach to managing knowledge is taken by Beazley *et al* (2002), who point out that organisations can encounter problems when employees leave and take their knowledge with them. With this in mind they argue that organisations must use 'knowledge continuity management', which is essentially concerned with knowledge transfer between different generations of employees. Bee and Bee (2005, p101) define knowledge continuity management as:

> The efficient and effective transfer of critical operational knowledge – both explicit and tacit, both individual and institutional – from transferring, resigning, terminating or retiring employees to their successors.

This definition illustrates how the key focus of knowledge continuity management is putting processes into place which can harvest critical operational knowledge from employees, and then systems that transfer this knowledge to successors. Perhaps the simplest example of this is a handover with a new employee. This need only be a week or two in duration for most roles, but will allow the new employee to quickly grasp the way things are done in their new setting. It has been said that this method of knowledge exchange is more effective than in-depth classroom-based training courses.

Beazley *et al* (2002) also note that even if an organisation has the best knowledge management system in the world, it does not mean that it will be used effectively. They argue that many early knowledge management systems were designed to make knowledge available without giving the same thought to encouraging their use. Beazley *et al* propose that knowledge sharing activities should form part of performance management systems in organisations, and that effective knowledge sharing should be recognised through reward systems. Thus, it is important to have an integrated approach to knowledge management rather than simply 'bolting it on' to existing systems and processes.

One organisation that uses systems to capture knowledge from leavers is Airbus, part of the knowledge-intensive aerospace industry. The case study below shows how Airbus has recognised that employees who leave the firm can leave gaps in its capabilities. For this reason the organisation works in partnership with HR to capture knowledge from all leavers by creating a 'transfer cell' around the employee.

 Capturing knowledge from leavers at Airbus

CASE STUDY

The essence of competitiveness for a high-technology company resides in the knowledge and capabilities of its employees. The departure of highly skilled employees, whether because of retirement or other reasons, can create holes in the capabilities of an organisation, and over time can become a major threat to its survival. The issue, then, is how to transfer technical knowledge and (largely tacit) experience from the leaver to relevant colleagues who can both appreciate and use this knowledge.

Aircraft manufacturer Airbus attempts to address this issue roughly six months before the scheduled departure of an employee. A 'transfer cell' is established, comprising the leaver, four or five colleagues who are closely related, and a knowledge management facilitator. The facilitator need not be a technical specialist: rather, he or she

needs the skills to facilitate the transfer of relevant knowledge from the leaver to other members of the transfer cell.

An initial meeting is held to discuss and clarify expectations for the knowledge transfer. This usually leads to a series of one-to-one interviews between the leaver (knowledge-giver) and the facilitator, from which key knowledge transfer topics are identified and mind-mapped, sometimes aided by written diaries and logs. Discussions with all members of the transfer cell then take place to identify what knowledge and information is likely to be useful and should be transferred to the relevant people. A transfer plan is agreed, using methods proposed by the facilitator, who then monitors the progress of the transfer, ensuring that the planned actions happen. A final step is a formal

| closure meeting to review achievements. | Source: Easterby-Smith and Mikhailava (2011) |

EXPERT SYSTEMS

The next approach to knowledge management is the concept of 'expert systems'. Bocij *et al* (2003, p706) describe expert systems as being:

> used to represent the knowledge and decision-making skills of specialists so that non-specialists can take decisions. They encapsulate the knowledge of experts by providing the tools for the acquisition of knowledge and representation of rules and their enactment as decisions.

This definition indicates that expert systems are computer-based systems that enable individuals with little or no specialist knowledge to make decisions that would otherwise require detailed 'expert' knowledge. It also shows that expert systems hold knowledge and enable others to access it. Expert systems can be found assisting in medical diagnoses, credit decisions, investment decisions and fault-finding in equipment. Let's explore a brief example to obtain a more complete understanding of it.

Assume that an individual wants to take out a new loan from a bank. In the past this person would have had to make an appointment to see their bank manager to make such a request, but now a call can be placed to one of the organisation's call centres where a bank employee can invariably grant the request by the end of the conversation. During the call the customer service representative will input information provided by the individual, such as loan amount, repayment period, existing monthly commitments and so on, into a computer system which will either grant or refuse the loan. This is an expert system and allows the bank to empower lower-skilled employees to make relatively routine decisions while being guided by the knowledge contained in the computer database.

COMMUNITIES OF PRACTICE

The final approach to knowledge management is the **'community of practice'**, which Hislop (2009, p167) defines as:

> a group of people who have a particular activity in common and as a consequence have some common knowledge, a sense of community identity, and some element of overlapping values.

Thus, a community of practice must have some sort of activity in common that provides the foundation for knowledge-sharing. Because the group shares an activity, they also share some common knowledge. For example, if an HR practitioner was to participate in a community of practice at a CIPD branch event, there would certainly be areas in which their HR expertise would overlap with that of other group members.

Despite the use of the word 'group' above, it is very important to recognise that groups are very different from communities of practice. It is correct to say that a community of practice is a group, but a group is not always a community of practice. Some of the differences between the two are discussed below.

Hislop (2009) notes that work groups or teams in organisations are often formed around some sort of specific service or product, with formalised divisions of labour and hierarchical structures. The performance of a team is measured against set objectives, and rewards are often attached to the achievement of particular goals such as producing a new product within a specified time period. On the other hand, Hislop suggests that communities of practice operate without hierarchies and structures and that communities manage themselves without the need for formal goals or targets. Communities of practice are also voluntary arrangements and evolve around the focus of sharing knowledge and information.

 REFLECTIVE ACTIVITY

Can you think of any examples of communities of practice within your organisation?

Perhaps you yourself operate within a community of practice? If you meet fellow members of your HR team, perhaps over a lunch break, and discuss HR issues, then you are likely to be in a community of practice. Other examples could include IT staff discussing technology problems or issues as an informal group. It is important to recognise that these groups are characterised by informality and an *ad hoc* nature. As soon as an organisation imposes some form of control or measurement, communities of practice become traditional work groups or teams.

Communities of practice: a critical perspective

It is important to also think critically about the drawbacks of communities of practice. One of the main critiques of many knowledge management theories is that they pay insufficient attention to issues of organisational power and conflict, and although communities of practice embody co-operative relationships between willing colleagues, issues relating to power and conflict cannot be ignored. For example, one individual could seek to dominate a community of practice for their own advancement, and this would inevitably be at the expense of group knowledge-sharing.

Hislop (2009) suggests that communities of practice often have inherent tensions. Existing members of these communities will have more 'community knowledge' and experience than newcomers, so an unequal distribution of power exists from the outset. The uneven distribution of knowledge can create conflict and allow informal hierarchies to form within the community.

A further limitation to the smooth functioning of communities of practice is that 'blinkered' or inward-looking communities can develop very quickly within organisations. Hislop argues that there are potentially negative consequences if the bonds between group members in communities are too strong. These bonds can lead to 'outsiders' being excluded from the community of practice and their input and knowledge being ignored. Communities which ignore new knowledge and ideas quickly lose their innovativeness because they are unable to absorb new stimuli from their external environment.

BARRIERS TO KNOWLEDGE MANAGEMENT

Perhaps the most important variable that affects knowledge management in organisations is organisational culture. Armstrong (2006, p303) defines this as:

the pattern of values, norms, beliefs, attitudes and assumptions that may not have been articulated but shape the ways in which people behave and things get done.

A key point in this definition is that culture can shape the way in which individuals behave, and so can act as a form of control, helping managers to guide employees through various situations. While 'effective' cultures may have positive effects on knowledge management, it is important to recognise that knowledge management can be compromised by cultures which are dominated by information-hoarding, secrecy and power-play. In situations where knowledge is seen as a source of power – for example, where there are financial bonuses attached to the production of new ideas or sales totals – employees will naturally be reluctant to share their knowledge with their co-workers.

In such situations there is likely to be a lack of trust between employees. Trust is an important precondition for knowledge-sharing activities inside organisations. It is also important to consider the type of information that is to be transmitted within knowledge management systems and processes. Referring back to the discussion of explicit (i.e. tangible, written) and tacit (i.e. intangible and intuitive) forms, it is important to understand that different types of knowledge respond to different forms of transmission. For example, whereas tacit knowledge might be best shared within a community of practice, explicit knowledge might be managed most effectively within an expert or Internet-based database system.

SUMMARY

This chapter has shown that knowledge is becoming an increasingly important part of organisational life. Knowledge itself can take a number of forms in our organisations and various approaches to its management are available. If organisations do not develop an effective approach to knowledge management, it is likely that they will lose ground to their competitors or, in the case of public sector organisations, fail to provide an effective service. Equally, organisations must think carefully about how their approach to knowledge management links with the type of information that they are transmitting. If this link is not made, it is unlikely that organisations will be able to effectively manage their knowledge. As organisational structures and systems develop, approaches to knowledge management will inevitably evolve. Effective HR professionals will understand the core concepts of knowledge management and think carefully about how they can weave appropriate systems and policies into the fabric of their organisations.

Shell's approach to knowledge management

Knowledge management at Shell

When Shell Brazil needed help retrieving broken tools from a borehole, engineers turned to their international colleagues for help. Within 24 hours, ideas were flooding in from all over the world via a global knowledge network devoted to wells, and Shell Brazil was able to save the well and US $7 million to boot.

The wells network is one of 11 global-knowledge communities set up by Shell International Exploration and Production (SIEP) between 1998 and 2002. Between them they cover the core business in SIEP, plus support functions such as HR, IT, finance and procurement. They have also become a major learning tool within Shell.

'This is a very knowledge-intensive business because there are so many variables, but there are lots of commonalities too,' says Arjan van Unnik, a founding member of New Ways of Working, the department set up to develop and sponsor these communities.

Learning in the pipeline

The Shell Open University was originally set up in December 2000 as an online course catalogue, but it has developed into a tool to help Shell employees manage their own personal development.

It now has 11,000 registered users and offers around 600 courses, some delivered online, some classroom-based, some delivered solely by Shell, and some together with its learning partners.

'Before we set up the Open University, we used a paper system with paper learning guides and nominations faxed and emailed through. Employees who don't have access to the Shell intranet can still do that, but anyone who does have access is expected to go through the open university site.'

'Operating units have what we call a commitment controller,' site manager, Rachel Shaughnessy says. 'That's a line or personnel manager who has to approve nominations. When we receive a nomination, an email is automatically sent out to the commitment controller for their approval.'

Originally the site was developed for the use of SIEP only, but its range is now being extended to include a lot more IT courses, for example.

Source: *People Management* (2002)

Questions:

1   Indicate whether the knowledge Shell is trying to manage is tacit or explicit.

2   Evaluate whether Shell's approach to generating knowledge (through its Open University) is likely to help the organisation support its market position.

3   Which of the broad approaches to knowledge management is depicted in the first part of the case study?

REFERENCES

ARGYRIS, C. (1992) *On Organisational Learning*. Cambridge, MA: Blackwell.

ARGYRIS, C. and SCHÖN, D. A. (1978) *Organisational Learning*. Reading, MA: Addison-Wesley.

ARMSTRONG, M. (2006). *A Handbook of Human Resource Management Practice*, 10th edn. London: Kogan Page.

BEAZLEY, H., BOENISCH, J. and HARDEN, D. (2002) *Continuity Management*. New York: Wiley.

BEE, F. and BEE, R. (2005) *Managing Information and Statistics*, 2nd edn. London: Chartered Institute of Personnel and Development.

BOCIJ, P., CHAFFEY, D., GREASLEY, A. and HICKIE, S. (2003) *Business Information Systems: Technology, development and management for the e-business*. Harlow: FT/Prentice Hall.

EASTERBY-SMITH, M. and MIKHAILAVA, I. (2011) Knowledge management in perspective. *People Management* [online]: http://www.peoplemanagement.co.uk/pm/articles/2011/06/knowledge-management-in-perspective.htm [Accessed 1 June 2012].

HISLOP, D. (2009) *Knowledge Management in Organisations*. Oxford: Oxford University Press.

MILLER, R. and STEWART, J. (1999) Opened university. *People Management* [online]: http://www.peoplemanagement.co.uk/pm/articles/1999/06/4147.htm [Accessed 1 June 2012].

NONAKA, I. and TAKEUCHI, H. (1995) *The Knowledge Creating Company*. Oxford: Oxford University Press.

PEDLER, M., BURGOYNE, J. and BOYDELL, T. (1991) *The Learning Company: A strategy for sustainable development*. London: McGraw-Hill.

PEOPLE MANAGEMENT (2002) Oiling the wheels. [online]: http://www.peoplemanagement.co.uk/pm/articles/2002/06/6961.htm [Accessed 1 June 2012].

SADLER-SMITH, E. (2006) *Learning and Development for Managers*. Oxford: Blackwell.

SENGE, P. (1990) *The Fifth Discipline: The art and practice of the learning organisation*. 1st edn. London: Doubleday.

SENGE, P. (2006) *The Fifth Discipline: The art and practice of the learning organisation*, 2nd edn. London: Random House Business Books.

SEWELL, G. (2005) Nice work? Rethinking managerial control in an era of knowledge work. *Organisation*. Vol. 12, No. 5. 685–704.

SLOMAN, M. (1999) Seize the day. *People Management* [online]: http://www.peoplemanagement.co.uk/pm/articles/1999/05/4270.htm [Accessed 1 June 2012].

WARD, J. and PEPPARD, J. (2002) *Strategic Planning for Information Systems*, 3rd edn. Chichester: Wiley.

CHAPTER 7

Improving Organisational Performance

Patricia Rogers, Michelle McLardy, Raymond Rogers and Susan Barnes

CHAPTER CONTENTS

KEY LEARNING OUTCOMES

By the end of this chapter, you will be able to:

- Analyse the conceptual frameworks and complexity of high-performance working and its contribution to sustainable organisation performance.
- Evaluate the business case for creating an HPWO.
- Examine the contribution of the PM process to high levels of performance.
- Evaluate the role of line managers in the PM process.
- Examine how to create and sustain a community of practice to build a high-performance culture.

INTRODUCTION

This chapter examines historical and current academic debates on performance management (PM) and how organisations can drive sustained organisational performance by creating a high-performance work organisation (HPWO). It also speculates on how both theory and practice might develop in the future and, based on that, what challenges could be faced by professional practitioners in various contexts. A number of themes are explored to examine the impact of line management commitment and involvement in organisational performance, competitive advantage, and employee engagement and well-being. It is important to state that the themes are merely a useful organising device and that other devices are possible. The separation implied by the device used here does not represent reality and the themes overlap and connect in various ways, some of which cannot be identified. So it is important to bear in mind that the structure of the chapter is simply one way of thinking about the content.

ABOUT PERFORMANCE MANAGEMENT (PM)

SCIENTIFIC MANAGEMENT AND PERFORMANCE MANAGEMENT

Some of the well-documented methods of managing people are rooted in the thinking of mass-production methods. Particularly noteworthy is the Ford Motor Company before World War I. The importance of increasing productivity and performance was the central focus of Ford in the early 1900s when demand for motorcars exceeded supply. 'Taylorism' or 'Scientific management' was developed by the engineer F. W. Taylor before World War I as the method that organisations should adopt if they wanted to increase productivity and performance. Weak management methods were, in Taylor's view, the cause of poor performance. He felt that decisions over working methods should not be left to individuals whose interest was only themselves and keeping their jobs.

Scientific management principles sought to transfer workers' job knowledge into the hands of managers, and contributors to his study saw less skilled workers as lower-paid workers who were easier to control and observe. Taylor's plan had an impact on productivity which, when introduced to Ford in the USA, made the organisation the most productive car manufacturer in the world. His ideals for the management of workers led to accusations of de-skilling and dehumanising the labour force, but no one questioned this because what was required at the time was high productivity.

Harry Braverman (1974) extended some of the critiques that followed Taylor's approach and noted that the popularity of the approach was sustained because it perpetuates the status and power of management while leaving workers feeling degraded, alienated and demotivated. In recent years there have been widespread discussions concerning the shift away from Taylorism towards a new production paradigm premised upon techniques of high-performance management (HPM), high-performance working (HPW) and high-performance working practices (HPWP) leading to a **high-performance working organisation** (HPWO). These concepts are central to the discussions in this chapter, and the chapter attempts to capture the historical developments and analyse the conceptual frameworks and complexities surrounding the concepts. It attempts to illustrate links between the concepts and organisational culture, working practices, the environment external to organisations and the management of people to demonstrate how these concepts contribute to sustainable organisational performance.

DEFINITIONS OF PERFORMANCE MANAGEMENT

There is no one simple definition of PM because it can include various aspects of managing people. It is worth noting that it has evolved through successive stages (Sparrow 2008):

- Cost-effectiveness (exerted in the form of a top-down system based on narrow specifications of performance as measured through outputs such as objectives) in the 1980s.
- A more developmental agenda focused around the enablement of competence and broader performance specification by the early 1990s.
- By the late 1990s, greater concern about the need for mutual employer–employee understanding about, and commitment to, performance often in the context of change programmes (what has now been called 'engagement').
- Finally by the early 2000s, concerns about broad strategic imperatives that might be hindered by a poorly designed performance management system (PMS) and attention given to the need for coherence between the PMS and other HR agendas such as talent management and total rewards management.

'Performance management' as a term was first used by Beer and Ruh in the 1970s, but it was in the 1980s that it became recognised, and later this recognition was reinforced by the Institute of Personnel Management (known today as the Chartered Institute of Personnel and Development), who produced the following definition (Armstrong 2009, p22):

> A strategy which relates to every activity of the organisation set in the context of its human resources policies, culture, style and communication systems. The nature of the strategy depends on the organisational context and can vary from organisation to organisation.

Armstrong and Baron (2006, p2) define performance management as follows:

> Performance management aims to make the good better, share understanding about what is to be achieved, develop the capacity of people to achieve it, and provide the support and guidance people need to deliver high performance and achieve their full potential to the benefit of themselves and the organisation.

A general assumption of PM is that if you raise the performance levels of individuals, the organisation's overall performance will increase. Although we might agree with this view, there are a number of factors that might contribute to an increase in organisational performance that might not be attributed directly to an increase in individual performance. Also, raising the performance of individuals should not be trivialised because this could involve concepts from the areas of motivation, trust, work security, reward, task design, commitment, engagement and flexibility. Improving performance has been an obsession of the UK and the rest of the Western world for decades. However, there is documented evidence that the Wei dynasty (AD 221–265) apparently had an 'imperial rater' to evaluate the performance of the official family, and that centuries later, Ignatius Loyola developed a system of rating members of the Jesuit Society. Nolan and O'Donnell (1991) noted that the productivity and performance of the UK has been the subject of long-standing controversy. Historically, Britain has underperformed, leaving successive post-war governments the problem of trying to improve the situation. However, by the mid-1980s this opinion of performance had changed somewhat, when government-commissioned research revealed that Britain's performance was top of the league table in Europe, ahead of the USA and on a par with Japan for the first time. The competitiveness theme has been identified by many authors (Connock 1992; Storey and Sisson 1993) as the main reason for the increased concern about PM in organisations and for research. Over the years we have seen the development of league tables for schools, hospitals, police, councils and universities and in the private sector. The term 'league table' might not be used, however, for the media and research publications, document market leaders and high pre- and post-tax profit organisations in, for example, banking, manufacturing, retailing and pharmaceuticals.

PM is often focused on the leading and developing of people within an organisation. It is also crucial to enable managers to manage effectively with long-term and overall goals in mind. Foot and Hook (2008) suggest that PM is 'basically a shared process between managers, individuals and teams in which objectives are agreed and jointly reviewed, and aims to integrate corporate, individual and team objectives'. This particular view emphasises the macro view of 'performance appraisal', a term for the process which is sometimes confused and used interchangeably with 'performance management'. The purpose is to evaluate the employee's job performance, usually annually or biannually, and the outcome of the process can include employment decisions such as continued employment, salary increases, bonuses, improvement and training plans. Performance appraisals should be used as part of a PM strategy and are inherently linked to each other. The macro view evaluates employees in the context of wider organisational issues and takes into consideration corporate performance. Foot and Hook advised that they should not be used as merely a motivational tool but as a means of integrating the corporate and the informal culture of an organisation.

Foot and Hook note that PM can be viewed as an important element of team-building through, for example, 'quality circles' and as part of a Total Quality Management strategy. In addition to this, the elements of employee engagement and rewards can be included in definitions to emphasise the holistic approach to the introduction of PM in an organisation. Williams (1998) proposed three types of PM system: one for managing employee performance, another for managing organisational performance, and a third that combines both employee and organisational performance so that systems interlock and everyone is engaged in working together. The integration of PM and HRM practices in improving an organisation's performance is explored later in this chapter. Cardy and Leonard (2011) also argue that PM is a critical and necessary component for individual and organisational effectiveness, and is needed for improvements to occur; without assessment and feedback (normally associated with performance appraisal and discussed later in this chapter), there is no formal mechanism for focusing efforts to improve.

THE DEVELOPMENT OF HRM AND LINKS WITH PM

Over the last 20 years a considerable amount of research has attempted to confirm the links between HRM and performance. However, with a lack of longitudinal studies, certain core questions about the relationship are still not answered (Guest 2011). The combination and expansion of research in this area has made a valuable contribution to our understanding of the growing relationship between HRM and performance. This part of the chapter chronologically maps the developments in this area.

The majority of published research demonstrates an association between HRM and performance (Boselie *et al* 2005). With the development of HRM in the 1980s we saw the *first phase* of research linking HRM and performance. A series of articles and books which included research by Miles and Snow (1984) started to make the links between business strategy and HRM; others contributed by inviting a shift from control to commitment, and noting the importance of 'external' and 'internal fit' and organisational behaviour as the basis of contemporary HRM (Walton 1985; Schuler and Jackson 1987). Prior to these studies Peters and Waterman (1982) started to provide evidence of successful organisations that seem to apply the 'high-commitment' HRM principles.

The *second phase* of research development was in the early 1990s, when the first survey-based, statistically analysed study of HRM and performance by Huselid (1995) provided evidence of the association between higher performance and HRM practices. A *third phase* emerged at around the same time and saw a rise in research surrounding the measurement of HRM practices and performance. It demonstrated that the published studies used different HRM practices and measurement techniques, therefore questioning the claims about the link (Dyer and Reeves 1995; Becker and Gerhart 1996). The *fourth phase* saw Becker *et al* (1997) exploring the links between the theory of HR practice and the outcomes. They both supported an approach that drew on expectancy theory (Vroom 1964) to determine core HRM content and its link to performance. The approach was widely adopted and further developed by researchers into the Ability, Motivation, and Opportunity (AMO) model, which covers practices designed to build and retain human capital and influence employee behaviour. Further development in the same phase focused on investment in human resources and in promoting superior performance and competitive advantage.

The *fifth phase* of research development focused on the 'role of workers and the importance of workers' perceptions and behaviour in understanding the relationship between HRM and performance' (Guest 2011, pp3–13). The voice of employees was neglected in earlier research, but in recent years this has been remedied by the developing use of employee surveys by a number of organisations along with the Workplace Employment Relations surveys (WERS) of 1998 and 2004, which provided national data on workers' perceptions. The *sixth phase* identifies growing sophistication and complexity in the theory and research on HRM and performance. Studies by Bowen and Ostroff (2004) showed that the relationship between HRM and performance can be considered at the individual and organisational level and continued further research which point to the importance of HRM implementation. They seem to suggest that to understand the HRM–performance link we need to understand the processes involved and ensure that HRM practices are implemented. An emerging theme from this phase is the development of line managers in implementing HRM policies and improving performance, which is discussed later in the chapter.

 REFLECTIVE ACTIVITY

Summarise the key phases of HRM and PM, making links to key theorists.

HRM POLICIES AND PRACTICES

There is a growing consensus that along with HRM policies, individual employees can, if properly configured, contribute to improving organisational performance. Although each individual within an organisation might have little impact on organisational performance, scholars have begun to argue that, collectively, a firm's employees can provide a unique source of competitive advantage (Huselid 1995). HRM practices in the area of recruitment, selection and development can make a significant contribution to an organisation's performance by selecting the right individuals and designing mechanisms that will monitor and support them through, for example, training and developing programmes to meet the organisational objectives. However, the effectiveness of highly skilled employees is limited if the right conditions and supporting mechanisms are not in place – i.e. appraisal systems, rewards systems, flexibility and engagement strategies. This list is not inclusive and a body of research has used the phrase 'bundles of practices', suggesting that groups of HRM practices improve an organisation performance. However, little empirical research exists which points to specific groups of practices that achieve, or support organisations to achieve, competitive advantage. There is research that focuses on individual HRM practice to the exclusion of overall HRM systems (Huselid 1998).

Over the years we have seen the development of the concept of 'high-performance work practices' (HPWP) in supporting the establishment of 'high-performance work organisations' (HPWO). The literature in this area refers to 'high-performance organisations' and 'high-performance systems'; for the purpose of this chapter HPWP is used and includes high-performance systems. Similarly, references to HPWO include high-performance organisations.

HIGH-PERFORMANCE WORKING ORGANISATIONS (HPWOS)

The challenge for organisations today is to deliver instantly flexible, new, high-quality products and services in order to respond to changes in demand from clients. As mentioned above, standardisation and specialisation are characteristics of traditional work organisations where work is divided into different segments from preparation to support roles and workers specialise in order to maximise productivity. This is suitable when a constant demand for standardised products applies, but it does not work for fast-changing, demanding markets, making companies look for new forms of work organisation.

An HPWO concentrates on enlarging employee influence on the business as well as the impact of processes, methods and the physical environment, including the technology and tools that enhance their work. HPWOs also implement a holistic organisational approach, which means flat hierarchical structures, job rotation, self-responsible teams, multi-tasking and a greater involvement of lower-level employees in decision-making. An HPWO invests in its human resources and supports their technical, innovatory and social skills; this promotes good interpersonal relationships in the workplace from which the organisation will benefit. This type of organisation is different from the Taylorist work organisation, which is based on task specialisation, a hierarchical structure and the centralisation of responsibilities.

Appelbaum *et al* (2000, pp7–8) identified three components at the core of an HPWO:

- Work is organised to permit front-line workers to participate in decisions that alter organisational routines.
- Workers experience greater autonomy over their job tasks and methods of work and have higher levels of communication about work matters with other workers, managers and experts (e.g. engineering, accountants, maintenance and repair personnel).
- Front-line workers are required to gather information, process it and act on it.

Organisations with these characteristics allow employees to use their initiative, creativity and knowledge to progress and develop the organisation. Empirical studies of HPWOs (Ramsay *et al* 2000) have identified some of the following practices:

- information-sharing
- staff briefings
- management-employee meetings
- employee surveys
- suggestion schemes
- consultative committees
- employee consultation on organisational change
- problem-solving groups
- formal teams.

HIGH-PERFORMANCE WORKING PRACTICES

HPWP are deliberately introduced to improve organisational performance and can be attributed to employer responses to changes in market and technological conditions – for example:

- global market competition
- consumer demand for a broad range of high-quality products and services
- developments in information and communication technologies.

These conditions could demand:

- more flexible, skilled and committed labour
- indirect and subtle management control strategies
- worker participation
- continuous development of staff
- employee commitment
- teamwork
- problem-solving groups
- employee consultation.

With these conditions in place along with a set of complementary HRM policies and practices – e.g. generous training provision and job security – it is believed that employees can contribute to a positive performance outcome for an organisation (Appelbaum *et al* 2000; Sung and Ashton 2005).

Although the concept of HPWP might be new to individuals, the practice is long-established and is considered to be 'common sense good practice' to improve the performance of organisations. Organisations that adopt HPWP are referred to as HPWOs. The notion of HPWP seems to suggest that there exists a system of work practices that leads to superior organisational performance. There are three key concepts that are embedded in this suggestion: performance, work practices and systemic effects – these concepts are examined below.

SYSTEMIC EFFECTS

MacDuffie (1995) referred to the 'bundling' of working practices as being critical to HPWOs. Bundles consist of a combination rather than individual practices which shape the pattern of interactions between managers and employees. The term was first used by Appelbaum and Batt (1994) as a general label for a range of 'post-Taylorist' or 'post-Fordist' practices; this included quality circles, worker participation schemes and autonomous work teams. Godard (2004) stated that for HPWP to be deemed successful they need to enhance cost-effectiveness: if the financial benefits do not exceed the costs, HPWP are not economically rational for organisations. A challenge for organisations in adopting HPWP is whether employees exhibit specific behaviours – i.e. are flexible, proactive, and enthusiastic and committed with regard to innovation. HPWP should be judged on whether they provide the high-performance results as demonstrated by increased profit, higher productivity, reduced costs and reduced staff turnover. In the longer term, judgement of the practices should be based on whether they encourage innovations that improve the quality of products, service delivery and processes because all of these impact on profits and productivity.

Research carried out by Sung and Ashton (2005) identified 35 HPWP defined within three broad areas outlined below in Table 7.1. However, this is not universal: Becker and Huselid (1998) used 30 practices in their US study, and Guest (2000) only 18 practices in his UK study. It was suggested that more than one practice can have an impact on performance. For example, flexible working arrangements could have an impact on employee commitment and turnover. Sung and Ashton surveyed 294 companies in 2005 and found that 95% were using HPWP. The study confirmed that companies adopting more than 35 HPWP had greater employee involvement and were more effective in delivering training provision, motivating staff, managing change and providing career development opportunities. The findings also stated that where more than 35 HPWP were utilised, more employees earned over £35,000 and fewer earned less than £12,000. It was also clear from the study that some of the bundles of HPWP work better than others, and that particular bundles were more widely used by some sectors. For example, companies in the financial services sector were more prominent in using financial incentives, while manufacturing and business organisations made more use of involvement practices.

Table 7.1 High-performance working practices

HPWP	Examples
High employee involvement practices	Self-directed teams, quality circles and sharing/access to company information
Human resource practices	Sophisticated recruitment processes, performance appraisal, work redesign and mentoring
Reward and commitment practices	Various financial rewards, family-friendly policies, job rotation and flexi hours

Sung and Ashton (2005) also placed importance on leadership and culture in the effective implementation of HPWP. The notion of HPWP has sparked widespread interest. According to Ramsay *et al* (2000) strategies would entail management allowing employees a degree of control over their work and supporting the introduction of progressive methods which increase employees' welfare. These involve measures such as employee involvement programmes, teamworking, enhanced training and development and performance-related rewards systems. The literature also points to two important supporting factors First is **high-commitment management** (HCM), which stresses the importance of progressive practices that contribute to enhancing employee commitment. This is said to be where management practices work to improve autonomy and intrinsic satisfaction, thereby contributing to superior organisational performance through improved motivation and effort, reduced need for managerial control and reduced staff turnover. The second variant, **high-involvement management** (HIM), is where the management style supports involvement practices in pursuing organisational goals and improving performance. It is clear from a number of studies that the role of the manager makes a valuable contribution to the introduction and sustainability of HPWP.

Bamberger and Meshoulam (2000) noted that the development of strategic HRM adopted a resource-based or a control-based approach to measuring HPWP. This, they say, is the internal development of employees such as training, career development and, in contrast, the control-based approach measuring HPWP through directing and monitoring methods (Snell 1992; Delery and Doty 1996). Bamberger and Meshoulam, while not totally convinced with the two approaches, further attempted to divide the two methods into three HR subsystems: people flow, including staffing, employee mobility and training; appraisals and reward, including performance appraisal, compensation and benefits; and employment relations, including job design and participation. They seem to suggest that an integrated measure of HPWP should assess selective staffing, extend skills training, broaden career paths, promote from within, guarantee job security, have result-oriented appraisal, introduce extensive and open-ended rewards, have broad job descriptions and flexible job assignments, and encourage participation. They conclude that HPWP are characterised by the combination of single practices collectively impacting on organisational performance and that organisations carefully selecting high-performance HR practices – for instance, extensive skills training, retention and job security strategies, promotion from within, result-oriented appraisal and broad career paths – can signal an organisation seeking to establish a long-term exchange relationship with its employees.

The model in Figure 7.1 attempts to give a holistic view of what should be taken into consideration in developing HPWOs and illustrates the relationship and the important interaction between HPWP, the culture of the organisation and the external environment. Deal and Kennedy (1982) state that creating a strong organisational culture is a powerful tool in improving organisational performance, so the model, in addition to the culture and the external environment, takes into consideration the importance of the HRM department in developing and driving through practices and developing the organisational culture that supports the appropriate practices, along with the role of the line manager in executing these developments.

Figure 7.1 A holistic focus on HPWO

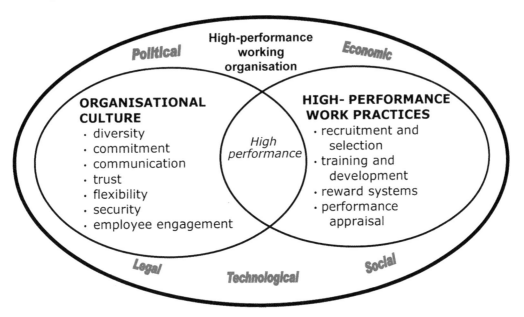

THE EXTERNAL ENVIRONMENT

The organisational environment is dynamic and complicated. It is essential that organisations understand their external environment – i.e. political, legal, economic, social and technological factors. An organisation must foresee the changing forces in the environment and adapt to achieve organisational goals and perform well against its competitors. HPWOs monitor their relationships with the environment continually and so are able to adapt rapidly to changing environmental forces. As threats and opportunities are identified, the organisation is able to review and amend current strategies.

The *political environment* consists of political and legal forces that could impact on the performance of organisations, and involves politicians in the business world through the development of policies and laws which could impact on an organisation's survival, competitiveness and performance.

 REFLECTIVE ACTIVITY

Retirement age and union rights are two examples of political intervention. Retirement age in the UK for many years was 65 for a man and 60 for a woman – a contentious issue that has long been debated. However, the government in 2010 changed the law so that the 65- and 60-year markers have now been removed, with the expectation that employees will work beyond these age markers.

To remain HPWOs how should organisations plan for this political intervention?

Political policies can shape the *economic environment*. Two of the key economic policies that influence organisations are:

- *monetary policy*, concerned with money supply (the borrowing and lending of money by banks to organisations), interest rates and credit availability. It influences the level of spending through interest rates. Cheap money reduces cost and expensive money increases cost
- *fiscal policy*, concerned with the use of taxation (taxation rates or levels are set by the government) and government expenditure to regulate economic activities. Taxation on income, expenditure and capital has an important influence on management decisions.

Classic indicators here are the availability of loans to organisations from the banks and changes in taxation made by governments in an effort to either dampen down or stimulate the economy. An organisation's ability to perform as it wishes is affected by the actions of the banks in two ways. The first is in terms of the cost of capital – i.e. the interest rate charged: the higher the rate, the more expensive it is to borrow, and the lower, the less expensive. The second is by either granting or rejecting loan applications. Organisations have to review and adjust their strategies in relation to these actions to ensure that their performance is not affected.

Technological development refers to inventions and innovations in technology which could impact on skills, methods, systems and equipment, and which could change jobs, products, production methods and processes and impact on organisational performance. The *social environment* refers to changes and development in the population. An understanding of demographics can shape the way organisations develop and impact on strategic planning – i.e. the ability to resource an organisation with skilled labour.

REFLECTIVE ACTIVITY

Referring to an organisation with which you are familiar, explain how the external environment impacts upon HPWP.

THE INVOLVEMENT AND COMMITMENT OF LINE MANAGERS IN IMPROVING PERFORMANCE

The term 'line manager' (LM) here refers to the first level of management that employees report to. The involvement of LMs in HRM has become more prominent in recent years due to a devolvement of HR practices (see Figure 7.2). It is a pattern that has been dominant in Europe for some time whereby the work of HRM is shared between HR and LMs. According to Brewster and Larson (2000) cited in Renwick (2003), there are several reasons for this:

- to reduce costs
- to provide a more comprehensive approach to HRM
- to place the responsibility for HRM on those managers most responsible for it

- to speed up decision-making
- as an alternative to outsourcing the HR function.

It is therefore the LMs' role to integrate HR into the organisation's daily work and lead the way in creating a partnership between employees, their LMs and HR itself which should, in turn, impact on and improve organisational performance.

Figure 7.2 HR practices developed for line managers

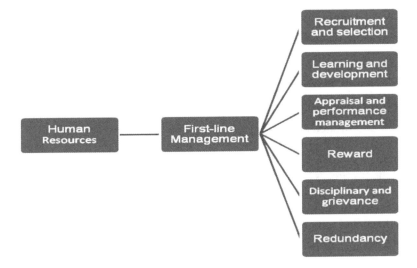

The purpose of PM is to allow LMs to demonstrate what is expected of individuals and teams and to manage expectations – both theirs and those of the employees – to meet organisational needs and objectives. LMs are expected to achieve results and where possible improve organisational performance through the people in their department or teams. They are expected to manage their staff through the PM cycle, sometimes referred to as the 'performance appraisal' process (outlined below), monitor achievements against objectives and, where necessary, provide feedback and coaching for their staff. Whereas it is considered relatively straightforward to create a PM system, the implementation of it is not so simple and requires LMs to have the capability, desire, motivation, competence and training to carry it out. It is important to note that LMs themselves also undergo the PM process, sometimes with the same criteria, although in other cases they may be measured against alternative objectives.

Research in this area suggests that although LMs have been involved in HRM practices their role, particularly in PM, brings into question their capability and commitment to HR practices. It has been argued that the degree to which an LM commits to the process affects the outcome – that is to say, if an LM feels that the process is simply a paper exercise and has no impact on the employee, he or she will not spend time undertaking the process properly and this in turn can affect employee engagement. LMs need to ensure that they treat all employees fairly and provide the same level of feedback and support because this has an impact on the level of trust and employee satisfaction in an organisation.

PERFORMANCE APPRAISALS

LMs play an important role in improving performance in organisations, and the performance appraisal (PA) process is one of the key activities that formally focus on the performance of individuals in developing an HPWO and achieving organisational objectives. PM and PA are sometimes used synonymously. However, Armstrong and Baron (2005) see PM as a comprehensive yet continuous and flexible approach to the management of teams and individuals, and PA as a more limited process which involves LMs in making an assessment of employees. But there are other authors and many organisations that argue for a closer link between the two processes.

PAs are potentially a controversial HR tool because the objectives for their introduction can sometimes be a reason for concern amongst employees who might fear for the security of their job if their performance is considered to be below par. It is therefore important that the objectives of any appraisal system are clearly communicated and understood by everyone involved and that, where possible, everyone is given the opportunity to feed back on the process so that improvements can be made. It is important for organisations to decide on the aims of the PA process. A common purpose is to enable a formal assessment of employees, which could be against pre-set objectives, or it might be by rating job competencies. However, although assessment is a core element of PA, it is not always the main fundamental objective. Fletcher (2008) outlines some of the aims of PA as:

- for making reward decisions – i.e. the development of equitable distribution, whether pay, promotion or as a method of comparing people
- for improving performance through facilitating learning – an accurate assessment of performance is likely to bring to light training and development needs
- for motivating staff – employees can be motivated in a number of ways: giving feedback has been observed to motivate individuals, along with making explicit performance standards and applying them consistently and giving people a fair hearing. Setting targets and seeing improvements on previous performance is also said to motivate employees
- for succession planning and identifying potential – identifying good and poor performers through the PA process allows the organisation to focus on resource planning and identify individuals for promotion.
- for promoting line manager and subordinate dialogue
- for formal assessment of unsatisfactory performance – although it might appear negative, unsatisfactory performance is documented and can be used in evidence in the disciplinary process.

REVIEWING PERFORMANCE

It is important that, where possible, LMs meet annually with individual members of their team to provide feedback. However, this assumes a traditional organisation structure is in place together with conventional ways of working. Organisations could organise individuals on a project basis, in remote teams regionally or internationally, and in some circumstances individuals could have more than one LM in one year. In non-traditional structures the HRM department, the use of technology and joint assessment plays an important part in gathering and feeding back information to employees. Regardless of the organisation, the process should:

- have clear aims and measurable success criteria linked to the organisation and department/local objectives
- be designed and administered in a manner that focuses on the coaching aspect of evaluation
- maintain a focus on performance improvement
- be closely allied with a clear and adequately resourced training and development infrastructure
- have clear and easy-to-use documentation
- provide training for all on how to use the system
- be reviewed regularly by all involved so that improvements can be made
- adopt a clear appraisal methodology that is suitable to the organisation: although appraisal by an LM is widely used, there are other methods – for example, self-assessment, peer, customer, upward and 360-degree.

The reviewer in the formal PA system is referred to as the appraiser. McGregor (1957) had some reservations about the use of PAs and noted that most LMs were reluctant to take on the role as appraiser because managers prefer to treat their subordinates as colleagues rather than as inferiors upon whom they are required to pass judgement. This is referred to as the 'top-down' style or 180-degree appraisal. The 1990s saw the development of a continuous feedback process by which the individuals concerned talk with each other and try to share their perceptions in a mutual way; the annual appraisal meeting thus becomes a review and summary of a series of discussions over a determined period.

THE APPRAISAL INTERVIEW

The formal appraisal interview should take place annually or biannually and should be planned and managed well in order for both parties to achieve interview objectives. These should include providing feedback on previously set objectives, discussing performance issues, identifying training and development needs, and setting new objectives for the following year. A poorly conducted appraisal interview can demotivate employees, create uncertainty for the appraisee and affect the confidence of and relationship between LM and subordinates. Ideally the interview should be recorded and both parties should sign a declaration that they agree with the completed form. It is good practice to allow the employee to see the completed form and add any comments. It is important also to end the interview with a plan for follow-up review meetings.

MULTI-LEVEL MULTI-SOURCE FEEDBACK

In an attempt to improve the quality of feedback the introduction of multi-level multi-source feedback systems have been introduced in organisations. *Self-assessment appraisal* enables employees to evaluate their own performance prior to the appraisal meeting, and gives the opportunity for a two-way discussion. The appraisee may become a more active participant in the process. *Peer appraisals* require the appraisee's colleagues to provide feedback based on the appraisal criteria selected, which is used non-judgementally as a teamworking developmental tool and helps colleagues to better understand each other and improve performance. *Customer appraisals* involve internal and external customers providing feedback on individuals; a wider strategic picture of a person in context may emerge from the process. *Upward appraisals* encourage employees to review their own manager. A person's managerial style and competences can be exposed by the opinions and provide useful information in circumstances where there is high staff turnover. Developed from this is the *360-degree appraisal* in which an individual is rated by subordinates, peers, superiors and sometimes clients or customers, as well as completing a self-assessment.

REFLECTIVE ACTIVITY

Managing PA expectations

A local council office, which employs 38 people, runs very efficiently. The team works on the financial planning for the city as well as following up with clients and customers, processing orders and managing small budgets. Each member has a clearly defined role and mistakes are very rare. Communication is clear and concise across the office and everyone takes pride in their work, so details are invariably correct.

There are four teams with a team manager and one general manager for the whole office. A few of the line managers are seeking promotion but unfortunately, due to the current economic climate and public sector job cuts there is no room for growth or career development.

Roger is a team manager and has been in the role for 10 years with consistently positive feedback from colleagues and his team – indeed, he meets and sometimes exceeds the performance targets set by the council. He believes that the time has come for a promotion and has arranged a meeting with the office manager. If Roger doesn't get the expected promotion he is after, he will leave and seek employment elsewhere.

1   Imagine you are the office manager. How would you manage Roger's expectations and advise him of the possible options presently available?

2   How would you deal with this in the short term (six months) and in the medium term (one to two years)?

In order for an appraisal system to be effective it is vital that LMs are committed to the promotion and implementation of appraisals. The organisation should provide LMs with sufficient time and resources to undertake interviews with employees, complete paperwork and follow up action points. The role of HR is to ensure that managers are fully trained and in possession of the appropriate interpersonal skills – i.e. interviewing skills, assertiveness skills and the ability to manage reward decisions. Fletcher (2008) suggests that at the start of the process an LM must become familiar with the employee's job role by looking at the job description and gathering feedback from a variety of sources. He also suggests that the employee should complete a pre-evaluation of his or her performance and be notified of the appraisal weeks in advance.

Coaching is important during the performance review process. It provides critical checkpoints towards achieving goals and objectives, thus creating opportunities to adjust them so as to attain the objectives of the employee and organisation. It provides managers with the opportunity to adapt their communication styles to match those of each individual employee. In addition, management must continue to develop their coaching and evaluation skills and emphasise consistency within departments (more information on coaching is to be found in Chapter 3). The PA system itself must undergo continuing evaluation in terms of the effect it has on employee productivity, performance and morale, obtaining constructive feedback from LMs and employees for improvement.

REFLECTIVE ACTIVITY

Outline the learning and development needs of an LM to support the principles of HPWP.

HRM PRACTICES SUPPORTING THE PERFORMANCE APPRAISAL PROCESS

REWARDS

Performance management also brings with it the issue of rewards. Employees need to trust their LMs to treat them all the same and, using criteria set within the PM process, measure them accordingly and provide a suitable reward. This in itself can cause issues because research has shown that some LMs find it difficult to criticise their employees and are unable or unwilling to handle difficult situations. There have been cases where LMs, particularly in times of recession, may be forced by senior management to distribute the financial rewards evenly, based not on performance but instead on the limited funds available.

Performance-related pay (PRP) is now implemented not only in the private sector but increasingly in the public sector. Once again, this implies that all employees will be treated fairly and assessed according to their performance. However, some LMs are very poor at dealing with underperformers, at criticising their staff and at handling potentially confrontational situations, and therefore endeavour to avoid these situations.

REFLECTIVE ACTIVITY

What skills do LMs need to carry out the PA process?

TRAINING

As part of the PM process it is important that organisations ensure that they look to develop talent. In addition, organisations should, through HR and LMs, use the right tools and techniques to maintain high-performance working practices.

A lack of training in handling HR issues is a key factor in the inconsistent application of HR policies. Devolving HR tasks to LMs can therefore produce some difficulties which range from dealing with skills gaps and resource deficiencies in managers to identifying the same in their employees through the PM or appraisal process. It is the capability and commitment of LMs that can determine the effectiveness of workplace learning. As mentioned above, feedback is vital for HPWOs, and it is important that when feedback is given to individuals and teams it is not just about the performance of employees but the performance of the organisation and its management. Feedback creates opportunities for learning, and individuals should be trained in giving constructive feedback in both formal and informal settings to ensure that learning and development take place.

RECRUITMENT AND SELECTION

The resourcing of the organisation, while important for all organisations, must be viewed strategically for organisations intent on being HPWOs. Replacing employees should start with a detailed analysis of the roles, skills and individuals required, along with how the organisation attracted similar candidates in the past, what characteristics and behaviours the recruiter looked for and the performance of individuals who were appointed against those criteria. Organisations should fully review the recruitment methods and selection tools used and not feel restricted in using and evaluating new opportunities in these areas.

Attracting the right person into an organisation is critical, and if it is not done well, even the best selection method will not generate future talent for the organisation. In recent times HR staff have been inspired to borrow techniques from the marketing of goods and services in competing for staff in the marketplace. Many employers have looked to position themselves as 'employers of choice', with a view to attracting the best candidates from their competitors. Central to this is the development of a positive 'brand image' of the organisation as a highly desirable employer. HPWOs with good HPWP – e.g. flexible working, career development, job security, teamworking, etc – can make good use of these practices in attracting individuals. Looking to existing employees is one way of finding out about practices that are considered beneficial, and this information could be gathered through regular staff attitude surveys.

It is important in recruiting individuals into the organisation that HR ensures that the right support mechanisms are in place so that individuals are inducted, supported, developed and rewarded and are then able to contribute to improving the performance of the organisation. Such support mechanisms should be planned before the selection process takes place, confirmed straight after the selection process is completed, and monitored using the appropriate procedures throughout the life of the post.

ORGANISATIONAL CULTURE

The idea of culture in relation to organisations has been documented from the early nineteenth century through the initiatives of reformers such as Robert

Owen. He introduced organisational culture into industry alongside Joseph Rowntree and Edward Cadbury. Even Taylor's 'scientific management' had cultural objectives, which threatened the subcultural influence of both organised labour and management. From the 1920s it was recognised that the social dimension of work and employee well-being had become an important element in improving performance and effectiveness in organisations through, for example, what are known as the Hawthorne Studies. Since these studies, a number of authors have reported results which note positive outcomes after the culture of the organisation is taken into consideration. This section identifies a number of initiatives that can be adopted by organisations looking to invest in a culture that supports the development of an HPWO.

DIVERSITY

Fostering an organisational culture that supports diversity can effectively improve an organisation's performance. The general view behind diversity initiatives is that given the current shortage of skilled labour, the effective use of diverse skills within an organisation makes good business sense. A survey of 15 Fortune-100 companies by Robinson and Dechant (1997) (reported in Cassell 2006) revealed that the main business reasons for engaging in diversity initiatives included:

- better utilisation of talent (93%)
- increased marketplace understanding (80%)
- enhanced breadth of understanding of leadership position (60%)
- enhanced creativity (53%)
- increased quality of team problem-solving (40%).

Diversity is based on the concept of difference, and Kandola and Fullerton (1994) provide a definition which states that diversity 'consists of visible and non-visible difference which will include factors such as gender, age, background, race, disability, personality and work style …'. The effective management of difference is most important to organisations looking to achieve high performance and competitive advantage in the marketplace, and is linked to an organisation's culture and values. For diversity to be successful Kandola and Fullerton (1994) suggested the MOSAIC vision, which is an acronym for:

- Mission and values
- Objective and fair processes
- Skilled workforce – aware and fair
- Active flexibility
- Individual focus
- Culture that empowers.

These key characteristics clearly highlight the importance of maximising the potential of all individuals within an organisation regardless of any group they may belong to.

SECURITY

Employment security is seen by a growing number of writers as important in promoting employee commitment to managerial policies and practices, thus contributing to improving organisation performance and relaxing the constraints placed on the adoption of HPW (Liu *et al* 2009). Particular advantages of employment security can be summarised as:

- It provides long-term security for all employees.
- Continued employment with the organisation is almost guaranteed.
- Employees should share in the financial success of the company.
- Employees should be given a chance to enhance their employability.
- Employees should be kept informed about all business matters.
- Feedback should be sought from all employees.
- The skills and competencies of all employees should be systematically developed.

Although it is not difficult to argue with the point above, concepts of, for example, 'the flexible firm' (Atkinson 1984) have illustrated that some groups of workers may never benefit from long-term employment security because of the need for cost-effectiveness, competitiveness and response to changes external to the organisation. Employees' sharing in the success of the organisation could imply job security for all. Although we know that this is not always the case, financial incentives – for example, employee share-ownership schemes and share incentive plans – are said to increase the feeling of employment security in organisations.

COMMUNICATION

Good-quality communication mechanisms are vital for HPWOs and should be designed to encourage vertical and horizontal feedback. Where possible, organisations should provide regular updates on the performance of the organisation and publish information on any foreseeable changes that could impact on the performance and general survival of the organisation. There should also be mechanisms in place that capture, evaluate, feedback and action employees' views – for example, about management, working methods and conditions, and on suggestions for new ideas. This is said to support the development of employee engagement in organisations.

EMPLOYEE ENGAGEMENT

Employee engagement is when employees are committed to the organisation and its values. Such commitment is important in achieving improved business performance. There is a clear body of research that links the way people are managed, employee attitudes and organisation performance. When employers and employees deliver on their commitments, it builds trust and a sense of fairness amongst both groups. Alfes *et al* (2010) describe employee engagement under three headings:

- *intellectual engagement*, or thinking hard about the job and how to do it better
- *affective engagement*, or feeling positively about doing a good job
- *social engagement*, or actively taking opportunities to discuss work-related improvements with others at work.

They also note that 'meaningfulness', which is linked to effective engagement, is considered to have the most impact on how individuals feel about their working life in general. If employees believe that their work is important and that what they do can make a difference, it promotes a positive perception about their job and the working environment.

LMs are important in helping individuals find meaning in their work. One way to support and develop this is through regular communication about the organisation's vision and future objectives and by creating a common framework to help employees see a bigger picture in their daily work. In addition, LMs can support meaningfulness by designing jobs in which individuals are able to experience positive feelings during their work. Job enrichment is just one of the effective techniques that enable organisations to create meaningful jobs.

Alfes *et al* (2010) provide evidence in their study which suggests that levels of employees' engagement are affected by their perceptions of management style. Where management provide opportunities for upward feedback and greater participation – thus providing greater understanding of wider organisational issues as well as personal involvement – the level of engagement is high. It is also suggested that when managers are interested in employee well-being and have effective leadership skills, engagement and related behaviours are enhanced. Building an engaged workforce requires:

- measuring employee attitudes
- supporting employees in understanding how their work contributes to improving the organisation
- providing opportunities for employees' views to be communicated upwards
- keeping employees well informed about what is happening in the organisation
- fairness in dealing with problems
- building a culture in which individuals feel valued and involved
- employees' feeling they have the opportunity to develop their job
- employers to be concerned for employees' health and well-being.

REFLECTIVE ACTIVITY

1 What are the key elements of employee engagement?

2 How does employee engagement impact upon HPWP?

TEAMWORK

Teamwork is a very important HPWO factor because it affects employees and the quality of their working life. The work performance of teams is higher than individual performance when the work requires a broader scope of knowledge, judgement and opinion. The advantage of teamwork is productivity growth that requires creative solving of different tasks, a high degree of adaptability and operational management. Teamwork also creates an environment that facilitates knowledge and information exchange. Other advantages include an increased potential for innovation that could add value to products and services; increasing the employability of workers through multi-skilling; job autonomy; greater employee responsibility; improved job satisfaction; and greater competencies in problem-solving and communication.

TRUST

Trust is a vital component of a successful organisation: if there is a lack of trust, there are serious consequences for both organisations and society as a whole. There are four distinct components: ability, benevolence, integrity and predictability. HR policies and processes lie at the root of creating and maintaining trust and provide clues as to the trustworthiness of the organisation. The implementation of these practices by HR makes the intentions of the organisation tangible for the employees.

According to research conducted by Harris (2001), LMs are able to see the value and benefit of having a formal appraisal system in place if for no other reason than to have a written record of the decisions made by them should they be required to defend them. However, there is a general feeling that the formal recording process of an appraisal or PM review has taken priority, which takes away from the purpose of a PM system which should be about 'investing in the quality of personal interactions and gaining commitment through high-trust relationships between manager and employee'.

There are five aspects to how organisations in the UK build and sustain trust:

● trust in each other
● trust in leaders
● trust in the organisation
● trust in external relations
● trust in the direct line manager.

However, the results of a survey commissioned by the CIPD (Hope-Hailey *et al* 2012) showed that poor communication, high levels of conflict and limited opportunities for staff to develop and progress are key factors in reducing trust. The main issue is whether employees trust LMs to attend to all aspects of their well-being. Employee response to HR practices is at the heart of all HRM performance-related models (Purcell and Kinnie 2006) because it is the link between employee reactions and their resulting behaviour which is vital. These responses are often measured against employees' level of job satisfaction and organisational commitment.

CREATING A SUSTAINABLE HIGH-PERFORMANCE CULTURE

Challenging economic environments result in the closure of major organisations, the loss of jobs and job insecurity for those remaining in employment. It might therefore seem difficult for organisations to focus on what makes employees happy and enthusiastic at work. In addition, research by Spreitzer and Porath (2012) shows that happy workers are more productive than unhappy workers over a period of time and are more likely to:

- turn up for work
- stay with the organisation
- go the extra mile for the organisation
- attract people who are just as committed to the job

Spreitzer and Porath found that organisations in which individuals are satisfied, are high performers and are engaged in creating the future of the organisation are more likely to sustain high performance. They identified learning as one of the key contributors supporting this. They state that individuals and organisations grow from gaining new knowledge and skills, and that employees who are developing their skills and abilities are more likely to believe in their potential for further growth. Organisations can support the development of individuals through providing electronic performance support systems (EPSS), which reduce the cost of training staff while increasing productivity and performance. Using EPSS, new employees in particular are not only able to complete their work more quickly and accurately, but also learn more about the job and the employer's business.

To create a culture for sustainable high performance it is important that organisations allow decision-making discretion, share information, and provide good performance feedback. Empowering employees to make decisions that affect their work gives them a greater sense of control; this includes giving them the opportunity to contribute to decisions and to bring forward new ideas for the organisation, and identifying them as the experts in the job they are employed to do and as people to be consulted on any related developments. It is important that managers are sensitive and careful not to capture ideas and claim them as their own because this could damage trust between managers and employees. The use of team decision-making is important, as mentioned above, in contributing to high performance and engaging employees. The challenge for managers is not to cut back on empowering individuals when people make mistakes. Mistakes create the best conditions for individuals and teams to learn from.

Illustration of practice

At Facebook, the motto is 'Move fast and break things', which is about encouraging employees to make decisions and act. The organisational decision-making discretion is fundamental to the culture of Facebook.

Methods used to encourage sharing of information are important in sustaining high performance in organisations. People can contribute more effectively if they can see how their work fits with the organisation's mission and strategy. However, it should be noted that sharing information should be accessible and understandable by all. Complex financial data or storing the information online with limited or no access for a number of individuals will hinder this. Offering good-quality feedback is discussed above.

SUMMARY

The concept of improving organisational performance has been an obsession in organisations for a number of years. For any organisation to achieve high performance it is noted that a number of HR practices must be in place, supported and executed by LMs. Each HPWO requires a different bundle of HR practices in order to be effective – however, it is evident that a number of HPWP exist, and research has continued in this area to identify precisely which ones they are. There is evidence that people management practices relate to high organisational performance, but there has been some criticism of the approach, mainly surrounding the methods used. For example, no account is taken of how the practices are implemented, of organisational strategy or how success is measured – i.e. do profitable organisations report more success because they can afford to implement more practices?

While PM and PA systems are important in developing organisational performance, the approach taken should also be holistic, to include an understanding of the external environment in which the organisation operates; the development of a culture which attempts to understand and maintain the psychological well-being of employees; and the development of HPWP by the HR function supported and implemented by line managers.

 Future Electric Transport Cars Ltd

CASE STUDY

Future Electric Transport (FET) Cars Ltd is a manufacturer of small electric cars that also carries out researches into future means of low-emission transportation. It produces less than 1,000 units a year and supplies only to the UK at present, but it is part of a larger parent organisation which also manufactures electric cars and public transport vehicles across Europe. Its office, which is the UK base, is in the Midlands and employs approximately 500 staff, of which 450 are factory-based production operatives, with a further 50 based in the office, undertaking support activities including finance, marketing, sales, product development and research, HR and logistics.

The company recently appointed a new HR director following the retirement of his predecessor who had been in the role for approximately 10 years. The newly appointed HR director did not come from a traditional HR background but rather from production management in one of FET's sister companies.

One of the first responsibilities of the new HR director was to allocate to the HR manager the task of introducing an appraisal system for all employees on site. An appraisal system was borrowed from a sister company and implemented at FET because the HR director wanted something simple that could be implemented straight away without cost or fuss.

The HR manager obtained copies of the relevant appraisal system which was more complicated than expected, particularly as the system in the sister company not only contained annual assessment against the company's yearly objectives but also an evaluation of each employee's performance in key competency areas, which seemed inappropriate within FET.

FET's sister company had trained its managers on how to carry out the appraisals, having produced a comprehensive guide. The HR director decided to save valuable time and money by circulating copies of the training material, along with copies of the relevant paperwork, in November to all appraising managers with the instruction that all employees were to have received an appraisal by the end of December, by which date all documentation was to have been returned to the HR department. The HR director did not expect to provide training because he believed experienced managers should know what they were doing.

The first stirs of opposition started almost immediately when some of the managers raised questions over who they were supposed to be appraising. Certain departments had a shared resource pool of secretaries and administrative staff, and it had never been made clear who reported to whom.

The HR manager raised his concerns with the HR director, who suggested that they let events take their course, as he was certain that the majority of managers would comply with the requirement to have all appraisals completed by the end of the year. The HR manager left it until after the Christmas break before he counted the returned appraisal paperwork. Fewer than 45% had been returned. Early in the new year the HR director and HR manager sat down to review events. 'Where did we go wrong, and how could we have managed this better?' was his question.

Question:

1   You are the HR manager. Prepare your notes for the meeting with the HR director, including how to implement a new appraisal system and how to rectify the current situation.

FURTHER READING

BOOKS

ARMSTRONG, M. (2009) *Armstrong's Handbook of Performance Management: An evidence-based guide to delivering high performance*, 4th edn. London: Kogan-Page. A good comprehensive text with practical examples throughout.

ARMSTRONG, M. and BARON, A. (2006) *Managing Performance: Performance management in action*, 2nd edn. London: CIPD. A concise easy-to-read practical text.

FLETCHER, C. (2008) *Appraisal, Feedback and Development*, 4th edn. London: Taylor & Francis. A comprehensive guide to the appraisal system.

WEBLINKS

Performance Appraisal: Resource summary. CIPD Factsheet. Available at: http://www.cipd.co.uk/hr-resources/factsheets/performance-appraisal.aspx [Accessed 6 June 2012].

Shaping the Future: The drivers of sustainable high performance. CIPD survey. Available at: http://www.cipd.co.uk/shapingthefuture/_stnhiprf.htm [Accessed 6 June 2012].

REFERENCES

ALFES, K., TRUSS, C., SOANE, E. C., REES, C. and GATENBY, M. (2010) *Creating an Engaged Workforce.* London: Chartered Institute of Personnel and Development.

APPELBAUM, E. and BATT, R. (1994) *The New American Workplace.* New York: ILR Press Audit Commission.

APPELBAUM, E., BAILEY, T., BERG, P. and KALLEBERG, A. L. (2000) *Manufacturing Advantage: Why high-performance work systems pay off.* Ithaca: Cornell University Press.

ARMSTRONG, M. (1996) *A Handbook of Personnel Practice*, 5th edn. London: Kogan Page.

ARMSTRONG, M. (2009) *Armstrong's Handbook of Performance Management: An evidence-based guide to delivering high performance*, 4th edn. London: Kogan Page.

ARMSTRONG, M. and BARON, A. (2006) *Managing Performance: Performance management in action*, 2nd edn. London: Chartered Institute of Personnel and Development.

ATKINSON, J. (1984) Manpower strategies for flexible organisation. *Personnel Management.* Vol.16, No. 8. 28–31.

BAMBERGER, P. and MESHOULAM, I. (2000) *Human Resource Strategy.* Newbury Park, CA: Sage.

BECKER, B. and GERHART, B. (1996) The impact of human resource management on organizational performance: progress and prospects. *Academy of Management Journal.* Vol. 39, No. 4. 779–801.

BECKER, B. and HUSELID, M. A. (1998) High Performance work systems and firm performance: a synthesis of research and managerial implications, in FERRIS, G. R. (ed.) *Research in Personnel and Human Resources Management.* Vol. 16. Greenwich, CT: JAI.

BECKER, B. E., HUSELID, M. A., PICKUS, P. S. and SPRATT, M. (1997) HR as a source of shareholders' value: research and recommendations. *Human Resource Management.* Vol. 36, No. 1. 39–47.

BOSELIE, T. P., DIETZ, G. and BOON, C. (2005) Commonalities and contradictions in research on human resource management and performance. *Human Resource Management Journal.* Vol. 15, No. 3. 67–94.

BOWEN, D. E. and OSTROFF, C. (2004) Understanding HRM–firm performance linkages: the role of the 'strength' of the HRM system. *Academy of Management Review.* Vol. 29, No. 2. 203–21.

BRAVERMAN, H. (1974) Labor and monopoly capital, New York: Monthly Review Press, in LEGGE, K. (1995) *Human Resource Management: Rhetorics and realities.* Basingstoke: Macmillan.

CARDY, R. L. and LEONARD, B. (2011) *Performance Management: Concepts, skills, and exercises,* 2nd edn. Armonk, NY: M. E. Sharpe.

CASSELL, C. (2006) Managing diversity, in REDMAN, T. and WILKINSON, A. (eds) *Contemporary Human Resource Management: Text and cases.* Essex: Prentice Hall.

CONNOCK, S. (1992) The importance of 'big ideas' to HR managers. *Personnel Management.* Vol. 21, No. 11. 52–6.

CULLY, M., WOODLAND, S. and O'REILLY, A. (1999) *Britain at Work: As depicted by the 1998 Workplace Employee Relations Survey.* London: Routledge.

DEAL, T. E. and KENNEDY, A. A. (1982) *Corporate Cultures: The rites and rituals of organisational life.* Reading, MA: Addison-Wesley.

DELERY, J. and DOTY, H. (1996) Modes of theorizing in strategic human resource management: tests of universalistic, contingency, and configurational performance. *Academy Management Journal.* Vol. 39, No. 4. 802–35.

DYER, l. and REEVES, T. (1995) Human resource strategies and firm performance: what do we know and where do we need to go? *International Journal of Human Resource Management.* Vol. 6. No. 3. 656–70.

FLETCHER, C. (2008) *Appraisal, Feedback and Development,* 4th edn. London: Taylor & Francis.

FOOT, M. and HOOK, C. (2008) *Introducing Human Resource Management*, 5th edn. Harlow: Pearson Education.

GODARD, J. (2004) A critical assessment of the high-performance paradigm. *British Journal of Industrial Relations*. Vol. 42, No. 2. 349–78.

GUEST, D. (2000) HR and the bottom line – 'Has the penny dropped?' *People Management*. Vol. 6, No. 15. 26–31.

GUEST, D. (2011) Human resource management and performance: still searching for some answers. *Human Resource Management Journal*. Vol. 21, No. 1. 3–13.

HARRIS, L. (2001) Rewarding employee performance: line managers' values, beliefs and perspectives. *International Journal of Human Resource Management*. Vol. 12, No. 7. 1182–92.

HOPE-HAILEY, V., SEARLE, R. and DIETZ, G. (2012) Organisational effectiveness: how trust helps. *People Management*. Available at: http://www.peoplemanagement.co.uk/pm/articles/2012/02/organisational-effectiveness-how-trust-helps.htm [Accessed 6 June 2012].

HUSELID, M. A. (1995) The impact of human resource management practices on turnover, productivity. and corporate financial performance. *Academy of Management Journal*. Vol. 38, No. 3. 635–72.

HUSELID, M. A. (1998) The impact of human resource management practices on turnover, productivity and corporate financial performance, in MABEY. C., SALAMAN, G. and STOREY. J. (eds) *Strategic Human Resource Management*. London: Sage.

KANDOLA, R. and FULLERTON, J. (1994) *Managing the Mosaic: Diversity in action*. London: Institute of Personnel and Development.

LIU, W., GUTHRIE, J., FLOOD, P. and MCCURTAIN, S. (2009) Unions and the adoption of high performance work systems: does employment security play a role? *Industrial and Labour Relations Review*. Vol. 63, No. 1. 109–27.

MACDUFFIE, J. P. (1995) Human resource bundles and manufacturing performance. *Industrial and Labor Relations Review*. Vol. 48, No. 2. 197–221.

MCGREGOR, D. (1957) An uneasy look at performance appraisal. *Harvard Business Review*. Vol. 35, No. 3. 89–94.

MILES, R. E. and SNOW, C. C. (1984) Designing strategic human resource systems. *Organizational Dynamics*. Vol. 36 (summer). 52.

NOLAN. P. and O'DONNELL, K. (1991) Restructuring and the politics of renewal: the limits of flexible specialization, in POLLET, A. (ed.) *Farewell to Flexibility*. Oxford: Oxford University Press.

PETERS, T. J. and WATERMAN, R. H. (1982) *In Search of Excellence: Lessons from America's best run companies*. New York: Harper & Row.

PURCELL, J. and KINNIE, N. (2006) HRM and business performance, in BOXALL, P., PURCELL, J. and WRIGHT, P. (eds) *The Oxford Handbook of Human Resource Management*. Oxford: Oxford University Press.

RAMSAY, H., SCHOLARIOS, D. and HARLEY, B. (2000) Employees and high-performance work systems: testing inside the black box. *British Journal of Industrial Relations*. Vol. 38, No. 4. 501–31.

RENWICK, D. (2003) Line manager involvement in HRM: an inside view. *Employee Relations*. Vol. 5, No. 3. 262–80.

ROBINSON, G. and DECHANT, K. (1997) Building a business case for diversity. *Academy of Management Executive*. Vol.11, No 3. 21–31.

SCHULER, R. S. and JACKSON, S. E. (1987) Linking competitive strategies with human resource management practices. *Academy of Management Executives*. Vol. 1, No. 3: 209–13.

SNELL, S. A. (1992) Control theory in strategic human resource management: the mediating effect of administrative information. *Academy of Management Journal*. Vol. 35, No. 2. 292–327.

SPARROW, P. (2008) Performance management in the UK, in VARMA, A., BUDHWAR, P. S. and DENISI, A. (eds) *Performance Management Systems: A global perspective*. Abingdon: Routledge.

SPREITZER, G. and PORATH, C. (2012) Creating sustainable performance. *Harvard Business Review*. Vol. 90, No. 1/2. 92–9.

STOREY, J. and SISSON, K. (1993) *Managing Human Resources and Industrial Relations*. Milton Keynes: Open University Press.

SUNG, J. and ASHTON, D. (2005) *High Performance Working Practices: Linking strategy and skills to performance outcomes*. London: CIPD and DTI.

VROOM, V. (1964) *Work and Motivation*. New York: Wiley.

WALTON, R. (1985) From control to commitment in the workplace. *Harvard Business Review*. Vol. 63, No. 2. 77–84.

WILLIAMS, R. (1998) *Performance Management*. London: Thompson Business Press.

WERS (1998): see CULLY, M. *et al* (1999).

Conclusion: Future directions in developing people and organisations

Jim Stewart and Patricia Rogers

INTRODUCTION AND OVERVIEW

Our closing comments have two purposes. First, we will attempt to identify some significant themes that emerge from the chapters of this book. Second, an attempt will be made to predict how these themes may develop in the future and to anticipate some consequences and implications for the professional practice of HRD. These purposes therefore have direct connections. Given the speculative nature of these purposes, we have not formulated or stated specific objectives here. We have also not included any reader activities. We hope, however, that readers will join in our speculations and that those provided here will inform and stimulate both thought and debate.

It needs to be acknowledged that as an edited text we cannot include the views of all of our contributors. Therefore, the conclusions and speculations that we write here are our views and not necessarily the views of those who authored the chapters. We hope that none of our contributors will oppose, violently or otherwise, to what we say here, but they may well disagree and wish to dispute or debate our views. That is perfectly healthy and no doubt some of you will have similar reactions as you read on. The important point to make is that we make our own arguments and not those of our contributors.

SOME SIGNIFICANT THEMES

Drawing out significant themes from the book is both a difficult and an arbitrary task. This is due to the complexity of the range of topics covered and the range of writers involved in authoring these chapters. We are aware, therefore, that our ideas are simply that - ideas. However, we can use the broad structure of the book and its associated logic to organise speculation on some significant themes. These are the overall contexts of developing people and organisations.

THE OVERALL CONTEXT

There are a number of points to make under this heading. First, that the context is ever changing. This is not necessarily new but developments in, for example, knowledge management illustrate the increasing rate and impact of change. The point is further illustrated by contemporary developments in HRD. There are a range of developments that demand different responses and roles from HRD professionals, both now and in the future. In part, this is also related to changing views on organisational design and what works in changing circumstances.

Another point relates to the sources of ideas informing HRD practice. We saw in Chapter three the ways that traditions in African cultures are now informing both coaching and mentoring. Ideas and experience from Asian countries are becoming more commonplace in professional practice. So, the context of, and for ideas is no longer limited to the well established Anglo-American axis of academic hegemony.

Globalisation is mentioned in relation to performance management but also in other chapters. This is an example of the changing context and also part of the explanation of widening sources of ideas to inform practice. The processes and consequences of globalisation were apparent in the financial crisis and economic recessions experienced by many countries in the first decade of the century. It is clear that globalisation is a significant feature in the context of developing people and organisations.

So what are the implications of these factors shaping the context for the future practice of developing people and organisations? We suggest at least three. First, the processes of globalisation calls into question the relevance and appropriateness of established approaches to designing and developing organisations. Organisation designs relevant to the twentieth century are, we would argue, being increasingly shown to be inappropriate to the twenty-first century. So too are the behavioural science-based approaches to organisational development. These pay little attention to changing social and cultural circumstances and, in any case, are firmly based in Anglo-American models of human behaviour.

A second implication is the need to utilise opportunities created for developing both people and organisations through continued and continuing advances in information and communications technology. E-learning hardly captures the scale and nature of those developments and associated opportunities. M-learning or 'mobile-learning' may come a little closer to capturing what is now possible, but what will be possible in the future? We see a definite need for HRD practice and so HRD professionals need to keep abreast of ICT developments and to research how they can enable and support HRD practice. This will not be easy and perhaps requires closer partnerships and working between HRD and ICT specialists than has been the case so far.

The final implication is even less concrete than globalisation or ICT but has clear connections with both. The rise of Critical HRD captures the need to question the purposes and values of work organisations. The consequences of globalisation and use of ICT to enable location-free work and employees, increases the diversity of workforces. They both also to some extent 'free' employees from direct managerial control through, for example, 'virtual' teams spread across the globe and time zones. This may well result in new and different approaches being required for performance management. Employees' expectations and demands of employment and employers are changing and may well continue to change in directions not conducive to compliant behaviour. Critical HRD may well have a contribution to respond to these changing expectations and demands through promotion of mutual goals rather than exclusively economic returns for shareholders.

DEVELOPING PEOPLE

The contextual factors and implications discussed so far also apply when considering developing people. Professional practice is going to be faced with increasingly diverse employees drawn from increasingly diverse ethnic backgrounds and cultures. People needing development are also going to have new, different and diverse expectations of development. HRD professionals are also going to be faced with an increasingly wide and complex range of decisions on development methods. Methods such as coaching and mentoring are not only going to be informed by new and diverse models of practice; they are going to be capable of delivery through new and different modes and technologies.

A related theme is the understanding of how and why people learn. Established theories informing design of people development are likely to be increasingly questioned and challenged. This, in turn, will question and challenge long standing principles underpinning design of learning and development interventions.

An additional point is that if Critical HRD increases influence in response to changing demands and expectations of employees, then the focus and measures commonly used to evaluate interventions will also have to change. There will be a move away from economic and financial indicators such as ROI and new ways will have to be found to assess success against social and cultural criteria.

These new criteria for evaluation will also have implications for performance management of individual employees. Standard criteria related to economic contribution to a department or organisation will no longer be acceptable as the only measures of performance. Neither will established methods used within performance management, such as appraisal. In any case, increasing use of 'virtual' teams and widely geographically spread workforces with varying expectations and demands of employment are not likely to be conducive to traditional approaches to performance management. So, both the content; i.e. what is measured; and the process; i.e. how it is measured; of performance management are likely to experience major and significant changes in the future.

DEVELOPING ORGANISATIONS

We have already said that new organisational forms will be both needed and demanded in the future. While Taylorist forms are still prevalent in the twenty-first century, we predict their demise as the century progresses. It is the case that such forms have adapted to changing circumstances in the past; moving application from their manufacturing origins to service industries such as the care and hospitality sectors, for example. It is also arguable that so long as capitalism survives then so too will its associated and most successful (to date) form of work organisation. However, economic and financial crises experienced in the twenty first century are likely to bring significant modifications to the capitalist model of market economies.

Related to this is the changing nature of production, and so wealth accumulation. We have seen historical moves from land to capital being the most significant factor of production. More recently, there has been an arguable move from capital to labour being the most significant factor which is likely to accelerate in the future. This is associated with a related move within the value of labour from physical labour to emotional labour; significant in the service as opposed to manufacturing-based economy. The move now is away from emotional to intellectual labour as discussed in the knowledge management chapter, and a shift to knowledge economies.

This latest move also challenges the basis of capitalism as labour becomes the basis of wealth creation and accumulation. The rise of knowledge work and knowledge workers will continue in the future and will in turn demand new organisational forms and ways of developing them to improve performance. Employees are becoming less a factor of production than production itself. Knowledge is the basis of value and that knowledge used and applied by individual knowledge workers creates added value.

A final implication of the rise in the importance of knowledge is the question of what will actually constitute an organisation. We already have current illustrations of this phenomenon of new 'organisation'; internet companies for example that have no employees, no customers buying goods or services but which can be valued at more than companies with hundreds of employees and hundreds of thousands of customers. The practice of organisational design and organisational development, as well as meeting the development needs of employees in an employment relationship with an organisation, has yet to respond to this question. We predict the question will be asked more and more in the future.

SUMMARY

To summarise, we have argued in this section particular views on what factors will affect and influence developing people and organisations in the foreseeable future. These are a constantly and ever-changing context within which globalisation and related factors such as widening sources of ideas to inform practice, are most significant. We have also suggested some implications that will increasingly face and occupy the attention of HRD professionals when developing people and organisations. These implications include changing organisation forms, changing employee expectations and demands, changing opportunities associated with ICT and the increasing importance of knowledge as an economic resource.

We hope our speculations provide food for thought and a basis for debate. However, we offer our thoughts with little certainty. This is not because of a lack of confidence in our knowledge base or in our ability to analyse what we know. Rather, our lack of certainty springs from a view of the nature of the future. We do not believe it is a given and waiting for us to discover as time passes. That is not the nature of the future. We believe the future has to be and will be created by human choice; by the choices you, we and others make.

Glossary

360-degree feedback: Performance appraisals with data from multiple relevant sources.

Action research: Reflective approach to problem-solving aimed at bringing about organisational change (see also Systems approach).

Appreciative inquiry: Identifying what is working well in organisations (the positives) in order to address what is going wrong or less well (the negatives).

Client system: The person, group or organisation that is the object of the change process –often known simply as 'the client'.

Coaching culture: 'A culture where people coach each other all the time as a natural part of meetings, reviews and one to one discussions of all kinds' (Clutterbuck and Megginson 2006).

Community of practice : Group of people who have a particular activity in common and as a consequence have some common knowledge, a sense of community identity, and some element of overlapping values.

Consultant: Individual acting as a change agent helping an organisation to become more effective.

Contracting: Agreeing a contract that usually identifies roles, expectations, resources and other information to successfully carry out, for example, the consultation process.

Corporate university: Arrangements within, owned and controlled by work organisations which may or may not have links with a formally constituted university. Corporate universities are 'in-house' universities in work organisations.

Corporatism: Approach that seeks participation and consensus from all key stakeholders, usually employers and their representatives, employees and their representative trade unions, and representatives of providers, eg education institutions.

Critical human resource development (CHRD): A learning perspective considered to be an alternative to conventional views of HRD as a 'tool' of management justified only in helping to meet managerial goals and objectives.

Data: Facts that have been obtained by observation or research and have been recorded.

Diagnosis: Process of collecting information about an organisation and working collaboratively to understand how the organisation currently functions.

Double-loop learning: Situation in which an individual, organisation or other entity is able, having attempted to achieve a goal on different occasions, to modify the goal in light of that experience.

Entry: In HRM, the process by which an organisational development practitioner first encounters and establishes a relationship with a client.

Ethnocentric: Describing an approach which assumes the superiority of one particular culture or ethnic group to the exclusion of others.

Eurocentric: Approach which takes a pointedly European perspective and focus on issues of race and culture.

Explicit knowledge: Knowledge which can be found written down in official documents such as manuals, procedures and guides.

External consultant: A change agent outside an organisation contracted to help the organisation to become more effective.

'Freezing': Embedding and reinforcing change so that it becomes accepted as part of the culture of the organisation; sometimes referred to as refreezing (see Lewin 1951, and 'Unfreezing').

High-commitment management: Progressive practices that contribute to greatly enhancing employee commitment.

High-involvement management: Management style that supports involvement practices in pursuing organisational goals and improving performance.

High-performance working organisation (HPWO): A focus in an organisation on increasing people's influence on the business as well as increasing the impact of processes, methods, the physical environment, technology and tools that enhance their work (Burton et al 2005).

HR development: Frameworks for helping employees develop their personal and organisational skills, knowledge, and abilities.

HR practitioners: HR professionals undertaking HR tasks. These professionals might be undertaking a generalist role or a more specialist role, such as in reward or learning and development.

Human resource management (HRM): The running and maintenance of strategies to manage people to achieve optimum organisational performance.

Internal consultant: A member of the organisation who acts as a change agent helping an organisation to become more effective.

International human resource development (IHRD): Broad term that concerns any process that addresses the formulation and practice of HRD systems, practices, and policies at the global, societal, and organisational level.

Intervention: In HRM, any planned and deliberate action based on valid information on the part of a change agent.

Key performance indicators: Specific measures that identify goals and help organisation achieve them.

Knowledge: Information that has been fully processed or has had managerial experience applied to it.

Knowledge workers: Workers with enhanced knowledge in particular areas.

Learning: Qualitative change in a person's way of seeing, experiencing, understanding and conceptualising something in the real world – processing change (Marton and Ramsden 1988).

Learning debate: Question whether the purpose of HRD is to improve organisational performance through enhancing individual and collective competence or to enhance individual development, growth and potential through learning.

Learning organisation: Organisation in which people continually expand their capacity to create the results they truly desire, where new and expansive patterns of thinking are nurtured, where collective aspiration is set free, and where people are continually learning how to learn together.

Line manager: First level of management in an organisation, to whom other employees report.

Mentoring: 'Mentors are established managers who provide support help and advice for more junior members of staff – ideally not a direct line manager' (Price 2011).

National human resource development (NHRD): Policies and interventions of mainly national governments to promote, support and shape investment in education and training undertaken by employers and citizens. The term can also encompass similar activities of supranational bodies such as the European Union and the United Nations.

Open systems: View which suggests that organisations are open systems in and out of which people, information and resources flow, rather than closed systems.

Organisational culture: Loosely described as 'the way we do things around here', rganisational culture has three main components: values, norms and artefacts (Schein 1990). Organisational design: The study and application of how an organisation's work is designed, whether deliberately or by default.

Organisational development: Process of facilitating planned organisational change applying across the whole organisation using behavioural science knowledge.

Organisational performance : the measured outcomes of an organisation as in comparison to the inputs and goals. There are various areas of organisational performance such as: financial, growth and development, etc.

Performance appraisal: Method of evaluating an employee's job performance, which should be carried out at regular intervals – eg annually or biannually – and result in formal or informal feedback and/or coaching and training.

Performance management: Strategic development and application of systems for the people within an organisation in order to deliver and sustain the performance and ultimately the success of the organisation in general.

Performance-related pay: Reward given in the form of a financial payment that is linked to an individual employee's performance in a set time period, usually a year.

Planned change: Generic term used to describe all systematic efforts to improve organisational effectiveness.

Process consultation: Set of activities on the part of the change agent that helps the client to understand and act upon the processes within the organisation.

Psychoanalytic theory: Conceptualisation of the self that centres on the Freudian notion of personality and suggests that the self (specifically the ego and superego) is socially situated and constructed through social relations with others.

Psychological aspects of organisational design: Emotive human factors, such as job satisfaction and employee engagement, which affect, and are affected by, the way in which the organisation is designed.

Psychological contract: Unspoken deal between employer and employee concerning the perception of the two parties of what their mutual obligations are towards each other.

Scientific management: Based on the work of F. W. Taylor, a pervasive approach to organisational design in which each job is broken down into its component elements and analysed to achieve maximum efficiency.

Stakeholder: Person or group who has a vested interest in the organisation.

Strategic human resource development: HRD policies and activities that are aimed at shaping and supporting implementation of corporate strategies.

Strategy: In HRM, the overall direction of an organisation, as decided upon by senior management teams on behalf of the sponsors of the organisation.

Systems approach: Cyclical approach to change management which involves identifying the problem, identifying the changes that need to be made to solve the problem, implementing the changes, and monitoring and evaluating the process (see also Action research).

Tacit knowledge: Intangible knowledge which is typically intuitive and located within people's (notably, employees') heads.

Talent management: An approach to managing human resources that emphasises the identification, recruitment, development and retention of key talent in the form of individual employees defined as talented and/or positions and roles which are critical to organisational success.

Total quality management: Style of management that focuses on quality in an organisation through a process of constant improvement at all levels of the organisation.

Transfer of learning: Implementing training/learning into the workplace.

'Unfreezing': Preparing for the process of organisational change through an acknowledgement and acceptance that change is necessary (see Lewin 1951, and 'Freezing').

Vocational education and training (VET): Policies and interventions of national governments to promote, support and shape investment in and approaches to education and training undertaken by employers and citizens. An alternative term for NHRD.

Voluntarism: Describing a low amount of government influence or control. It seems to be peculiarly UK in origin, and the term 'non-interventionism' is often used elsewhere.

Index

Also from CIPD Publishing . . .

International Human Resource Management:

A Cross-cultural and Comparative Approach

Edited by Paul Iles and Crystal Zhang

International Human Resource Management offers balanced coverage of international, comparative and cross-cultural HRM.

- This title is ideal for students taking international HRM for the first time or studying in their 2nd language.
- A cohesive co-authored text, with contributions from experts on specific countries and regions.
- A title grounded in theory but balanced with cases and examples.

Order your copy now online at cipd.co.uk/bookstore or call us on 0844 800 3366

Paul Iles is a Professor of Leadership and HRM at Salford Business School, the University of Salford, and was previously Running Stream Professor of HRD and Course Leader of the DBA at Leeds Business School, where he provides academic leadership in HRD , leadership, talent and change management.

Dr. Crystal Zhang is a senior Lecturer in Human Resource Management and Organisational Behaviour at Leeds Business School, Leeds Metropolitan University.

| Published March 2013 | ISBN 978 1 84398 300 2 | Paperback | 340 pages |

The Chartered Institute of Personnel and Development is the leading publisher of books and reports for HR and L&D professionals, students and all those concerned with the effective management and development of people at work.

Also from CIPD Publishing . . .

Performance Management:

Theory and Practice

By Sue Hutchinson

The essential core text for any student taking a performance management module at undergraduate or postgraduate level.

- The only text designed for and completely mapping to the CIPD advanced Performance Management module.
- Critical, academic and theoretically balanced with examples that demonstrate how to apply learning in practice.
- Contains examples from a range of sectors and sizes of organisation, reflecting reality.
- An international perspective with case studies and examples from around the globe, including a dedicated chapter on this.
- Excellent range of student-friendly learning features and online resources to fully engage students with the subject.

Order your copy now online at cipd.co.uk/bookstore or call us on 0844 800 3366

Sue Hutchinson is Principal Lecturer of HRM at University of West of England where she is also Programme Director/Manager of Postgraduate and Professional HRM programmes. She has written extensively for both academic and practitioner audiences.

| Published February 2013 | ISBN 978 1 84398 305 7 | Paperback | 400 pages |

The Chartered Institute of Personnel and Development is the leading publisher of books and reports for HR and L&D professionals, students and all those concerned with the effective management and development of people at work.

Student resources

Your dedicated online area giving you all you need, when you need it. Helpful factsheets to guide you in revision and preparing for exams, practical tools, online journals and much more can be found at **cipd.co.uk/studyresources**

Students can **save 20%** on textbooks

Plus **save 10%** on CIPD training, online subscription products, conference tickets, publications, DVDs and Toolkits.

To find out more, call us on +44 (0)20 8612 6208 or visit cipd.co.uk/memberbenefits